I0644556

Liberated by God's Grace

Edited by
Anne Burghardt

Bibliographic information published by the German National Library

The *Deutsche Nationalbibliothek* lists this publication in the *Deutsche Nationalbibliografie;* detailed bibliographic data are available on the internet at http://dnd.dnd.de

Printed in Germany · H 7924

This book was printed on FSC-certified paper

Editorial assistance:	Department for Theology and Public Witness
Layout:	Department for Theology and Public Witness
Design:	LWF-Office for Communication Services
Printing and Binding:	Druckhaus Köthen GmbH & Co. KG

Published by Evangelische Verlangsanstalt GmbH, Leipzig, Germany, under the auspices of
The Lutheran World Federation
150, rte de Ferney, PO Box 2100
CH-1211 Geneva 2, Switzerland

Parallel editions in German and Spanish
ISBN 978-3-374-04160-2

Contents

Preface

Martin Junge

The year 2017 marks the 500th Anniversary of the Reformation. Churches in the Lutheran tradition take 31 October 1517 as the starting point of the Reformation. It was on that date that Martin Luther is said to have nailed his Ninety-five Theses opposing the sale of indulgences and what he perceived to be clerical abuses attached to this practice on the door of All Saints' Church in Wittenberg. Since then, the Reformation has made an impressive journey. Today, Lutheran churches can be found in all four corners of the globe, with a steadily growing number of Lutherans living in the global South. The Lutheran World Federation, a world-wide communion comprising 144 churches, today represents over 70 million Lutherans in seventy-nine countries.

The churches' diverse formative experiences, social and cultural backgrounds make it virtually impossible to talk about "the" Lutheran identity. For some churches, the year 1517 does not necessarily have special significance since they associate different dates with the beginning of the Reformation. For several LWF member churches, for instance, the introduction of Christianity in their local context represents the key date that is being remembered as constitutive of their self-understanding and identity. However, the commemoration of this quincentennial anniversary offers an excellent opportunity for all Lutheran churches to reflect on the ongoing relevance of the questions that triggered the Reformation and to discern its societal impact.

The four booklets included in this collection aim to contribute to such an in-depth review. The discussion is shaped around the overarching theme of the 500th Anniversary and the Twelfth Assembly, "Liberated by God's Grace," with its three sub-themes that help to elaborate different aspects of the main theme: "Salvation– Not for Sale," "Human Beings–Not for Sale," and "Creation—Not for Sale." The booklets include essays by bishops, pastors, academics, members of the LWF Council, representatives of different LWF networks and ecumenical partners from all LWF regions. The wide range of authors and topics gives the reader a glimpse of the wide variety within the communion and some aspects of the LWF's programmatic work. The three questions at the end of each essay seek to encourage further reflection and discussion.

It is our hope that these booklets can be used in bilateral discussions between partner churches to trigger a dialogue on the message and role of churches in different contexts. Furthermore, they will hopefully provide significant impulses for our deliberations as we prepare for the Twelfth Assembly that will take place in 2017 at Windhoek, Namibia.

Last but not least, I would like to express my gratitude to all those who have contributed an essay to this publication and for making these comprehensive and meaningfully diverse. I would like to encourage readers carefully to study these booklets and hope that they will lead to meaningful and worthwhile conversations on their content.

Introduction

Anne Burghardt

"Liberated by God's Grace"—the Lutheran World Federation's main theme for the 500th Anniversary of the Reformation—is closely linked to the doctrine of justification by faith which, in the Lutheran tradition, has also been called "the doctrine by which the church stands or falls" (*articulus stantis et cadentis ecclesiae*). The central insight of this doctrine, namely that in Christ God's grace is given to us as a free and unconditional gift, evokes a response of gratitude, expressing itself in the loving and caring engagement with human beings and the whole of creation. This understanding is as pertinent today as it was in Luther's times and continues to impact all aspects of theology. The essays in this booklet explore the topicality and influence of this Reformation insight from different perspectives.

In his article "Liberated by God's Grace—From What, To What?" Gottfried Brakemeier argues that in today's world the concept of grace/mercy is becoming increasingly suspect. A world without grace would end up being an inhumane world. A theology centered on justification by faith holds on to the concept of grace since, in biblical terms, justification promises God's unconditional acceptance of human beings. Showing love is the response to God's abundant love for human beings, not an attempt to "earn" God's love by "good deeds." Referring to Luther's writing "On the Freedom of a Christian, 1520," Brakemeier shows how Luther's two sentences, "A Christian is a free lord of all, and subject to none" and "A Christian is the most dutiful servant of all and subject to everyone"[1] belong closely together.

[1] Martin Luther, "The Freedom of A Christian, 1520," in Helmut T. Lehmann, *Luther's Works*, vol. 31 (Philadelphia: Muhlenberg Press, 1957), 344

> "A Christian is a perfectly free lord of all, subject to none."[2] This is his [Luther's] first sentence. Anyone who has God as lord cannot serve other lords (cf. Mt 6:24). Serving God frees us from serving humans. All pressures fall away as soon as people entrust themselves in faith to God's grace. However, this freedom would be thoroughly misunderstood as arbitrariness. So Luther adds: "A Christian is a perfectly dutiful servant of all and subject to all."[3] That is his second sentence. The two belong together. Freedom destroys itself if it is not in a position to take on obligations. Above all, however, love is betrayed. It is essentially "serving the neighbor." Without diakonia, faith also becomes false as there is no "Christian" faith that does not take action in love (Gal 5:6).[4]

The rediscovery of the gospel's liberating message, which Luther discovered through his profound study of the Holy Scriptures, was at the center of the Reformation. This powerful and liberating message needs to be heard anew at different times and in different contexts. In his essay, Hans-Peter Grosshans, a member of the LWF's hermeneutics network, points to the diversity of human life and the fact that through the medium of the Holy Scriptures God speaks to individuals' and communities' concrete lives.

> Hearing God's Word is therefore not followed by some sort of imperial anti-individuation process but by a song praising the manifold grace of God (1 Pet 4:10), expressed in the diverse and many-hued lives of Christians and churches—in "the freedom of the glory of the children of God" (Rom 8:21).[5]

The fact that the significance of hearing and understanding the Word of God has been highlighted since the beginning of the Reformation gave rise to many new translations of the Bible which, in several cases, noticeably impacted the further development of certain national languages. Comprehending the actual meaning of the text has a lot to do with the hermeneutical key that is being used. Elżbieta Byrtek describes the importance of education in Lutheran churches throughout the centuries, which originated in the desire more widely to engage with the Scriptures and their meaning. True engagement with the Scriptures implies posing questions, listening to different "readings" and voicing one's concerns and doubts.

> Faith that is not afraid of posing questions, seeking answers and staying in dialogue with those who do not share one's own opinion, is a living faith, one that

---

[2] Ibid.

[3] Ibid.

[4] Gottfried Brakemeier, in this publication, 24.

[5] Hans-Peter Grosshans, in this publication, 58.

> will be able to survive in today's multilateral and complex world. A world where "right" answers given by external authorities do not necessarily speak to people but where Christians, liberated by God's grace, have a responsibility to talk about this grace to others and to be ready to engage in difficult dialogues.[6]

The Reformation was a catalyst for the renewed understanding of the church's role in society. Luther valued ordinary work, both in- and outside the home. Thus everyday work acquired a new dignity since he explicitly considered it to be an essential part of serving both God and the neighbor. This perception laid a fruitful basis to the later concepts of active citizenship. In his article about the church's calling in society, Kjell Nordstokke points out that, according to Luther, God has called the church to be a "living word" in the world.

> The call to be "a living word" is an exhortation to active citizenship. Luther radically changed the understanding of Christian vocation, shifting the focus from the internal life of the church, to serving in the world—being Christian citizens who love and care for their neighbor.[7]

Using the example of Norway, Norstokke identifies four areas of action for diakonia: loving one's neighbor; creating inclusive communities; caring for creation; and struggling for justice.

In 2013, the LWF approved the Gender Justice Policy (GJP), a document that helps to raise awareness about questions pertaining to inclusiveness and gender roles in the churches. Using the example of the Murut people of Sabah, Malaysia, Au Sze Ngui describes how the liberating power of the gospel has brought about a change in the perception of gender roles among the Muruts. In her article, she also draws on the theological argumentation and methodology outlined in the GJP. Ngui explains how the Christian understanding of the equality of all human beings before God has empowered Murut women in the church to take on responsibilities that traditionally would have been within the male domain. She refers to the gospel's liberating power when it comes to revisiting certain traditions, which despite the rhetoric that is sometimes being used, do not correspond to the actual message of the gospel.

> Liberation from the bondage of sin is the beginning of our striving for justice: we are free; we are forgiven; we are the recipients of God's grace. We are free to

[6] Elżbieta Byrtek, in this publication, 77.

[7] Kjell Nordstokke, in this publication, 33.

> change and to change the world. There are many examples of how Christianity has been an agent of change by supporting the revision of some "traditional" practices.[8]

"Freed by God's Love to Change the World" is the motto of the LWF's Global Young Reformers Network that was formed within the framework of the commemoration of the 500th Anniversary of the Reformation. Inspired by this motto, Monica Villarreal picks up the question about faith's liberating power from the perspective of youth. Being liberated, being freed by God always implies the question what we are actually liberated or freed from and to. Villarreal quotes Caroline Huth from Argentina, a member of the steering group of the Global Young Reformers Network, who expresses the idea of an ongoing reformation by explaining how her faith has freed her for creating new space:

> As Lutherans we believe that while traditions are not necessary for salvation, they are sometimes good for order, tranquility and common practice. But when they do not serve their purpose, when people are uncomfortable and the church is no longer inviting and God's message does not reach everyone, then we may need to consider reorganizing the pews.[9]

The ecumenical voice in this volume belongs to Tim Harris who, in his article, refers to both the profoundly personal as well as ultimately global character of Martin Luther's discovery of God's grace. This rediscovery

> not only addressed his own need for personal assurance from his spiritual angst, it sparked a movement of ongoing reform, the heart of which must always be shaped by and draw us back to a deeper appreciation of the great gospel message of grace and peace. [10]

The rediscovery of the gospel's greatness nonetheless also reminds us of our own limitations in understanding the gospel as our cultural blinkers and blind spots sometimes tend to make the gospel smaller than it is. "The gospel is bigger than any and every culture, and no ethnic grouping, nation or culture can claim any supremacy in their particular expression of the gospel."[11] In the spirit of ongoing reformation, there is thus always the need to "translate" the gospel "into the many and varied expressions of gospel articulation, proclamation and lived realities that are part and

[8] Au Sze Ngui, in this publication, 66.
[9] Monica Villarreal, in this publication, 82
[10] Tim Harris, in this publication, 96
[11] Ibid., 89

parcel of human life,"[12] keeping thereby in mind our own limitations in understanding it.

In his contextual Bible study on Isaiah 55:1-2, Zephania Kameeta addresses the pressing issues of poverty and hunger in Africa and Namibia in particular and unfolds the liberating message of Isaiah in this context.

> The text of this Bible study does not say, Come so that you can be counted or registered or so that research can be done why you are thirsty; but just simply, come and drink. This is what is needed in this hour of need. Those in need want help now before they perish. Now is your hour and your moment. Budgets and money is now not in question, come, eat and drink, so that you can live.[13]

The three sub-themes: Salvation—Not For Sale; Human Beings—Not For Sale; Creation—Not For Sale

The three subthemes elaborate the various "not for sale" dimensions of the main theme, "Liberated by God's Grace," and question practices and theological concepts that stand in the way of the gospel's liberating message. Attempts to commodify salvation differ widely, ranging from prosperity gospel to attempts to "guarantee" salvation by following certain practices, rituals etc. The salvific aspect of consumerism as well as questions regarding from where and under what conditions "salvation" is expected in the secular context, are also crucial.

The renewed relationship between God and human beings inevitably provides a deeper insight into the creation of human beings in God's image and the understanding that human beings will be renewed through God's grace. Human beings cannot therefore be regarded as commodities whose value can be measured in terms of profit only.

Today, in light of the massive exploitation of natural resources, it is vital that we pay attention to God's creation beyond human beings. We read in Genesis that God considered creation to be "good" and entrusted it into human care. The notion of "dominion" in Genesis 1:26 has often been misused and it has been overlooked that God declares all creation to be "good," quite apart from its usefulness to humans. The renewed relationship between God and human beings therefore also has implications on how humans relate to the rest of the creation since creation primarily belongs to God and is only entrusted into our hands.

[12] Ibid.

[13] Zephania Kameeta, in this publication, 103.

Diverse reflections on different aspects of the three sub-themes can be found in the respective booklets included in this collection. Hopefully they will help to trigger conversations around the liberating message of the gospel as together we journey towards the 500th Anniversary of the Reformation.

Liberated by God's Grace—From What, To What?

Gottfried Brakemeier

A concept in crisis

Grace and mercy (German: *Gnade*) have become rare words occurring only in exceptional cases, such as in the "plea for mercy" of those condemned to death. Or we say that the sun is beating down "mercilessly," drying out the land and ruining the harvest. Above all, wars are "merciless." They are unrelenting; the enemies' vengeance fearsome, raging without regard for guilt and innocence, believing it does not need to worry about right and wrong. Destruction, rape and murder are rife. That is repeated in the "law of the street." Many young delinquents have long forgotten the word "mercy," if they have ever heard it at all. Even if the victim has already been knocked down, they keep on beating and kicking—"mercilessly."

It is significant that we only become aware of mercy when it has disappeared. The term only carries weight in the negative meaning of "merciless." Whoever knows no mercy is thus "merciless," is regarded as ruthless, unscrupulous and brutal. Otherwise the concept has disappeared from everyday life. Gone are the days when rulers understood their authority as being their divine right and legitimized their rule as being by the "grace of God." In a democracy all state power emanates from the people. The ballot paper decides on how the government is formed. Parliamentarians are "representatives of the people." That has nothing to do with God's grace. Also God has become superfluous. During their installment ceremony, many politicians have even stopped using the phrase "So help me God." A secular world is uneasy about the term "mercy" and does not know what it is good for.

What is more, the very word is suspect. No one wants to depend on anyone else's mercy. Anyone needing mercy is a weakling. We want to stand on our own feet, earn our own living and owe no one anything. People strive to steer clear of grace and mercy. It is ultimately a question of prestige. Children do not want to be a constant burden on their parents and depend on them for their keep. As soon as they can, they move out and take their lives into their own hands. It is a disgrace if that does not work out. The same applies to the relationship with the state. Long-term unemployed people suffer from feeling superfluous and having to live at the expense of the community. Many consider them to be parasites. The jobless do not want to be beggars and live on handouts all their lives. Who could condemn that? It is better to manage without mercy.

After all, mercy makes slaves of us. There are countless examples of this. The generosity of the masters creates a crowd of humble servants who do not dare to object to unreasonable requests. Favorites and lackeys are not free. "He who pays the piper calls the tune," says the proverb. That has always been the way dictators have cemented their power. They have granted privileges and thereby guaranteed loyalty. That is no different even under "democratic" conditions, since voters can often be bought. Politicians can win supporters by making promises to the electorate. Gifts create an obligation, even those given only at Christmas. The concept of "mercy" is unattractive because it sounds hierarchical. It would seem to establish dependencies. There remains a gap between giver and taker, between them ("up there") and us ("down here"), with the former always setting the tone as benefactors and patrons.

It appears that mercy is an obstacle to the human striving for freedom. Unfortunately, the church has often understood it that way as well. Movements committed to freeing people from undignified bondage have not always received the necessary support. In this respect, "liberation theology" highlights unusual elements, although they are not entirely new. God is on the side of the oppressed and leads them out of the house of slavery, as God led the people of Israel out of Egypt. God is in solidarity with the poor and sides with them in the struggle for justice. Many view this theology with suspicion and accuse it of being an inadmissible politicization of the gospel. However you react to this charge, the fact is that Latin American liberation theology and its related currents on other continents have starkly outlined the old question about how mercy relates to freedom. How can we talk about God's liberating mercy without disempowering people and plunging them into new dependencies? And how can we represent human autonomy without making it seem that talking about mercy is superfluous?

A world without mercy?

It does not call for much imagination to envisage a world without mercy. This is already reality on a large scale. The horrific news from our immediate neighborhood or from distant countries testifies to this, as does the social inequality in society. No animal can be crueler than the human being. Bestial murders, blind destruction or the distress of millions of refugees in areas of hunger and crisis are illustration enough. The nation responsible for the Holocaust had always been proud of its culture. Civilization is no guarantee for protection from genocide, as is shown by other examples from the past and the present. We only need to remember the history of suffering of the indigenous population in the Americas. Native Americans were brutally decimated and eradicated except for a small remnant. The wrong done to the slaves imported from Africa is just as tragic. The list of crimes committed by the human race is long. It began with Cain and Abel and found a shocking expression in the crucifixion of Jesus. Violence has been the trademark of humanity from time immemorial. "[T]he inclination of the human heart is evil from youth," says Genesis 8:21. A world without mercy is cold, inhumane and murderous.

Besides the above, there are less spectacular types of brutality, such as economic exploitation. Anyone who falls into the debt trap will find it hard to get out. Banks know no mercy; they are about profit, bonuses and return on investment. Many people have been stripped of their assets due to speculation and false promises. In a thoroughly capitalist system life is commodified. Everything can be bought or sold, including religious goods. Stock prices determine business activity and, again, there is no room for mercy. Social concern, compassion and goodness disappear with it. Greed displaces consideration of the neighbor. Selfishness becomes a virtue. A struggle for jobs begins, often resorting to bullying and similar methods. You have to be "clever" and on the side of the winners. A well-known proverb aptly sums up this spirit: "Everyone for themselves and God for us all." Social considerations are pushed into the sole responsibility of God. That is convenient and at the same time cruel. Such behavior can occur in many guises and yet they are all equally inhumane.

In addition, people do not see that a world without mercy exposes us to fatal dangers. The decline of compassion does not remain without consequences. It provokes hatred of those who were not able to hold their own in the general competition, those who were excluded or oppressed. The "survival of the fittest" is a principle unsuited to the human community. After all, the losers are still able to take terrible revenge on their opponents. A match is enough to start a huge conflagration. Being indifferent or even hostile toward socially vulnerable milieus, religious and ethnic minorities and other national groups means risking serious social conflicts. It is no surprise when children who have always vegetated on the margins of society and never experienced affection develop a cynical attitude to life and turn to crime.

The precondition for peace is inclusion, not exclusion. But being inclusive presupposes looking favorably at the neighbor. I must grant them a place in society even if they are different and do not match with my ideals. You do not necessarily have to have the same opinions as your partners to extend them the hand of friendship. Mercy is capable of a tolerance that recognizes the right to exist but must not slip into arbitrariness. Crime cannot lay claim to the principle of tolerance. Yet mercy, rightly understood, does not limit people's living space. On the contrary, it protects and extends it. Only those capable of compassion belong to the peacemakers blessed by Jesus (Mt 5:9). Without mercy, humanity is likely to be crushed by its conflicts.

Finally, we must admit that imagining a world without mercy would be a gross delusion. Everything that the concept "mercy" stands for—kindness, acceptance, gratuity, readiness to forgive, etc.—can be suppressed and betrayed. And yet mercy remains part of reality. Human beings are inconceivable without mercy. Anyone who disputes that is blind. In his "Small Catechism," Martin Luther puts this in masterly fashion in his explanation of the first article of the creed:

> I believe that God has created me together will all that exists. God has given me and still preserves my body and soul: eyes, ears, and all limbs and senses; reason and all mental faculties.[1]

We do not owe ourselves to ourselves. Nor are we the product of a genetic accident or biological manipulation. All of that may have played a role. But it is not enough to explain the mystery of a person. People are not manufactured, they are created and therefore have an inviolable dignity. Their life is a gift, as is every new day. Mercy is present at the beginning of life and thereafter remains a basic need. Every person has to be supported in their own way with their own errors, weaknesses and guilt. They need consideration, forgiveness, love. Who could do without that?

The faculty of reason that characterizes human beings has been perceived to be their distinguishing feature. We differ from other living beings in that we can think, speak, plan and shape the world. For Martin Luther reason is also "in comparison with other things of this life, the best and something divine."[2] It is a force that shapes culture, he adds. Although reason is not protected from entering the service of evil, it raises us above

---

[1] Martin Luther, "Small Catechism," in Robert Kolb and Timothy Wengert (eds), *The Book of Concord: The Confessions of the Evangelical Lutheran Church* (Minneapolis: Fortress Press, 2000), 354.

[2] Martin Luther, "The Disputation Concerning Man, 1536," in Helmut T. Lehmann, *Luther's Works*, vol. 34 (Philadelphia: Muhlenberg Press, 1960). 137.

all other creatures. It would still be wrong to make reason the exclusive criterion of the human. Rationality is linked to irrationality, spirituality, the emotions. And they are unpredictable. It has been proven that decisions are more frequently emotional than rational; human beings are complex and cannot be explained on the basis of simply decoding their genome.

Precisely for that reason, the Christian faith will insist on the fact that mercy is part of our humanity. That was always clear to Martin Luther and he emphasized it often. It is empathy that makes a person a person. We would remain a machine if we could not show compassion, sympathy and love. The apostle Paul said this most clearly. "[...] and if I have not love" all my abilities, however great, are worth nothing (1 Cor 13:1f.). Jesus himself recalled that God prefers mercy to burnt offerings (Mt 9:13f.). Religious ceremony is just as worthless as intellectual brilliance if it bypasses other people and their needs. If we sum all that up in the concept of mercy we find that human nobility basically consists in being merciful. All else is secondary.

God's humanity

Jesus knew he had been sent in the name of a God who is love in person (1 Jn 4:16). This God differs from all gods that legitimize murder and killing, allowing—or even requiring—violence in their name. Gods are not all the same. You have to have a good look and distinguish between the gods. They are recognized by their demands, their commands and their works. Some of them are real tyrants, placing heavy burdens on their worshippers and taking away their reason. They sow hatred and strife, and insist on crusades and holy wars. Religions can be as barbaric as any person. Terrible crimes have been committed in their name, and still are. Frequently religion has blocked progress and development and believers have clung to obsolete behavioral patterns. Religious people are often backward, old-fashioned, suspect. Religion has therefore fallen into discredit among many of our contemporaries. Some dream of abolishing it. It is not only superfluous but downright harmful. Religious fanaticism with its typical disposition for violence has become one of the greatest sources of danger in the global world. Who will curb this religious madness?

At a time when talk about God is losing plausibility, faith has to be accountable for its discourse. Christianity believes in the God whom Jesus called his father and whom his congregation may also address as Our Father. The name stands for a trusting relationship. God could just as well be called mother, as the Bible indicates at some points. Unlike earlier prophets up to John the Baptist, Jesus does not preach an angry God, whose retributive justice will soon descend on the world, but a merciful God, who turns to the lowest, the outcast and the guilty.

In so doing, Jesus caused offence to those who held themselves to be righteous and therefore claimed privileges. The table fellowship Jesus kept with tax-collectors and sinners (Lk 15:1f.), is a scandal in their eyes. It reverses their view of the world, which values only merit and performance. If God is what Jesus proclaims, they will have to change. Yet they are not willing to do so. They react to the patience of the rabbi from Nazareth with the "unworthy" as though it were an act of aggression. Jesus has eyes for the sick and the vulnerable, for those living on the margins, for the poor and despised. They are the ones he tries to bring back into the community of the children of God. His attention and concern are unconditional. Gratuity is the main feature of his actions. That means that Jesus understands himself to be an advocate of a gracious God, who does not reject sinners and gives the lost a chance.

It is well known that the Reformation started with a change in the understanding of God. Martin Luther discovered the merciful God who accepts human beings without regard for merit and worthiness. Justification, biblically speaking, means just this: promise of the right to life without proof of performance, unconditional acceptance, showing love. Martin Luther had been tormented by scruples because of his repeated defeats in the fight against evil in himself; these doubts were suddenly overcome when he discovered that God justifies the sinner "by grace and faith alone." His frightened question, "How can I get a merciful God?," was thereby answered. It would be wrong to interpret this as a time-bound expression of a bad conscience. It is the human question *par excellence*. Where is there mercy in this world? A merciless God is more of a Moloch than a father. Such a God threatens infernal punishment and spreads fear and terror. No consolation can be had from such a god. Denying God is also no solution. Atheism is just as "dismal" as a cynical religion. With the father of Jesus Christ things are different. This God offers shelter, refuge, protection from meaninglessness.

> With these words God wants to entice us, so that we come to believe he is truly our Father and we are truly his children, in order that we may ask him boldly and with complete confidence, just as loving children ask their loving father." God would thereby tenderly urge us to believe that he is our true Father and that we are his true children, so that we may ask him confidently with all assurance, as dear children as their dear Father.[3]

If you ask where this conviction comes from, the reply is easy. It originates in Jesus Christ, in whom God came the closest ever to human beings. "No

[3] Op. cit. (note 1), 356.

one has ever seen God" (Jn 1:18), but God is revealed in Jesus. The congregation confesses him as the revelation itself. There are signs of God in nature and history, but they are not unequivocal. Anyone speaking of God's love cannot bypass Jesus of Nazareth. This love is expressed in his words and deeds, and also in his suffering. Jesus dies on the cross as a victim of his enemies. All the evil in the world pours down upon him, but even in this hell, Jesus remains true to his mission. Instead of cursing his tormentors, he prays for their forgiveness (Lk 23:34). He prefers to die himself than to wish the death of others. Jesus consistently refrains from seeking reprisals. For the Christian community, this story allows the behavior of the heavenly father to shine through. God forgoes vengeance on his enemies (Rom 5:10). Instead he forgives their debt. He gives reconciliation (2 Cor 5:18ff.). No peace can grow from revenge.

Jesus witnesses to the God who seeks human salvation, including that of the godless and "unbelieving." The New Testament speaks of his love of humanity (Titus 3:4). In Jesus Christ God shows solidarity with suffering creatures, in order to wrench them out of their hardship. The God of Jesus Christ is "human," knowing "compassion" and thereby showing mercy. The latter comes to a head at Easter. Sin, suffering and death do not prevail. The Crucified One is experienced as living, and in possession of the key to death and hell (Rev 1:15). The resurrection of Jesus Christ frees us from the captivity of transience and gives us a future, even in the face of death. The end of all things is not just nothing, meaninglessness, absolute annihilation, but a new beginning (Rev 21:1ff.). The kingdom of God becomes the all-defining reality.

The imperative of the gospel

Under such circumstances it is not surprising that the will of God is best expressed in the command to love. God sets the standard with divine action and God's own being. Again we must point to Jesus Christ, in whom this love appeared (Rom 8:39). "Be merciful, just as your Father is merciful," says Jesus (Lk 6:36). And when asked about the supreme commandment he replies "[...] 'you shall love the Lord your God with all your heart [..] [and] your neighbor as yourself'. There is no other commandment greater than these" (Mk 12:29ff.). They are two commandments in one. Loving God and the neighbor is not the same. Loving the neighbor is not loving God or vice versa. These two cannot be confused. Loving God is shown in the fact that God alone is worshipped. The liturgy belongs to God alone (Mt 4:10). Any human "personality cult" is reprehensible. By contrast, diakonia is for the neighbor. They need assistance, solidarity, attention. The principle is: "Bear one another's burdens" (Gal 6:2). So we need to differentiate. Love has many faces. And yet there is ultimately only one single command—about love, i.e., the attitude that can only want what is good.

This command is not just one among many, but a criterion for ethics in general. "On these two commandments hang all the law and the prophets" (Mt 22:40). And Paul will say, "Love is the fulfilling of the law" (Rom 13:10). If a precept contradicts the command to love, it must be reworded or abolished. We can observe this in the discussion between Jesus and the Pharisees on observing the Sabbath. But that is only one example among others. At any rate, God wants a humane world. And this is not to be had without a minimum of "love." Although "love" is an over-used word, it cannot be done without. Indeed, it needs to be protected from abuse. Biblically speaking, love is not primarily a feeling but rather an intention. Whether I love my neighbors or not, ultimately depends on my intentions in their regard. I can also feel the best for my enemies, without actually liking them. We owe salvation to God's love of the enemy. God's mercy is addressed to all people without distinction. It calls the sinners back into God's community.

That happens without pressure and coercion. Love creates no dependences, if it is authentic. It grants freedom. It must almost amaze us that the father in the parable of the prodigal son raises no objections when his son decides to leave his father's house and demands his share of his inheritance (Lk 15:11f.). His father lets him go. Similarly, Jesus does not bind his disciples to himself. He leaves it up to them to turn away if they do not agree with him (Jn 6:66f). Genuine discipleship is based on a free decision. Mercy without love serves its own purposes and is thus humiliating for the recipient, unlike mercy that comes from love. It wants the neighbors to be its partners, not subordinates. It refrains from patronizing them and telling them what to do. "Legalism" contradicts the command of love. It establishes religious dictatorship and turns mercy into coercion. Love, by contrast, gives greater value to human beings and allows them to take responsibility. To do so, they have to be able to think, and to practice recognizing "whatever is true, whatever is honorable, whatever is pure, whatever is pleasing, whatever is commendable [...]" (Phil 4:8). Love needs guidance but no regulations; coercion destroys it.

Above all, however, it needs motivation. Love does not spring up by order. That is why the New Testament explains the imperative to act with God's action. We are to love because we were loved by God."We love because he first loved us," says the first letter of John (4:19). Jesus himself puts it similarly in the parable of the unforgiving servant (Mt 18:21f.). The duty mutually to forgive one another arises from God's forgiveness of debt. That applies to ethics as a whole: each time the command is preceded by the memory of God's merciful action. Experiencing mercy inspires us to do good. Here is the source on which the imperative draws. "You wicked slave!" says the lord in the parable, "I forgave you all that debt because you pleaded with me. Should you not have had mercy on your fellow slave, as I had mercy on you?" (Mt 18:32f). Any benefactor must feel foolish if the recipient remains hard-hearted. That is precisely what the Apostle Paul asks: "Or do you despise the riches of his kindness and forbearance and patience? Do you not realize that God's kindness is meant to lead you to repentance?" (Rom 2:4). The issue is how to draw the right conclusions from this goodness.

Anyone who refuses to do that suffers considerable losses. Naturally you can argue that you owe something to God. Who or what is "God"? A modern trend wants religion without God. Apparently the concept is no longer appropriate. People want to believe but to do so differently than in the past. Indeed, we will have to be sure that mercy is not catapulted out of the world at the same time as God. Who, or what, do people want to believe in, if God disappears from life? There is a great danger that, in this case, one has to accept the meaninglessness of the world, likewise the general lack of love and the tragedy of a finite life. God is the decisive force that makes it possible to resist the negativity of life and the power of evil. The experience of preservation in difficult situations, even at the risk of death, becomes impossible under the conditions of the modern eclipse of God, wherefore combating God's reality must be seen as a major "risk factor" for successful life.

In addition, denying God's grace runs the risk of losing the sense of wonder, a feeling for the extraordinary. It therefore normally sees no grounds for gratitude. Everything threatens to go under in platitudes and, at the same time, to run automatically according to well-known laws. Who is responsible for the wonders of creation? You do not need to give thanks to "evolution." The very idea is absurd. Becoming dulled toward God's mercy leads to blindness toward dimensions without which life would be insipid. So remembering it can set a huge liberation process in motion. It opens our eyes to the justification of a prayer such as the Lord's Prayer. You have to be clear about what you are doing when you press the "delete" button on God's mercy.

Freedom

The Reformation understood itself as a freedom movement. "For freedom Christ has set us free," writes the Apostle Paul (Gal 5:1). That lent dynamic to the movement. It dared to rise up against foreign domination and appeal to the gospel as the sole standard. Accordingly, at the Diet of Worms in 1521, Martin Luther defied the Pope, emperor and the concentrated power of the church. He had already developed the theme in detail in "On the Freedom of a Christian, 1520." "A Christian is a perfectly free lord of all, subject to none."[4] This is his first sentence. Anyone who has God as lord cannot serve other lords (cf. Mt 6:24). Serving God frees us from serving humans. All pressures fall away as soon as people entrust themselves in faith to God's grace. However, this freedom would be thoroughly misunderstood as arbitrariness. So Luther adds: "A Christian is a perfectly dutiful servant of all and subject to all."[5] That is his second sentence. The two belong together. Freedom destroys itself if it is not in a position to take on obligations. Above all, however, love is betrayed. It is essentially "serving the neighbor." Without diakonia, faith also becomes false as there is no "Christian" faith that does not take action in love (Gal 5:6). That is the litmus test of faith.

It is worth reflecting at length on the two sentences of the Reformer. Martin Luther aroused the anger of the papal church because he denied its role as mediator in the salvation process. Faith alone suffices for justification. The church is witness to the gospel and thereby fulfills an essential task. But salvation comes exclusively from Jesus Christ. Humans do not need to work for their salvation anymore or strive to perform meritorious works. Instead, they are invited to accept it in confidence. Luther was able to appeal to Paul, who had stated "[...] no one will be justified by the works of the law" (Gal 2:16). Luther had personally experienced what that meant. It took a load off his mind when he realized that his sin did not disqualify him from the kingdom of God. He could again go through life with his head held high. God's mercy had freed him from the pressure to perform acts of religious merit. That pressure was not only strong in the medieval church. It is also present today, not least in non-Christian religions. Anyone who does not bow to the regulations is regarded as a "non-believer"' and is treated with hostility.

Even under altered conditions, the message of justification has no less relevance. Each person needs the experience of being accepted. It is a condition for mental health and finding identity. An undesired child has a hard time in life. Without the protection and care of mother and father the child cannot grow up. Later, too, recognition is vital—by a small group if not by the public at large. Everyone strives for praise, applause and approval. People must have the feeling of being someone, having some significance, having a place. But what happens if society rejects its own members including its own parents? I myself can belong to this society if I

[4] Martin Luther, "The Freedom of A Christian, 1520," in Helmut T. Lehmann (ed.), *Luther's Works*, vol. 31 (Philadelphia: Muhlenberg Press, 1957), 344.
[5] Ibid.

start to hate myself and develop an inferiority complex. Then I imagine that I am not worth much, I am a failure, I bear a stigma. That is a dangerous development that may end in suicide or outbreaks of violence.

God's mercy puts it differently. When everyone teases and humiliates you, driving you crazy, you remain God's beloved creature. You are no less important than anyone else. Do not envy the success of others. Justification means emancipation from social judgment. "Who will bring any charges against God's elect? It is God who justifies" (Rom 8:33), says the Apostle Paul. A person is always more than the sum of their actions or non-actions. What others think of me continues to be important. The image they spread cannot be indifferent to me. No one is immune to denigration and aggression, and defamation of character is rightly a crime. And yet, human judgments have lost their absolute validity. They have become "relative." The key thing is what the gospel says about me. Then I will manage better, with all my deficiencies. I will learn to accept myself with my errors and weaknesses without apologizing for them. The promise of justification has extraordinary psychological effects. It teaches us to recognize sin without plunging into despair.

Of course, justification resists pride. It thwarts the illusion of being able to manage everything and calls for a realistic image of what it means to be human. The Apostle Paul chastises the pride of the Corinthians with cutting words. He wants to know, "For who sees anything different in you? What do you have that you did not receive? And if you received it, why do you boast as if it were not a gift?" (1 Cor 4:7) The message of justification pricks the bubble of arrogance. It brings people down to earth with a bump and teaches them modesty. God's mercy is a stumbling block for the proud, the strong, the righteous, for those who think they do not need to be grateful for anything. Yet without God's mercy they would also be nothing. It is advisable not to deceive yourself. Society as a whole sets limits on God's mercy. Yet if the last judgment on a person is God's responsibility, all human judgment is subject to reservation. Society is thereby deprived of the final right of decision about its members. Human beings are God's property and as such enjoy God's protection. No one is an exception. All are invited to accept God's mercy in faith. Nevertheless the gift precedes human response. In a further sense, the message of justification is thus part of the grounds for human rights. Divine law focuses on respect for human dignity and the integrity of the human person.

This makes it clear that God's mercy towards human beings is not situated in a vacuum. It places individuals in fellowship with others. Hence the second clause of Luther's treatise on freedom has to follow the first one. There is no contradiction. We can learn that from Jesus Christ. The one who was free and felt exclusively responsible to his Father in heaven "emptied himself, taking the form of a slave" (Phil 2:7). He was not forced to do this, it was voluntary. In his own words, he "came not to be served but to serve and to give his life a ransom for many" (Mk 10:45). That is why: "Whoever wishes to be first among you must be slave of all" (Mk 10:44). Only the one who can serve is really free. "Freedom from" must correspond to "freedom to." Only then will it receive the seal of quality. Mere independence can be just as despotic as pure arbitrariness. It needs to be bound to what is good.

It is thus a tragic misunderstanding when people think that a Protestant does not need to do good works. While Catholics have to score well, Protestants can fold their hands in their laps. This is a popular misunderstanding one still comes across now and then. Anyone arguing like that has not read the confession the Lutherans published in Augsburg in 1530 that has retained its validity to this day. The Sixth Article reads, "Likewise, they teach that this faith is bound to yield good fruits and that it ought to do good works commanded by God [...]."[6] However, the Lutheran tradition distinguishes between works of love and works of the law. The latter are not just for the sake of the neighbor but to fulfill the law. However, that means performing an action that we can count as merit, which contradicts the spirit of love not concerned for its own glory but for the welfare of the neighbor. Jesus himself demonstrated time and again that it is the practice of love that counts, not formally fulfilling the commandments. Love does not boast of its good works; it does them without thinking of its own advantage.

Because love is service, Christians can subordinate themselves. They know that every community needs rules and depends on its members respecting them. For that reason there are ordinances, offices and authorities. The New Testament recognizes the state as a good institution of God and calls for obedience towards it (Rom 13:1f., 1 Pet 2:17). Every church is committed to its national constitution. Social peace is not possible without a basic social consensus. The church itself needs administrative and leadership structures. A Christian is not an anarchist. However, the required obedience is restricted by the higher principle that: "We must obey God rather than any human authority" (Acts 5:29). So a Christian can go into opposition. That will always be the case if the laws are not just. Liberation theology has correctly recognized that sin can take the form of unjust social structures, an insight that cannot be abandoned again. It is part of the church's task to name and denounce abuse. That happened for instance in 1977 at the Lutheran World Federation's Sixth Assembly in Dar es Salaam, Tanzania. The delegates declared that the system of apartheid was incompatible with the Lutheran confession; those who still clung to it

[6] "The Augsburg Confession—Latin Text—Article VI: Obedience," in op. cit. (note 1), 41.

placed themselves outside the community; racism was sin. But there are also other, less dramatic cases of structural criticism. Wherever necessary, the church will press for a change in prevailing laws. For love "does not rejoice in wrongdoings" (1 Cor 13:6). Christians can call for resistance on grounds of conscience. In any case, ministering to suffering people also includes a readiness to take political action.

Martin Luther himself is an impressive example of this. He was by no means an "unpolitical" person. The ills of his age provoked his displeasure and gave occasion for critical positions. The Reformer appealed to those responsible for his age and called for measures to improve social conditions in his "To the Christian Nobility of the German Nation Concerning the Reform of the Christian Estate, 1520."[7] But he spoke up resolutely on other occasions, as well. There is no such thing as a nonpolitical church. As long as Christians live in this world they are part of society, i.e., the polis, and co-responsible for its weal and woe. Certainly, church and state have their respective tasks. While the state is to look after law and peace, the church is entrusted with working for God's will and God's law. Precisely for that reason, the church cannot be indifferent to whether and how the state observes its mandate. It has to raise its admonishing voice and protest if injustice and violence become endemic ills. If ethical questions are up for discussion the church must not be silent. Conversely, the state should be interested in the church properly sowing faith, love and hope, and ensure that they are disseminated among the citizens. It has to guarantee the appropriate infrastructure.

The distinction between church and state means an unmistakable rejection of the idea of theocracy. Jesus himself clearly spoke out on this. We should neither give the emperor what is God's nor vice versa (Mk 12:17). Worldly power has its own law, although it is never released from its responsibility before God. Consequently, Lutheran theology does not want a theocracy but a state based on the rule of law. Theocracy is by its nature authoritarian and basically anti-freedom. It allows only one faith and forbids legitimate diversity. Instead we must expect that society can agree on a legal system that guarantees its members a maximum of freedom, peace and prosperity. Such consensus is also possible with non-Christians. Justice is a generally human postulate and is binding in religious and secular ages. The state based on the rule of law is not a Christian invention and yet it is a project the church must promote.

---

[7] Martin Luther, "To the Christian Nobility of the German Nation Concerning the Reform of the Christian Estate, 1520," in Helmut T. Lehmann (ed.), *Luther's Works*, vol. 44 (Philadelphia: Fortress Press, 1966), 115ff.

Naturally, the church of Jesus Christ must beware of being co-opted by party politics. It would lose its freedom and be incapable of critical distance. While individual Christians cannot avoid making their political choice and voting for a party, the church as an institution is prohibited from doing this. It has to commit all parties equally to promoting the common good and thus to press for them to be publicly accountable for their respective programs. The church should resist the temptation to want to control the state. But it has the duty to remind the state bodies of their responsibilities. That is part of its "political diakonia"' and proof of the freedom given them by God.

Questions

In the global world of the twenty-first century, tolerance is becoming a central condition for peace. Is it right to claim that the gospel ultimately liberates us from intolerance? How far may Christian tolerance go without becoming arbitrariness?

The church should not interfere in political matters. That is a frequent demand. It is grounded in the fact that people say the church has to care for people's salvation and the state for their welfare. Can salvation and welfare be separated so neatly?

Why must we actually talk of God's mercy? Is a humane world not possible without God? Many say that we should abolish religion in order to create peace in the world. What needs to be said in this regard?

The Church and the Public Space. A Lutheran Interpretation

Kjell Nordstokke

The Reformation and the Understanding of Being Church

The core message of the Lutheran Reformation is that justification by faith is the doctrine by which the church stands or falls. This position builds on Luther's reading of the Bible and his interpretation of the ministry of Jesus. It has often been presented as the five so-called *solae* or guiding principles of Lutheran theology: by Scripture alone (*sola scriptura*); by faith alone (*sola fide*); by grace alone (*sola gratia*); through Christ alone (*solo Christo*); and glory to God alone (*soli Deo gloria*).

At first sight these principles make no reference to the church. This may give us the impression that ecclesiology (the theology of the church) was not an important issue for Luther and his followers. This was clearly not the case; the Reformation started as a reaction against the late medieval model of the church and its concentration on economic and political power. According to Luther's view, the consequence of this way of being church was a silencing of the proclamation of the gospel. The church was therefore in great need of being reformed. It is the proclamation of the gospel that forms the church's being and sending into the world, and not the other way round. The church exists and has its mandate by Scripture alone, by faith alone, by grace alone, through Christ alone and to God's glory alone.

The state of the fifteenth-century church was such that many longed for reform. The Pope had become a political leader with his own army; bishops were local rulers and in control of enormous economic resources. The problem, however, was not only how the church exercised its political power. Rather, the Reformers criticized the way in which the Pope and the bishops used religious power in order to legitimize their position as worldly rulers. For instance, they would excommunicate political adversaries and in some cases impose an interdict on a country. This meant that a whole people were denied access to the sacraments and to a Christian funeral. The struggle for political power thus severely impacted ordinary people and their religious life. They feared for their salvation if they could not attend mass and use the sacraments as prescribed by the church authorities. In a similar manner, people adopted practices that the church had established with the purpose of increasing the church's income, such as for instance the selling of indulgences. Having observed how poor people, driven by fear, wasted their money on buying indulgences in order to escape the torments of purgatory, Luther wrote his Ninety-five Theses "on the power and efficacy of indulgences" in 1517. As we know, this was the start of the Reformation. On the one hand its point of departure was a reaction against the church that abused its power to exploit the poor; on the other, it questioned a church that instead of proclaiming the gospel offered believers confidence in a piece of paper that could be bought. Salvation in not an article that can be commodified; salvation is not for sale.

Luther did not only criticize such practices. Motivated by his theological conviction, he radically questioned this model of being church and challenged the political leaders of his time to take back the power that he believed the church to have wrongly usurped. The church's mandate is not to exercise power as a political ruler, he claimed. The "power of the sword," in Luther's words, belongs to those who God has rightly installed as kings and other worldly rulers. All citizens, also the church, should acknowledge their authority in obedience. The church has a different mandate: God has called it to exercise the "power of the word," the public proclamation of gospel in word and deed.

The Word as a powerful public word

This discernment between the power of the sword and power of the Word has led to the formulation of the teaching of the two kingdoms in Lutheran theology and to an intense discussion on how to interpret this teaching in times that politically and socially are very different from the context in which Luther lived.

First, it is important to note that the issue here is discerning, not separating. Luther emphasized that both kingdoms (Luther would rather say governments) are subject to God's will and judgment. All rulers are therefore responsible to God and, as good Christians, they should consider their task as a divine vocation and diligently use Word and sacrament to strengthen them in their duty as governors. This made sense in times when all citizens belonged to the church. Kings and other rulers were expected to be good Christians who regularly attended church and therefore were exposed to the "power of the Word."

Clearly, this doctrine must be applied differently today when in most places the church represents a mere section of society, perhaps only a minority, who are members of or go to a church. In addition, only very few political leaders today would consider their position as having been ordered by God; their mandate and power are regulated according to secular procedures with regard to selecting and performing leadership. How does this challenge the church to contribute to fostering responsible government and a social and political order that corresponds to God's will for creation and for human life?

A second point to be noted when interpreting the doctrine of the two kingdoms relates to another huge difference: the scandalous political and economic power that the church had accumulated at the time. The fact that such abuse of power may have been instrumental in the formulation of this doctrine may have contributed to an interpretation that warned against any mixing of church and politics. This was the position held by many church leaders during the time of Nazism. They claimed that the secular government should act according to its own legislation and should be recognized as the social order established by God and that therefore it needed to be obeyed. In a similar manner, a fair number of people rejected the idea that churches should involve themselves in the struggle against apartheid, maintaining that this was a political question, beyond the mandate of the church. Some would argue that dealing with these kinds of political issues could cause divisions within the church, as if that were a more serious sin than the kind of division apartheid had caused in the South African society.

It is quite clear that the doctrine of the two kingdoms does not foresee a withdrawal from the world. Rather, it urges the church to discern the basis for its public mandate. Today, the church no longer accumulates political and economic power—at least not in most parts of the world. The issue is therefore not so much to warn the church about the risks of striving for "the power of the sword," but rather of withdrawing from the world and limiting its concern to spiritual matters.

Luther did not interpret the "power of the Word" as a withdrawal from the world. On the contrary, he clearly understood it as a public word. According to him, the pulpit was a public arena from which to address the whole community, not only the inner circle of believers. In addition, his words were spread all over Europe thanks to the newly developed methods of printing. We can observe that Luther's concern when preaching and writing was not limited to spiritual matters, but very often related to politics and the economy. He advocated for the establishment of schools for all children, for services for the poor and helpless and severely questioned the practice of usury declaring it unethical. When reading these texts today, his ability to interpret the signs of the time impresses us, especially his courage to address public issues, even if we have to admit that some of his writings were most unfortunate, i.e., his statements about the Jews and his call to stop the rebellious farmers.

The third point requiring our attention is the fact that Luther had confidence in the power of the word. This follows his theological interpretation of the gospel as a living word (*vox viva evangelii*) and the church as a reality created by the word (*creatura verbi*). God created by words, "For he spoke, and it came to be; he commanded, and it stood firm" (Ps 33:9). In a similar manner, the gospel has the power to create what it names. Such power does not depend on political position or the use of arms in order to be effective. Nevertheless, the power of the word is strongly resisted by the "powers and authorities," an expression that not only refers to the worldly rulers, but even more to the power of evil, which according to the Apostle Christ was triumphed over "by the cross" (Col 2:15).

Luther believed God to have called the church to be "a living word" in the world. The proclamation of the Word on the one hand envisages faith in God's care and mercy in our daily life, and confidence in God's lordship and providence in whatever happens to us, as individuals and society. On the other, it calls us to be stewards of the gifts with which God has endowed us, as responsible citizens caring about the well-being of others.

In the following, we shall take a closer look at the ways of being "a living word" in the world. The first perspective will be the individual, how each Christian is called to serve God and the neighbor. This has often been presented as the Lutheran ethics of vocation and is today very much interpreted as a vocation to active citizenship. The next perspective relates to the church as a collective body–especially as a local community–to assume roles in the public arena. We shall present diakonia as one basic task within this mandate of being a public church, with advocacy as a specific focus area of this mandate. Finally, we shall reflect on the role of the church being a sanctuary in today's post-modern world as a new and challenging role, with roots that go back to the first centuries of Christian life and public service.

The vocation to be active citizens

The call to be "a living word" is an exhortation to active citizenship. Luther radically changed the understanding of Christian vocation, shifting the focus from the internal life of the church, to serving in the world—being Christian citizens who love and care for their neighbor. Luther sharply questioned the religious orders of his time and the idealizing of the vocation of monks and nuns who had distanced themselves from normal life and instead lived a secluded life in a monastery, devoted to religious practices. From his own experience, Luther knew that such understanding of vocation would often be self-centered. But, even more important, it would ignore the call to serve the neighbor.

Luther understood Christian vocation from the perspective of being in Christ, and the two basic directions this organic relation brings with it. First, in relation to God, in Christ we are saved from the power of sin and death. By God's grace we are liberated and set free, also from the law and the fear that God will reject us and exclude us from God's love and care. This is one dimension of being in Christ: the adoption to childhood in our relation to God, enjoying with Christ free access to our heavenly Father. There is, however, another dimension of being in Christ: as Christ was sent into the world, so we are sent for the sake of our neighbor. This is the main message in one of Luther's most important writings "The Freedom of a Christian, 1520," with its famous statement: "A Christian is a perfectly free lord of all, subject to none. A Christian is a perfectly dutiful servant of all, subject to all."[1]

The simultaneous relation to God and to our neighbor is fundamental in this understanding, as it is in Jesus' teaching on the greatest commandment of loving God and one's neighbor. Crucial to Luther's understanding is that out of our own strength we are not able to love God nor our neighbor as our vocation claims, but in Christ and empowered by God's Spirit this is not only possible but is what in fact it means to be a Christian. Luther sums up his reflections on the freedom of a Christian as follows:

> We conclude therefore that a Christian lives not in himself, but in Christ and in his neighbor. Otherwise he is not a Christian. He lives in Christ through faith, in his neighbor through love. By faith he is caught up beyond himself into God. By love he descends beneath himself into his neighbor. Yet he always remains in God and in his love [...].[2]

Luther expressed this view on being a citizen according to the way in which society was conceptualized at his time. It implied that every citizen should be faithful to their social role, as farmer, tailor or merchant, without any ambition of changing the way in which society was structured. If Luther would

[1] Martin Luther, "The Freedom of a Christian, 1520," in Helmut T. Lehmann (ed.), *Luther's Works*, vol. 31 (Philadelphia: Muhlenberg Press, 1957), 344.
[2] Ibid., 370.

have spoken about active citizenship it would have been within the confines of respecting what he would have considered to be the natural order of society and there finding opportunities for serving one's neighbor. Furthermore, he would hardly see any role for women outside the home. Nevertheless, what is new and radical is his positive evaluation of ordinary work—both in- and outside the home. Honest and faithful work is true service, more than observing religious practices. Sowing and harvesting the fields, building houses for people to live in, producing clothes and preparing food for hungry people—from the perspective of the Christian vocation all such activities are dignified and considered ways of serving God and of serving the neighbor.

This remains an important reminder to us today. Our life as Christians is not limited to what we do on Sundays and to how we relate to spiritual matters. Much more, it relates to how we live our lives throughout the week, and not least the way in which we perform our daily tasks, as caring family members, honest professionals in our work and responsible members of the wider community. At a time when work is conceived as a way of earning as much as possible the Lutheran ethics of vocation can orient us so that we see work in accordance with the perspective of serving God and our neighbor, and of promoting justice and well-being. In times when our lifestyles threaten the ecological balance this challenge gains a new dimension. Indeed, the concept of Christian vocation continues to be relevant and deserves to be lifted up as a core component of the Lutheran heritage, and it can help us to develop our understanding of active citizenship.

THE "LIVING WORD" AS DIACONAL ACTION

For Luther the "living word" referred in the first place to the preached word, and mainly from the pulpit. This does not, however, imply that he limited the understanding of "word" to what is orally expressed and can be registered by human ears. As a biblical scholar, Luther was well acquainted with the biblical concepts of "word" (Hebrew: *dabar;* and Greek: *logos*) that both express a living reality. Most notably this is articulated in the message of the incarnated Word, as reads 1 John 1:1: "We declare to you what was from the beginning, what we have heard, what we have seen with our eyes, what we have looked at and touched with our hands, concerning the word of life." In a unique way, Jesus not only announced the gospel; he himself incarnated the gospel. His ministry as the word of life encompassed both teaching and care for people in need. It would make no sense to separate between his words and deeds; they are an integral part of his mission.

The concept of Christian vocation referred to above can be interpreted as mission, following the example of Jesus. To be in Christ means to be sent as he was sent, and to serve in word and deed as Jesus did: "Whoever serves me must follow me, and where I am, there will my servant be also" (Jn 12:26). The Greek verb used for "serve" in this verse, is "*diakonein.*" Here it refers to the service of the disciples; on another occasion, Jesus uses it in order to explain the distinct meaning of his mission: "For the Son of Man came not to be served but to serve, and to give his life a ransom for many" (Mk 10:45).

When the New Testament was translated into Latin, the Greek word *diakonia* was rendered as *ministerium* and, later, as ministry in English. This indicates that diakonia basically means to be sent, to receive a mission, a task, or a vocation. The one who sends determines the content of the mission; which is expressed in the saying of Jesus: "Jesus said to them again, 'As the Father has sent me, so I send you' " (Jn 20:21). In other words, as disciples of Jesus Christ the diakonia of the church is to follow the example he gave in words and deeds.

Against this background, the concept of diakonia is widely used in churches today. In its *Plan for Diakonia* the Church of Norway defines diakonia as

> the caring ministry of the Church. It is the Gospel in action and is expressed through loving your neighbor, creating inclusive communities, caring for creation and struggling for justice.[3]

This definition clearly states that diakonia is more than a possible consequence of the gospel, as an optional activity when considered necessary because of external challenges. Diakonia is an integral part of the gospel. It is imperative to make God's living and liberating word visible in action and, as such, an integral part of what the church as the body of Christ is called to be and to do in God's name. Not by our own understanding or effort, as Luther states in the "Small Catechism"; "[...] but instead the Holy Spirit has called me through the gospel, enlightened me with his gifts, made me holy and kept me in the true faith, just as he calls, gathers, enlightens, and makes holy the whole Christian church on earth [...]."[4]

It is clear that Luther was not familiar with this way of understanding the concept of diakonia. He knew deacons who according to Roman Catholic tradition would later be ordained as priests, and mainly had liturgical tasks. Luther saw no reason for maintaining this tradition and soon the title of deacon disappeared in the churches of the Reformation. On one occasion, Luther wrote that the congregations very much needed real deacons that could care for the sick and the poor, but this never became a priority at

---

[3] **www.gammel.kirken.no/?event=dolink&famID=247**

[4] Martin Luther, "The Small Catechism," in Robert Kolb and Timothy J. Wengert (eds), *The Book of Concord. The Confessions of the Evangelical Lutheran Church* (Minneapolis: Fortress Press, 2000), 355.

his time. The pure proclamation of the gospel and a right administration of the sacraments remained the most urgent tasks.

This urgency made Luther appeal to the public authorities in matters of social care. They should establish services, for instance community chests, with the purpose of helping the poor, or providing homes for orphans. Luther considered it most efficient to impose these tasks on the worldly authorities, having in mind that all citizens then belonged to the church, and could therefore be expected to perform such services as good Christians. Without any doubt, this practice has strongly influenced the understanding of responsible political leadership in the countries that adopted the Reformation, and led to the development of public welfare services in these countries.

Nonetheless, it has also resulted in decreasing diaconal consciousness and practice in many churches. One may ask if the focus on Word and sacraments has engendered the development of a kind of pastor-centrism within Lutheranism, which has portrayed the congregation as passive receivers of Word and sacrament, rather than a living community endowed with gifts and ministries. Luther did not subscribe to the kind of ecclesiology that reduced the laity to objects of church services. On the contrary, his teaching on the "priesthood of all believers" claimed that all baptized were empowered to be "priests" in the sense of having access to God and being included in God's mission to the world. In that sense, it gives meaning to interpret "the priesthood of all believers" as the diakonia of all baptized.

In today's social and religious contexts, the model of "outsourcing" the diaconal mandate to public authorities is no longer viable, neither from a theological nor sociopolitical point of view. In a secularized society, the church cannot count on political leaders when it comes to the task of realizing its diaconal ministry. The church must organize its diaconal work–locally at the congregational level or by established organizations or specialized ministries that can operate nationally and internationally.

As the caring ministry of the church, diakonia may have many areas of action. The above mentioned plan of Church of Norway indicates four areas: loving one's neighbor; creating inclusive communities; caring for creation; and struggling for justice. They indicate the importance of lifting up these issues on the church's agenda in the form of initiatives rooted in the life of the congregation, such as visiting the sick and receiving people in challenging life situations, but also, whenever possible, establishing services for instance within the areas of health care or social welfare. In some instances, such services are organized in partnership with public offices or with other agents within civil society. This affirms that diaconal action envisages general well-being and the promotion of human dignity, justice and peace.

Diaconal action is both faith- and rights-based. It holds together our distinct identity as a caring and inclusive communion and our shared vocation to promote human dignity, justice and peace in the world. As we have seen, diakonia links to a theological interpretation of the gospel and of being church while affirming the vision of a public church and assuming the vocation to contribute to the well-being of society. This reflects the vision of embarking on a pilgrimage of justice and peace that the World Council of Churches formulated at its 2013 Assembly in Busan. Moreover, it is in line with the LWF booklet *Diakonia in Context* that points at transformation, reconciliation and empowerment as the basic directions of diaconal action.

Many churches, including those belonging to the Lutheran communion, are in the process of renewing their reflection on what it means to be church today and on how to understand and practice "the power of word." At Luther's time, the concept of vocation mainly referred to individual Christians and their service in the world. Today, we recognize the necessity of addressing the congregation as a whole and its communitarian call to serve and to be a visible "living word" in the world. Without any doubt, this is in line with the vision of *ecclesia semper reformanda,* of reformation as the continued self-questioning and renewal of the church.

Advocacy

The publication of the Ninety-five Theses in 1517 can be interpreted from the perspective of advocacy. As a pastor in Wittenberg, Luther had observed how people wasted their money on indulgences. His theses represent a vehement critique of the abuse of religious power that exploited ordinary people and manipulated their faith. At the same time, it sought to defend the dignity of the believer and their right to hear the Word of God freely.

There is a clear link from this historical moment of the Reformation to situations in today's world that challenge the churches to speak out against similar abuses of power, be they religious or political. Advocacy, the public voice of church in defense of victims of injustice, is an integral element of the church's mission for the healing of world, as reported in the LWF document *Mission in Context*:

> Mission as advocacy for justice denotes the church's praxis in the public arena as affirmation and reaffirmation of the dignity of human life, both as individual and as community, as well as a widened sense of justice, encompassing the economic, social and ecological spheres.[5]

[5] At **http://www.lutheranworld.org/sites/default/files/DMD-Mission-in-Context-EN-low.pdf**

Advocacy is different from lobbying that seeks to influence governments or other leaders for the benefit for one's own organization or interest. Advocacy is concerned with the situation of others, in the first place marginalized groups in church and society: those who are unable to defend their own interests, or for different reasons are silenced in society. This does not mean that advocacy is speaking for others, ignoring the voice of those it seeks to defend. On the contrary, advocacy presupposes listening and solidarity. A good example is the voice that many churches have given to people affected by the HIV and AIDS pandemic. From the day that the church gave space to people living with HIV and AIDS, to their stories and struggle for justice, its advocacy role grew in importance.

Advocacy can be seen as an expression of the prophetic ministry of the church. This ministry is largely modeled by the Old Testament prophets who criticized the religious and political leaders of their time, especially for the way in which they ignored their duty to protect the rights of the poor. Jesus' ministry also manifests his prophetic role—above all in the way in which he defended the dignity of marginalized people of his time, liberating them from bonds of stigmatization and shame, and including them in the new society that his disciples represented. The narrative of the healing of the man born blind in John 9 illustrates this dimension of Jesus' diaconal ministry.

As followers of Jesus the church is called to have a prophetic voice. This is how many heard the churches when they declared apartheid to be a heresy. However, not all churches raised their voice against apartheid. Within the Lutheran family of churches, some considered apartheid to be a political issue, which according to their interpretation of the two kingdoms belonged to the authority of secular powers. After apartheid had been dismantled, a number of churches admitted that they had failed to take sides in this conflict, or that they had wrongly supported the racist government. This leads one to reflect on why it is easier to confess sins committed in the past than to respond to the social and political challenges of the present. One reason is that churches, as well as their members, are constantly tempted to remain within their comfort zones and to stick to interpretations of the gospel that leave us in peace.

From this perspective advocacy also plays a role in keeping the church alert and able to read the signs of the times. Advocacy is frequently related to resisting the power of the mighty and their ideologies. In certain cases it may be a task also to address the church establishment in order to question how we are being "conformed to this world" (Rom 12:2) when dealing with burning issues of our time. Is it fair to say that the church has sometimes imitated structures of domination and exclusion? Has the church adopted a lifestyle of religious consumerism and ethical indifference instead of being profoundly provoked by the signs of growing poverty and injustice in the world?

Conformism is not in line with the Lutheran heritage. On the contrary, it subscribes to the principle of *reformatio continua*, or the need of constant reformation in the life and mission of the church.

Sanctuary

Luther's hymn "A Mighty Fortress is Our God" continues to be one of the most frequently sung hymns in the churches of the Reformation—not only by Lutherans. Based on Psalm 46 it expresses confidence in God's care and protection against all forms of evil. God provides sanctuary, a safe haven.

Throughout history, the church has interpreted this biblical message as an imperative to act likewise and to offer sanctuary to people in need. Asylum was given to refugees and also to helpless and homeless persons. The first hospitals were established within this tradition of practicing Christian hospitality. The Reformation was followed by decades of religious conflict that forced many to leave their homes. Among the Protestant refugees, many found asylum in Wittenberg, Strasbourg and Geneva. In many ways this has impacted the commitment of Christians, even today, for instance in supporting humanitarian assistance for refugees and in advocating for religious freedom.

The call to offer sanctuary may take different forms. Two recent examples from Norway illustrate this:

The first relates to the situation in 1993 when hundreds of asylum seekers from the former Yugoslavia had their application for permanent residency rejected and were told to leave Norway. Many then sought refuge in church buildings, and because the government acknowledged this space as sacred, the asylum seekers were not arrested by the police. Some stayed there for months, even years, and many had their cases reconsidered and were in fact granted asylum by the government. Others voluntarily returned to their country of origin. It is interesting to note that the secular government respected the sanctuary, although the same authorities criticized the church for promoting civil disobedience and for undermining legal procedures. It should also be mentioned that many ordinary people were mobilized in an effort to assist the asylum seekers in the churches by providing food, clothes and not least friendship.

The other is related to the terrorist attack in July 2011 when seventy-seven persons were killed in Oslo and on the island Utøya. In the days that followed, many churches, especially the Cathedral in Oslo, were filled with people. Some brought flowers, others lit a candle, and there were those who simply sat down in silence. Not many of them were active Christians, some were Muslims, and some said they had never been inside a church before. Clearly they were searching for a sanctuary, a holy space, where they could express their grief, anger and their terrified awareness of being vulnerable. Secular and post-modern society does not offer a similar space, and even secular persons sensed the importance of it.

Offering sanctuary does not mean absolute safety from the forces of evil. All 600 that had sought refuge in St Peter Lutheran Church in Monrovia, Liberia, on the night of 29 July 1990, were killed by rebels. Perhaps they had sung "A Mighty Fortress is Our God" as they were gathering in the church that evening, just as Luther and his friend had as they were entering the city of Worms on 16 April 1521 where the Diet had been summoned.

Sanctuary does not mean invulnerability, but care and solidarity; it does not promise unconditional happiness, but eternal blessing. "The Lord of hosts is with us; the God of Jacob is our refuge. (Selah)" (Ps 46:7), and, as Luther sings, "For God himself fights by our side with weapons of the Spirit. Were they to take our house, goods, honor, child, or spouse, though life be wrenched away, they cannot win the day. The kingdom's ours forever!"[6]

Public church

As we have seen, Lutheranism firmly situates the church in the public space. It is there where the Word is announced and practiced as a living and a visible word. This is in accordance with how Jesus refers to his public ministry: "'I have spoken openly to the world; I have always taught in synagogues and in the temple, where all the Jews come together. I have said nothing in secret'" (Jn 18:20). Similarly healings were performed openly, in the context of everyday life.

There are different ways of arguing for the public church and, consequently, different models of being a public church. One may be described as church-centered; it promotes Christian knowledge and values with the aim of Christianizing public space. As a strategy, it may also aim at recruiting new members to the church.

Another model may be presented as the universal; its point of departure is society and people's general welfare. The concept of civil society has added new facets to understanding this model, as it opens space to different actors, also churches, with the task of contributing to what is right, good and true for all citizens. In addition, this space offers a new opportunity for ecumenical and interfaith cooperation in an effort to construct a just and peaceful society.

[6] See Luther's choral *A Mighty Fortress is Our God*, verse 4.

There are strong traits within Lutheranism that point in direction of the second model. The teaching of the ethics of vocation as call to active citizenship points in that direction. The same applies to the understanding of diakonia as service in the public space, as well as the task of advocacy and of providing sanctuary. It is all about loving one's neighbor.

Consequently, Lutheranism emphasizes the theology of creation, as a result of which we may regard the public space as an arena of God's continued action in a way that calls all humans to participate in God's mission of promoting human dignity, justice and peace. Equally, it is strongly influenced by the theology of salvation, of Christ incarnated in the middle of ordinary human life; and last, but not least, it is nurtured by the theology of sanctification that announced that God's Spirit equips and empowers all baptized to love one's neighbor.

All three underpin the view that public vocation of the church envisages: transformation, reconciliation and empowerment, in a way that promotes human dignity and contributes to the construction of a just, participatory and sustainable society. At the same time, some will interpret the acts of this vocation as signs of God's love and gracious care and thank God for them and, eventually, when moved by God's Spirit, seek ways of growing in faith, hope and love.

Questions

How is active citizenship understood and practiced where you live? What are the challenges? In what way could the Lutheran ethics of vocation be activated in order to strengthen the concept of active citizenship? How could this topic become more integrated in teaching and preaching?

What kind of diaconal work is your church and local congregation involved in? How does this work express the theme of the Reformation Anniversary, "Liberated by God's Grace"? Do you agree with the statement that diakonia in an integral dimension of the church, its being and its mission?

Is the concept advocacy known and used in your context? Give examples of how your church/congregation is involved in advocacy, and discuss how this ministry can be strengthened. The LWF commemoration of the Reformation states that salvation, human beings and creation are not for sale. How can these statements motivate us to be more conscious of our role as public churches?

The Liberating Word of God. Reflections on the Lutheran Understanding of Holy Scripture

Hans-Peter Grosshans

God speaks to people and addresses them. This does not, however, go without saying. We ourselves do not speak just to anybody. Whenever we speak to others, we begin and maintain a relationship with them, and when we communicate with others, we always express our own selves in addition to any information being conveyed. Communicating ourselves, moreover, also entails revealing ourselves and we are therefore often cautious as to whom we address and what we communicate to them. We might wish to reveal ourselves only to a small extent and by no means entirely and do not wish to reveal ourselves to just anybody, nor to allow everyone to peer into our souls, minds, our lives. When God communicates with people, God expresses, reveals and thus shares Godself with them. It is indeed marvelous that we speak to one another and reveal ourselves to each other in conversation, offering a mutual glimpse into our souls, minds and lives. It is a great thing that God also reveals Godself to us when speaking to us, communicating with us, and allowing us to be in communion with God. So God is bound to God's Word; God is committed to it. Once God says something, God holds fast to it. God is precisely the one who comes close to human beings and reveals Godself to people in God's Word that is addressed to them.

It is particularly notable that God's words are first and foremost a promise. It appertains to God's divinity that God keeps promises. We therefore read that the "word of our God will stand forever" (Isa 40:8; 1 Pet 1:25). Thus, God is not only revealed through God's words but also committed to these words, saying: "I promise this to you!" This is why God's Word is emphasized in the Christian faith. God's Word forever establishes a reliable and everlasting promise to God's beloved creatures to be their God.

In all this it remains certain that God's Word comes from God. God is the true and original source of all the words through which God is committed to us. God is the source of everything that God has revealed to us, of all we know and can expect of God.

God did not only communicate, reveal and commit Godself in words, but also in creation, the history of Israel and the life and works of Jesus Christ. We no longer have direct access to any of these events, but can only encounter them indirectly as mediated by the written word. This is not, however, a matter of chance. It is not that these events represent God's actual communication with people and that the texts just happen to complement God's eventful presence here, so that we might also be able to dispense with them. It is all the more significant then that God's works are recorded and witnessed in words and texts with regard to the creation and the history of Israel as well as God's presence in Jesus Christ. God chose to be revealed in words and texts. It is through these words and texts that God communicates and is revealed.

Texts are therefore the central medium for our relationship with God. This makes Christianity a scriptural religion. The events that reveal God are witnessed in the texts of Holy Scripture (creation, the history of Israel, Jesus Christ, the church) and hence the revelation of God as it is articulated in those events.

The interest of Protestant Christians is of course focused on "God's Word." Faith centers on the living communication between each Christian and the community of Christians with the Triune God. This living communication between God and people is also served by Holy Scripture, which can also be treated like a normal book or a historical religious text. But, what matters for Christians is to read, interpret and understand Holy Scripture in such a way that it unfolds its potential to be the Word of God, speaking to us. Implied by God's words, through which God speaks and promises Godself to people, is their expression in Holy Scripture. God wishes to reveal Godself in God's words preserved in Scripture, and wants people to remind God of God's promise.

As we focus on Holy Scripture in the following, we will need to bear in mind the close connection between Holy Scripture and God's Word, involving God's living and salvific communication with people.

By Scripture Alone (sola scriptura)

The original area of interest

The Holy Scripture was emphasized particularly strongly by Protestant theologians of the Reformation for various reasons, even though the center of interest of Protestant Christians lay more in the "Word of God" than in Holy Scripture. This principle of "by Scripture alone," as expressed through the Latin phrase *sola scriptura*, was established in the sixteenth-century Reformation.

In his 1520 writing *Assertio omnium articulorum Martini Lutheri per bullam Leonis X. novissimam damnatorum* ("Assertion of all of Martin Luther's Articles Condemned by Leo X's Most Recent Bull"), Luther summarized his various thoughts on this principle in theology and the church:

> The primary principles of Christians should thus not be anything other than the divine words; the words of men should however be conclusions derived thereof, which must then be traced back to and held up to them.[1]

These divine words are to be found only in Holy Scripture. In his response to the papal bull condemning him, Luther insisted that one read and study the Bible as had been the case in the early church, when one could not refer to any interpretations of theological and church authorities, or as Luther put it, had not yet read either Augustine or Thomas. Luther indeed asked:

> Why do Augustine and the Holy Fathers, in their disputations and teachings, refer back to Holy Scripture as the primary principles of truth, and use their light and power to enlighten and strengthen their own darkness and weakness? Through this example they indeed teach that the divine words are more certain and clear than those of all men, even their own words, so that the words of men need be corrected, proven, completed and strengthened by Scripture and not these by the words of men. [...] How godlessly perverse are we indeed that we should wish not to learn Holy Scripture learnt through itself and its own spirit but instead through the words of men, in contrast to all the Fathers?[2]

By emphasizing Holy Scripture, Martin Luther was not leveling criticism along the lines that Holy Scripture had not been used and interpreted in previous centuries. Luther himself had worked intensively with biblical

[1] Martin Luther, "Assertio omnium articulorum M. Lutheri per bullam Leonis X. novissimam damnatorum. 1520," in *WA* 7, 98 (91–151). The Latin text reads: "Sint ergo Christianorum prima principia non nisi verba divina, omnium autem hominum verba conclusiones hinc eductae et rursus illuc reducendae et probandae." Latin or German texts of Luther are translated by the author there where no English translation is available. Luther has written four works to defend the propositions condemned in the papal bull in 1520. One of these works is translated into English, see Martin Luther, "Defense and Explanation of all the Articles, 1521," in Helmut T. Lehmann (ed.), *Luther's Works*, vol. 32 (Philadelphia: Muhlenberg Press, 1958), 7–99.

[2] Martin Luther, "Assertio omnium articulorum," ibid., 98.

texts in his exegetic lectures from the beginning of his teaching activity. Luther, moreover, shared this intensive occupation with Holy Scripture with many theologians of the centuries before him, just as he shared his appreciation of Holy Scripture with the church as a whole. The point of Luther's response to the papal bull lay more in his not wishing to base his reading and interpretation of Holy Scripture on the history of its reception within the church. Luther set Holy Scripture and its contemporary reading and interpretation against the church doctrine and practice based on this centuries-long reception history. Luther, by contrast, taught more of a "consequent exegesis"[3]—to use a term coined by Eberhard Jüngel.

The fact that Martin Luther and other Reformation theologians wished and were able to interpret Holy Scripture not only in a manner that built on previous interpretation and reception history within the church, but also in opposition to them, came as the result of very specific problems and areas of conflict. In the process, a methodology was established for dealing with controversial topics in the doctrine and practice of the church.

This can be illustrated with the following well-known example: In the papal bull *Exsurge Domine*, Luther's views are denounced as erroneous that "the Roman Pontiff, the successor of Peter, is not the vicar of Christ over all the churches of the entire world, instituted by Christ Himself in blessed Peter."[4] How is one to decide on the claim of the Bishop of Rome to lead the church and the reasons behind it? The claim of the Bishop of Rome to lead all of Christendom can be founded on purely historical terms: it developed that way historically—at least within the territory of the former Western Roman Empire. Yet, the condemnation of Luther's doctrine on this topic makes it clear that the Roman Catholic theologians and the Pope did not seek such a historical explanation, but instead a theological one founded on the claim of the Bishop of Rome to universal authority having been established by Christ. According to Luther, however, this justification of the universal headship of the Bishop of Rome is not evidenced in any direct reading of Holy Scripture. In light of the historical developments it is therefore clear that Roman Catholic theologians sought to legitimize the Bishop of Rome's claim to authority through the interpretation of biblical texts. Retrospectively, we can also add that the Bishop of Rome's claim to

[3] With his programmatic term consequent exegesis, Eberhard Jüngel characterized both the theology of Karl Barth and Rudolf Bultmann; cf. Eberhard Jüngel, "Die Freiheit der Theologie," in *Entsprechungen: Gott-Wahrheit-Mensch,* Theologische Erörterungen II (Tübingen: Mohr Siebeck, 32002), 11–36, here 19.

[4] Condemning the Errors of Martin Luther—Exsurge Domine. Bull of Pope Leo X issued June 15, 1520, at **www.papalencyclicals.net/Leo10/l10exdom.htm**

universal primacy was historically only possible by ignoring all of the Eastern churches that had emerged outside of the Western Roman Empire.

Luther's return to direct access to the Holy Scripture had a purifying effect that continues today: the Holy Scriptures could not and still cannot be used to justify anything and everything that has developed and established itself in the doctrine and practice of the church over the centuries—just as the view that the church departed too far from the gospel was founded on the Reformation's return to the Holy Scriptures: too much of what was supposedly "good" could lead to the churches being disloyal to Jesus Christ, their head.

With no substantive biblical justification, the question arises as to why such church doctrine and practice should continue to be maintained; or whether an alternative could be imagined that is better suited to Holy Scripture. The next question is whether one should not simply seek the most pragmatic solution to the problem within the current context which can be reconciled with the principles of God's Word.

Enough problems arise within the context of the churches for which there are no solutions in Holy Scripture. Solutions, then, need to be found that are conceived with God's Word in mind. These are, nevertheless, merely human solutions involving church doctrine and practice within a particular time and limited context.

Our example illustrates that the Protestant principle of *sola scriptura* is a church process used to address specific matters and problems that arise in church doctrine and practice. With its exclusive *sola*, it seeks solutions to problems that are chiefly or solely based on tradition and the interpretation and reception history of Holy Scripture and thus not on Scripture itself.

Martin Luther himself grappled with the standard objections, which were and continue to be raised, to this exclusive role of Holy Scripture to address issues and problems in church doctrine and practice.

Objections to sola scriptura

A number of objections have been sustained and questions posed regarding the Protestant scriptural principle during Martin Luther's lifetime. Three of these will be discussed here.

First, wherefrom does the Holy Scripture derive its authority and who can vouch for its truth if not the church, which formed the biblical texts into a canon, thereby authenticating the authority of Holy Scripture itself? How can Holy Scripture be set in opposition to church tradition when it is itself part of that tradition?

Luther raised the postulate of *autopisty* or the self-authentication of Holy Scripture, which stipulates that Holy Scripture has no other guarantors of its own authority than itself. The Second Epistle to Timothy attempts to support this with its explanation of the text's inspiration (2 Tim 3:16). In Luther's view, Holy Scripture does not derive its authority from such an internal claim, but by dint of its content, which can be summarized in Jesus Christ. The truth claims connected with Jesus Christ thus represent the authority that vouches for Holy Scripture. Nothing and nobody else can authorize Holy Scripture and its main areas of content. "The Gospel is not believed because the church confirms it, but because one senses that it is God's Word."[5] Holy Scripture is not authoritative and reliable for the faithful, because the church, as a community of people with knowledge of the truth, compiled and united the biblical texts into a Holy Scripture. Luther believed the relationship between Holy Scripture and the church to be precisely the other way around. It was not the church that granted authority to Holy Scripture, but Holy Scripture which lent authority to the church. The church derives its authority from Holy Scripture because it is the place and institution in which the truth of Holy Scripture is heard and able to unfold.

Second, are there not so many unclear areas in Holy Scripture that there can never be a reasonable interpretation of biblical texts without the binding interpretative decisions of the church?

Luther assumed that the self-authentication of Holy Scripture corresponded to the principle that Holy Scripture interprets itself. In his response to the papal bull, he wrote that Holy Scripture is "in and of itself most certain, most comprehensible, most manifest, its own interpreter."[6] Luther posited that the interpretation of biblical texts was not difficult as

---

[5] Martin Luther, "De potestate leges ferendi in ecclesia, 1530," in *WA* 30/II, 687 (677-690); in the original Latin: "Non enim ideo creditur, quia Ecclesia approbat, Sed quia verbum Dei esse sentitur."

[6] Martin Luther, "Assertio omnium articulorum, 1520," in *WA* 7, 97 (91-151). This view follows on Luther's understanding that each book is to be interpreted in light of the author's spirit. "Scripture is its own light. It is good when Scripture interprets itself" (Martin Luther, "Predigt am Jakobstage. 25. Juli 1522," in *WA* 10/III, 238 [235-241]). Luther supported this principle in opposition to all views that ascribe the authority of correct interpretation to individual people and church officials, whether on the basis of the charisma of office or extraordinary talent. Luther also emphasized the significance of the Holy Spirit in the interpretation of Scripture. The spirit, in which people are able to interpret Holy Scripture, thus does not have a different origin than Scripture itself. This is also the reason why Luther was suspicious of any allegorical, figurative interpretation of biblical texts, and instead emphasized that they were to be interpreted in a literal sense.

Holy Scripture was so clear within itself and always had a straightforward meaning,[7] which emerged from its primary subject, Jesus Christ.

Third, if Holy Scripture is easy to understand, would not everyone have to be easily persuaded of its veracity?

Luther was of course aware that many understood the biblical texts poorly, superficially, or just plain wrongly, and that many people would not even come to acknowledge the truth of the biblical texts. Luther therefore distinguished between the external and internal clarity of Scripture. One had to distinguish the external clarity of Holy Scripture, which was plain to see—especially for those who could read the original biblical languages—from the clarity "in the heart," which emerges when people hear, understand and recognize what God claims and promises in these texts. Martin Luther did this in his 1525 "On the Bondage of the Will" with the words:

> To put it briefly, there are two kinds of clarity in Scripture, just as there are also two kinds of obscurity: one external and pertaining to the ministry of the Word, the other located in the understanding of the heart. If you speak of internal clarity, no man perceives one iota of what is in the Scriptures unless he has the Spirit of God. All men have a darkened heart, so that even if they can recite everything in Scripture, and know how to quote it, yet they apprehend and truly understand nothing of it. [...] For the Spirit is required for the understanding of Scripture, both as a whole and in any part of it. If, on the other hand, you speak of the external clarity, nothing at all is left obscure or ambiguous.[8]

Here Luther spoke out against the viewpoint of Erasmus of Rotterdam, a prominent scholar of the time, that Scripture contained obscure and unclear passages that required interpretation by church authorities or in accordance with the church's interpretative tradition. Luther proposed, on the contrary, a distinction between the internal clarity (or obscurity) of the message of the biblical texts, anchored in the understanding of the human heart, in contrast with external clarity (or obscurity) in terms of the intellectual understanding of the symbols and meanings within the texts. If one reads biblical texts with an open mind, it follows that human reason will not find anything obscure or ambiguous although the message of the text can remain obscure and unclear to the heart of an individual person.

For Luther, Holy Scripture had a central position when it came to recognizing God, but also for the life, doctrine and practice of the church. He

[7] Cf. Martin Luther, "Ad librum eximii Magistri Nostri Magistri Ambrosii Catharini, defensoris Silvestri Prieratis acerrimi, responsio, 1521," in *WA* 7, 711, 5f. (698-778).
[8] Martin Luther, "On the Bondage of the Will, 1525", in Helmut T. Lehmann (ed.), *Luther's Works*, vol. 33 (Philadelphia: Fortress Press, 1972), 28.

presented theoretical arguments for this and practiced it in the development of his doctrine using biblical texts. Luther's theology was founded on taking the biblical message seriously in a radical and unconditional manner, inasmuch as they had as their content Christ and the gospel founded in him. For Luther, these messages of Holy Scripture had an unconditional validity and supplanted the empirical experience of people, their intellectual and philosophical convictions and their traditions.

The Protestant scriptural principle

In order to understand the principle of *sola scriptura* we need to go beyond Luther to look into its further development in post-Reformation Protestant theology as well. In post-Reformation "early Protestant orthodoxy," Holy Scripture would become the principle behind theology and thus also the decision-making processes of the church with regard to doctrine and practice, in the Aristotelian sense of the first principle—the primary source of the knowledge of anything. Holy Scripture is then seen as the foundational underpinning of theological and ecclesiastical knowledge. Holy Scripture thereby became the sole principle and criterion in Protestant theology, which is ultimately concerned with spiritual salvation and people's liberation from sin and death.

Johann Friedrich König (1619–1664), for example, phrased it in his standard textbook of his era: "That which Holy Scripture teaches is the sole source of knowledge, from which all theology ultimately needs to be derived, and to which all returns or is resolved in the end."[9] This citation clarifies a number of things. Holy Scripture is indeed a source in a number of respects. First, Holy Scripture is the source of understanding. In connection with Holy Scripture and God's Word, however, this never refers to the expansion of knowledge alone. If one is not to live on bread alone but by every word that comes from the mouth of God (Deut 8:3; Mt 4:4), this implies an understanding of God's Word that is termed life in a biblical sense, i.e., an existence from and for God. Holy Scripture is thus a source both of understanding and life. Holy Scripture is indeed the source of life for the church, if we are to understand the Christian church and the community of believers who exist from God and for God, and who therefore indeed live—in the biblical sense. Those who would obscure or even hinder this source of understanding would thus also misunderstand the church's

[9] Johann Friedrich König, *Theologia positiva acroamatica*, Rostock 1664, ed. and transl. Andreas Stegmann (Tübingen: Mohr Siebeck, 2006), § 46 (author's own translation).

source of life and would cause it to dry up; and those who would go as far as to bring alien waters into it, would bring about its very ruination.

We need to specify further what is meant by source here. The connotation of an effervescent source could lead to the naïve idea that the Bible already contains passages on church doctrine and practice. Theology would then only have to take these passages from the source, place them in order and systematically evaluate their dogmatic, ethical and practical use for the church. We can see that the theologians of post-Reformation early Protestant orthodoxy were well aware of this problem, as reflected in the König's quote, when he speaks of Christian doctrine, once derived from Holy Scripture, needing to be retraced to it in the end. Holy Scripture as a source of understanding thus acts to serve Holy Scripture as a source of life.

With regard to Holy Scripture the image of a source has yet a further dimension that first came into focus in later centuries. Holy Scripture is indeed also a source for historical awareness. As Gerhard Ebeling put it,

> in the historical sense, the source challenges us not merely to receive what it provides us with but to wring information out of it regarding its own origins. [...] In the historical treatment of sources suspicion, to a certain degree, looms large that the source is deceptive, or at least possibly silent, with regard to what one wishes to obtain from it historically. One makes use of a source [...] because one seeks information with regard to the historical reality behind the text and from which the text derives.[10]

Holy Scripture can thus be used today as a source of understanding and life with regard to theology and the church only when one engages with historical-critical knowledge. This in no way casts doubt on the truth and authority of Holy Scripture. On the contrary, the historical-critical interpretation of the Bible verifies the truth and authority of Holy Scripture. One can place much greater trust in what the historical-critical method is able to interpret as truth from the Bible as an original source, as it stands up to the methodologically required suspicion of historical knowledge instead of running away from it.

Holy Scripture is a principle of theology and hence of all church doctrine and practice as well as a source and origin in at least a threefold sense: it is a source of knowledge (with regard to church doctrine and practice), source of life and a historical source. Similarly, the church and theologians need to distinguish among the Bible, Holy Scripture and God's Word. Each indicates a different use of the same textual body and a different expectation of the

[10] Gerhard Ebeling, *Dogmatik des christlichen Glaubens*, vol. 1 (Tübingen: Mohr Siebeck, 2012), 39 (author's own translation).

texts. As the Bible, the texts are a religious book and a historical source. As Holy Scripture, in the usage of the church, the Bible is the source and principle of understanding of its doctrine and practice. As God's Word, the biblical texts are the means through which God expresses Godself to people and hence communicates life and salvation (as a source of life). Only God's Word can grant life and salvation in that it, as the law, confronts people with God's requirements for a true and perfect life, and in that it, as the gospel, invites all the burdened and downtrodden to find relief in Jesus Christ, while consoling all people with the reliable promise that they, as God's children, will have a firm place at the table of their father in heaven.

The 1577 "Formula of Concord" thus not only had Holy Scripture as its source, but also declared it to be the norm for all church doctrine, i.e., the standard for all doctrine of Christian truth and for every life in the truth of the Christian faith. The Formula of Concord states:

> We believe, teach, and confess that the only rule and guiding principle according to which all teachings and preachers are to be evaluated and judged are the prophetic writings of the Old and New Testaments alone [...].[11]

It is then explained that other writings of ancient or modern teachers should not be regarded as equal to Holy Scripture but need to be placed in a subsidiary role. This applied of course to the Reformers themselves. These other writings were instead to be viewed as "witnesses." The "Formula of Concord" expressly accentuates that the Protestant churches were to recognize the creeds of the early church (Apostles' Creed, Nicene Creed, Athanasian Creed), as the authentic and authoritative expressions of Christian faith, alongside the "Augsburg Confession" together with its "Apology," the "Smalcald Articles," and Luther's Small and Large Catechisms. It does however also emphasize that these creedal texts "are not judges, as is Holy Scriptures, but only witnesses and expressions of faith,"[12] and "show how Holy Scripture has at various times been understood and interpreted in the church of God by those who lived at the time."[13] The "Formula of Concord" thus did not grant precedence, and certainly no normative significance, to the creedal texts recognized by the Protestant churches when it came to explaining the Christian faith for the time. As was variously reiterated in the text, "Holy Scripture alone remains the only judge, rule, and guiding

[11] "Formula of Concord," in Robert Kolb and Timothy Wengert (eds), *The Book of Concord. The Confessions of the Evangelical Lutheran Church* (Minneapolis: Fortress Press, 2000), 486.
[12] Ibid., 487.
[13] Ibid., 487.

principle, according to which, as the only touchstone, all teachings should and must be recognized and judged, whether they are good or evil, correct or incorrect."[14]

In the interpretation of these texts from the "Formula of Concord," questions have frequently arisen and been the matter of lively discussion, including the matter of the canon of Holy Scripture (i.e., the question of what we exactly mean by Holy Scripture), and the question of the principles of interpretation. In the reading and interpretation of the individual scriptural texts within the Protestant churches, emphasis has been placed in particular on what "was Christum treibet" (what promotes Christ). From the early years of the Reformation, Protestant interpretation was indeed characterized by skepticism with regard to a chiefly ecclesiastic interpretation of biblical texts such as allegorical interpretations. The Reformers, by contrast, placed emphasis on the literal sense of biblical texts. Protestant theology in fact played a significant role in bringing about the development of a modern hermeneutics oriented toward the material form of the text. All of this contributed toward formulating the Protestant scriptural principle.

One moment of truth for this principle undoubtedly lay in the controversy over authority in the church and in theology. With one sole source and norm for church doctrine and practice and Christian life, all other possible "authorities" are relativized that could be considered for the formation of church life and the life of the faithful. However, the central and most important significance of the principle lay in providing a voice and asserting validity for the liberating, salvific and life-giving Word of God to a lost world. If it were to be reduced to its principal and normative status for church doctrine and practice, however, it would become false and sterile. It was thus of greatest importance to prevent this from happening so that the texts of Holy Scripture could be interpreted in accordance with their literal sense and applied to the lives of believers.

Interpretation of Holy Scripture

The Reformation returned authority to the Holy Scripture with regard to the life of the church and the lives of each and every believer. Martin Luther had a well reflected and nuanced understanding of Holy Scripture, its role within the church, as well as the rules and methods of its interpretation. From this starting point, Lutheran theology repeatedly treated the issues and methods involving the interpretation and understanding of biblical

[14] Ibid., 487.

texts. What are the main points that emerge in Protestant scriptural interpretation and Protestant-Lutheran hermeneutics?

First, the Reformers emphasized the literal sense of biblical texts, with human reason taking on a major role in the interpretation of Holy Scripture. The importance of reason in interpretation was developed further in *Clavis scripturae sacrae* (Key to Holy Scripture), written in 1567 by Matthias Flacius Illyricus (1520–1575), a second-generation Croatian Lutheran. Flacius agreed with Luther's view that those who read a biblical text can reach a plausible and biblically appropriate understanding if they follow generally accepted rules—rules involving the reading and interpretation of texts, which emerge from insights gained through the use of reason in the reading of texts, and of Holy Scripture in particular. Clearly one reaches the limits of reason when dealing with biblical texts. While reason can grasp the linguistic meaning of the texts and gain insight into their content, it has no access to their inner clarity and cannot persuade the heart to trust and follow the gospel and the message of the Old and New Testaments. This, the actual objective and ultimate purpose of biblical texts, to awaken and maintain people's trust in God, can only be brought about by God. God awakens trust by speaking to people through biblical texts.

One must, however, first understand intellectually what it says in the texts. When the Ethiopian court official read the words of Isaiah on his way home from Jerusalem, Phillip asked him, "Do you understand what you are reading?" (Acts 8:30). One cannot truly trust the message of a biblical text if one does not really understand it. This applies to an incorrect understanding of a biblical text as well, as it would then no longer be intellectually clear what God wishes us to trust in and follow. From a Protestant point of view, one must therefore, unquestionably, read and interpret biblical texts in full accordance with the (reasoned) rules of the art of reading and interpretation. Flacius pursued this course in his hermeneutics in *Clavis scripturae sacrae*. While he was fully convinced of the divine status of Holy Scripture, he still took into account the views of the other sciences of his time (and humanistic philosophy and its rules of interpretation in particular). At the 1546 Council of Trent, the Roman Catholic Church attacked the Protestant principle of the self-interpretation of Holy Scripture, supporting instead the doctrine that Scripture was hermeneutically incomplete and needed to be supplemented by tradition. The Protestant side then had to respond by showing that Scripture was indeed sufficient unto itself and could be understood on its own. To this end, the hermeneutical method and the tools required for the interpretation of biblical texts need to be clarified, under the assumption of the completeness and comprehensibility of Holy Scripture. Flacius's expansive work did precisely that. In his response to Roman Catholic critics, Flacius emphasized that the reason why Holy

Scripture (or parts of it) could not be understood was not because it was incomprehensible but in fact due to flaws in the interpreters' linguistic education along with their questionable interpretive methods. Taking the coherence of Holy Scripture for granted, Flacius underscored its normative autonomy by presenting all the elements involved in exegesis. With the help of philology, exegesis, rhetoric, logic and other scholarly knowledge, any biblical text can be rendered comprehensible within the Bible as a coherent whole. In addition to the coherence of Holy Scripture as a whole, Flacius also emphasized, in particular, the comprehensive perspective, i.e., the scope of all of the texts of Holy Scripture. This scope represents the goal pursued by the Bible as a whole and the golden thread that runs through all of its texts. This scope is not however clear from the beginning but is itself the result of interpretation of Holy Scripture as a whole.

Second, new foundational insights into the interpretation of Holy Scripture would follow in the course of the centuries following the Reformation. During the era of Europe's religious wars in the seventeenth century, the conviction that there was no single correct interpretation of biblical texts gained traction in Europe. A methodically developed interpretation of Holy Scripture thus did not need only one but often several plausible interpretations of biblical texts, whereas the different Christian churches had previously presumed that there was only one absolute meaning of Holy Scripture and its laws, with people resorting to armed conflict as a means of defending their own positions. The development of a methodical interpretation of Holy Scripture also paved the way for scholarly disputes over the appropriate and correct understanding of biblical texts. Confessional fighting on the battlefield could then, most sensibly, be replaced by scholarly discussions.

Third, according to Protestant understanding, the interpretation of biblical texts can only truly achieve its goal if people hear God speaking to them through these texts and are touched existentially by them. Protestant theology has consequently been confronted with the question of what exactly touches and connects with human beings in this way. Within the Lutheran churches, for example, Pietism was of the view that the interpretation of biblical texts should not only meet the academic standards of scholars and educated people but also contribute to deepening the piety of those who simply read the Bible or heard a sermon. In this context, human emotions, feelings and passions were of importance and had to be taken into account if one was to understand the spiritual stirring of the emotions of the authors of the biblical texts, and if the readers of biblical texts and hearers of sermons were truly to be existentially moved. The contexts and the lives of readers and listeners thus gained in importance in Pietistic scriptural interpretation. Fully understanding biblical texts means that readers and listeners need to be moved in their feelings, emotions and passions, i.e., in their concrete existence.

Fourth, for Protestant Christendom in general, Holy Scripture is one of the means through which God communicates with people in this world, and is indeed the main medium for this communication. This is not a matter of mere chance for Lutheran theology, which was and remains convinced that God purposefully seeks to express Godself through Holy Scripture, committing Godself to this particular medium. This then leads to the view that it is futile or even misleading to look for any other avenues through which God might communicate with us. This referred to church traditions that were not covered by Holy Scripture as well as the free action of God's spirit in the faithful, as God speaks directly into people's hearts. By focusing on Holy Scripture as God's chief medium, the Bible increasingly became the object of historical interest in Lutheran theology. But how exactly does God express Godself and God's will in these texts? And what do we discover about God when we experience how God expresses Godself in our understanding and our communication?

Time and again this entails tensions with regard to the interpretation of biblical texts. The historical-critical method was and remains the main challenge when it comes to the reading of and listening to the Bible in church. At times, the differences would appear to be quite radical between historical-critical exegesis and the Reformation interpretation of the Bible. The conviction thus gained traction that the texts of the Old and New Testaments were not the timeless Word of God but reflected historical events instead. The individual authors of the biblical texts always wrote from their own particular perspectives, just as the interpreters of the biblical texts interpreted the texts from their own particular perspectives as well. Their interpretations do not only take the biblical texts into account, but their own personal and historical situation. All of these insights into the process of scriptural interpretation make it increasingly clear that the God witnessed in the Bible did not only express Godself through a text (the Bible) but also through history, at a particular time and place, as needs to be taken into account when interpreting, so that God's message can be understood for our own time. This is the starting point for the historical-critical method of biblical interpretation. The method falls short, however, if it is only used to distinguish historical elements from the virtually timeless message and meaning of the texts. In the past, precisely those elements of the biblical message were often identified as timeless that were currently in vogue and generally accepted at that particular time and within that particular context. The Protestant relationship between history and scriptural interpretation has many more facets than does such a simple model.

Biblical texts are, first, to be recognized as historical texts written at a particular point in history and in a particular place in the world. One therefore needs to understand the historical conditions from which the texts emerged. Second, the text is placed before interpreters who are part of a particular interpretive tradition and who therefore already have an idea of how a particular biblical text is to be understood. Third, interpreters are located in a particular time and geographical place, which also influence what they are able to conceive of and what interests them about the text in particular.

Interpretation is thus influenced by the circumstances of the context in which interpreters live. One must therefore ascertain what people in each context experience as the truth. Scriptural interpretation from a Protestant point of view is always more than just a methodical reading and explication of a biblical text, but is also ultimately about the individual interpreters as a whole and their discovery of the possibilities provided by God for their own existence and lives in truth.

Fifth, the interpretation of biblical texts can succeed once interpreters are not only able to ascertain what the text actually seeks to express, but also when the text reveals the human condition in all its variety to readers and interpreters and raises the question of whether the life varieties expressed therein could be their own. The Lutheran New Testament scholar Rudolf Bultmann (1884–1976) considered[15] that we can only reach a true interpretation and understanding of biblical texts when we have listened to the questions the texts ask of us, and when we discover what it is that the texts demand of us. Only then can the texts open up new possibilities to us for our individual and collective lives by calling us away from ourselves and opening our eyes to the presence of God in our lives. In Bultmann's opinion, the entire interpretative process is a critical one: we are to analyze and interpret biblical texts critically in order critically to examine ourselves and our individual and collective lives. The main area of interest for modern Lutheran hermeneutics is the interpretation of biblical texts not with the goal of confirming our own selves and ideas but critically to listen to God's Word in respect to our own lives in our particular contexts and situations.

Sixth, it is part of the overall interpretation process that believers from different situations and contexts share with one another the insights that they receive from their individual and collective listening to God's Word. The resultant diversity of understanding of Holy Scripture bears witness to the lively and concrete nature of God's communication with God's people. The Triune God is not like an imperialistic ruler who, from a fitting distance, would uniformly send God's messages to people all around the world, and would expect that they all live their lives in the same homogenous way.

[15] Cf. Rudolf Bultmann, "Das Problem der Hermeneutik," in *ZThK* 47 (1950), 47–69.

Human life is diverse and God speaks through the medium of Holy Scripture to the particular concrete lives of individual people and communities. Hearing God's Word is therefore not followed by some sort of imperial anti-individuation process but by a song praising the manifold grace of God (1 Pet 4:10), expressed in the diverse and many-hued lives of Christians and churches—in "the freedom of the glory of the children of God" (Rom 8:21).

Questions

What expectations do you have when you read or hear a biblical text? Do you expect the biblical passage to tell you something meaningful for your personal life and your understanding of the world?

What role should the texts of Holy Scripture play in the formation and decision making of the church and its governing bodies today? What is the relationship between Holy Scripture to other contextual and scientific insights?

What is crucial in the interpretation of a biblical text, in sermons or Bible studies? Should the interpretation of biblical texts be adapted to contemporary understandings? How should we deal with different interpretations of the same biblical text in evangelical churches?

Implementing Gender Justice: An Asian Perspective

Au Sze Ngui

Testimony of the impact of God's liberating grace

In Jesus Christ, we are "liberated by grace." As we read in Romans 5:1-2, "Therefore, since we are justified by faith, we have peace with God through our Lord Jesus Christ, through whom we have obtained access to this grace in which we stand; and we boast in our hope of sharing the glory of God."

The Murut people of Sabah, Malaysia, used to be animists. When the gospel of Jesus Christ came to them, they were liberated from their beliefs. They had been subject to fears and omens that manifested themselves in daily life: if someone wanted to take a boat journey–the Murut mainly live on the banks of one of the large rivers in the interior of Sabah–they would have to wait for a sign. If a snake was seen on the river then it was a bad sign, meaning that the journey would be fraught with danger and the boat might capsize or they might meet with some sort of disaster. If they saw a series of birds flying in a certain direction, this would be a good omen and the journey would be a smooth and safe one. They were subject to fears of spirits and so never went out after dark as this could cause them to encounter some evil spirit who would harm or curse them in some way. They feared encountering anything out of the ordinary in their everyday lives for the extraordinary, be it an animal, insect or object, would not bode well for the person who encountered it.

After the Murut heard the gospel, they were set free from the fear that was manifested in their former beliefs and their lives were changed. This freedom not only liberated them from the bondage of fear but also from their traditional views and practices. The roles of Murut men, women and children had been strictly divided: the men were hunter gatherers, hunting, fishing and gathering fruits or vegetables to provide for their families. The women stayed home, looking after the children and their homes as well as doing the cooking, farming, growing vegetables and foraging in the surrounding jungle for basic supplements. Children were not given very much responsibility though they had to help with household chores and some of the simple farming activities. As they grew up they were taught certain hunting or cooking skills depending on their gender.

After the Muruts had encountered the Christian message of God's liberating grace the traditional roles of men and women and children changed. Although the Murut men still hunt and fish for their families and the women are still mostly in charge of the household duties, the women started to express their opinions, even if the men still had the greater voice in the decision-making process. Even though women are still the cooks and the homemakers, through the church they began to contribute to the social life in non-traditional and varied ways. The women started to become active in many areas in the church. They started to participate in the worship ministry by leading the singing in the church; they started to teach children at Sunday school, taking thus also key teaching roles.

The greatest change in gender roles took place at the level of the church leadership. Women are now elected as church leaders and their key role within the church is acknowledged. Even Murut men acknowledge that within the church the women are a force to be "reckoned with" and within Murut society the voice of women is being heard. For example, in a small church called Mansaso in the Tenom region in Sabah, Malaysia, a Murut woman chairs the church council. Traditional gender roles that confined women and men to limited spheres of action were transformed by the inclusive and liberating message of the gospel.

THE LWF GENDER JUSTICE POLICY (GJP) AND ITS RELEVANCE IN SPECIFIC ASIAN CONTEXTS

One of the core values of the LWF is inclusiveness. Since the Second LWF Assembly in 1952, women have been included in the LWF leadership structures as council members and with each assembly decisions were made to ensure inclusiveness. Today, the LWF has a policy of requiring the participation of forty percent women and men respectively and twenty percent youth in councils, symposiums and assemblies. Moreover,

> simply fulfilling quotas is not sufficient [...]. In order to be faithful to previous assembly commitments and achieve the goal of full inclusivity, there is an urgent

> need to be transformed as churches and as a global communion by the power that women and youth bring.[1]

Along the way, admitting that violence exists within churches and that measures need to be taken to combat such violence especially against women constitutes a confession of sin. The communion realized that injustice cannot be tolerated and needs to be addressed. Therefore, in 1997, at the Ninth LWF Assembly in Hong Kong,

> the commitment to gender equality was identified as one of the communion's core tasks: to speak on gender and power from a theological and biblically based faith perspective as a justice and relational issue and to address gender and power as issues of leadership.[2]

The GJP approved by the LWF Council in June 2013, outlines a set of principles and provides the basis for the communion to achieve gender justice. It implies the protection and promotion of the dignity of women and men who, being created in the image of God, are co-responsible stewards of creation. The goal of the gender justice policy is to strive towards actualizing the liberation brought by God's grace. The aim is to eliminate gender-based institutional, cultural and interpersonal systems of privilege and oppression, i.e., power systems that sustain discrimination. In order to achieve this goal, the GJP "seeks to provide political intentions and tools that contribute to fostering gender justice in order to achieve inclusive and sustainable communities and churches."[3]

According to the LWF's understanding, the theological foundation of the GJP is embedded in the biblical-theological notion of being justified by faith through grace: "to be justified is to be freed from that which binds us (cf. Rom 5)."[4]As Christians we believe that God created us (Gen 1:27); we are all sinners (Rom 3:23); Christ died once for all (2 Cor 5:14-15); we are all justified by faith (Rom 5:1–2). Therefore we are all equal in Christ Jesus and strive toward gender justice for all, precisely because of this common basis. Thus, gender justice is "a matter of faith"[5] for us in the LWF communion.

---

[1] At **www.lutheranworld.org/sites/default/files/DTPW-WICAS_Gender_Justice.pdf**, 9.

[2] Ibid., 18.

[3] Ibid., 9.

[4] Ibid., 24.

[5] Ibid., 11.

The methodology proposed in the GJP for implementing gender justice is: see–judge–act. This means to observe and read each reality and context and to use biblical, theological and universally agreed upon human rights concepts to discern this reality and the main issues arising from this particular context. After reading and discerning the reality, one needs to agree on actions that should be taken in this specific context.[6]

When applying the methodology proposed in the GJP, a first step requires that we "see" the reality in the Murut community and "judge" this reality in light of the principles of inclusiveness and justice as part of the teaching of the gospel.

The changes in the Murut community illustrate clearly how the message of the gospel liberated them from fears that were part of their former beliefs. Muruts began to see one another in a different light–in the light of God's grace–understanding that all are sinners, justified by their faith and redeemed by the blood of the Lord Jesus Christ. Therefore, all are equal in God's eyes. There is no greater sinner or better saint since "all have sinned and fall short of the glory of God" (Rom 3:23). Christ died once for all. Therefore, every sinner, whether man or woman, liberated from the penalty of their sins has a new birth and is a new person.

> [F]or in Christ Jesus you are all children of God through faith. As many of you as were baptized into Christ have clothed yourselves with Christ. There is no longer Jew or Greek, there is no longer slave or free, there is no longer male and female; for all of you are one in Christ Jesus (Gal 3:26-28).

Thus within our own families, communities, across cultures, nations, race as well as gender, we are one in Christ Jesus as children of God. Thus, if we are all children of God, liberated by God's grace, justified by faith, we are to be God's light and salt in this world.

Although we are children of God, we are still living in this fallen world and daily deal with consequences of sin in our lives. The Murut community is still undergoing change. While women are now given more space to speak out and take part in decisions regarding the family, the community and the church, they are still expected to fulfill certain expectations and live in accordance with the traditional understanding of a "woman's role." For example, during the visit of a group from an urban church group, a number of Murut men were rather shocked to see how youth of both sexes of the visiting church group helped with washing the dishes. Pointing at one of the youngsters, a man asked, "Isn't this women's or girls' work, why is he washing dishes?" One of the members of the visiting group, a teacher

---

[6] Ibid., 14.

by profession, replied that everyone is responsible for helping with the household chores, regardless of gender, especially when both women and men have responsibilities outside their homes.

The situation described above is a reality in many parts of the LWF communion. Within Murut culture and society, there is still inequality. Within the Murut Christian community, there is still institutional, cultural and interpersonal discrimination. How can churches and Christian communities eliminate discrimination and inequality?

First, we need to see each other in the light of God's grace, "For by grace you have been saved through faith, and this is not your own doing; it is the gift of God—not the result of works, so that no one may boast" (Eph 2:8). God's grace is what saves me, a woman. God's grace is what saves him, a man. God's grace saves not works, not gender, not class, not institutions, not culture. When I am saved by God's grace and you are saved by God's grace, we are all at the same level and this must bring everyone, regardless of culture, race or tribe under the umbrella of God's grace. When you look down at another person, you look down at Christ. Having been saved from our sins by Christ, can we do anything that would hurt the Lord Jesus Christ?

Second, allow me to return to the example of the visiting church group cited above. When the urban church group interacted with the Murut village community, they realized that there was an inequality in how labor was divided. During the Sunday service, the worship leader asked the song leader to come and lead the singing. Since the person was not present in the church someone else had to take over. Later during the service, the women of the congregation presented a song. With them was a woman who carried a small baby. She turned out to be the song leader whom the worship leader had been calling for earlier. Some of the visitors recognized this lady as one of the cooks who had prepared breakfast for them that morning. They realized that she had been so overburdened with different tasks that day since she had had to help with the visitors while, at the same time, taking care of her small child, that she had not been able to make it to the church on time. This example shows that in the Murut community, as in many member churches of the LWF communion, labor is not distributed equally.

Being liberated by God's grace calls for redressing this disparity and we should consider how together we can walk along on the road to holiness and Christlikeness. One way to do this is through discussing and considering what is proposed in the GJP: the liberating grace of God is a blessing for all—male and female.

Third, in the fight against discrimination and for inclusiveness, we must not consider this battle to be distant from each individual within the communion. Gender justice is justice for all, not just for women. Reformation is reformation for all and not just for some. The dissemination of the GJP will encourage discussion among men and women in the member churches of our communion and encourage our member churches to consider reformation in the area of gender in light of the upcoming 500th Anniversary of the Reformation. Liberating grace means looking at oneself, one's family, church, community and nation in a new light–the light of Jesus Christ. Liberating grace opens the door to reforming and renewing all relationships. The first renewed relationship is between human beings and God.

Through our justification by faith in Christ Jesus, we are granted the privilege of becoming God's children. God no longer holds us in debt for our sins. Romans 5:6-8 describes this transformed relationship:

> For while we were still weak, at the right time Christ died for the ungodly. Indeed, rarely will anyone die for a righteous person–though perhaps for a good person someone might actually dare to die. But God proves his love for us in that while we still were sinners Christ died for us.

This means that God's grace liberates us and our faith justifies us to have a relationship with God and the Holy Spirit dwells within us. We are changed for we now have God within us. Renewed relationships start between God and human beings and they need to permeate all relationships. The relationship of marriage must express this liberation by God's grace. There must be an equal division of responsibility and labor: husbands and wives share in the work that it takes to build a marriage, to build a home, to teach and nurture children, to look after parents and elders of the family without sacrificing completely their own spiritual lives as children of God. It is thus important that relationships are renewed within the institution of the family; there must not be favoritism. Our faith is grounded in justice and fairness and must therefore also permeate our family relationships. It is crucial that family relationships are brought under the liberating grace of God since the family, however it is understood and defined in different contexts, is the most basic social unit in the world. Justification by faith should thus become visible at the level of the family through the implementation of gender justice. Gender justice liberates members of a family to look for better ways to care for one another by assuming different tasks and roles that might not always correspond to "traditional" gender roles. It also implies that daughters are given the same educational opportunities as sons. This is still not self-evident in some parts of the LWF communion.

The cultural traditions of many nations are part of the communion of the LWF. These traditions and cultural mores, which sadly have not been renewed by God's grace, color the various member churches. Seventy-seven percent of the member churches ordain women. Yet, there are still twenty-three percent that do not.[7] This is an example of exclusiveness within our communion. The GJP calls on the member churches to study this policy together and to consider the importance of letting God's liberating grace permeate all areas of the church so that renewal and reformation might take place within "all of us" and that we, the communion of the LWF, may carry Christ visibly, and be the light and salt of this world, showing forth the Lord Jesus Christ and witness to the liberating grace of God.

In each of our societies we need to continue to preach about constantly renewing relationships because God has granted us grace and renewed our relationship with Godself. As God is inclusive, so we must also be inclusive; as God is just, so we must be just. We need to look at society as Christians and not as Kenyans, Germans, Chinese, Australians or Brazilians. We need to see ourselves as liberated to be the followers of Christ who carry God's grace into all parts of the world and all relationships. Heading towards the 500th Anniversary of the Reformation, we, as Lutherans within the LWF communion, need to reflect upon and evaluate our own church and society in light of liberating grace. If there is still discrimination, inequality and exclusivity then we fall short.

> Sometimes, it takes a catalyst from outside the community to effect change and it is the hope of the LWF that the GJP will be this catalyst, enhancing the "communion's journey towards inclusiveness."[8] When we are liberated by God's grace, doors are opened for change and reformation. If there is no grace, there can be no change for we will all be as we have always been. So if anyone is in Christ, there is a new creation: everything old has passed away; see, everything has become new! All this is from God, who reconciled us to himself through Christ, and has given us the ministry of reconciliation (2 Cor 5:17–18).

Just as the inclusion of male and female youth as dishwashers was an eye-opening event at a local level, so too it is hoped that the GJP will be the eye-opener for the LWF communion. I envisage the Murut community coming together, both men and women and youth, to study the GJP after it has been translated into the language they comprehend, and consider how gender inequality might be redressed within their community. Just as the liberating grace of God granted the Muruts liberation from fear and omens, it is my hope that the GJP will be God's liberating grace for the reformation of non-inclusive social, institutional, cultural norms. Discriminatory social norms limit and stifle a community's creativity as well as the contribution it might make toward Christ's body at large and the LWF communion.

---

[7] Ibid., 17.

[8] Ibid., 1.

THE REFORMATION AND CONTINUING THE REFORMATION OF INDIVIDUALS, COMMUNITIES AND INSTITUTIONS

"Gender justice refers then to both, women and men, together organizing life based on partnership and justice."[9] The Reformation did not happen outside but within the church. Martin Luther called for reform in order to correct what was wrong within the church. Today, we call for reformation within the LWF communion and for gender justice to prevail. We call for an end to discrimination and the inclusion of all. All this happens under the liberating grace of God which grants us renewal and reform.

As we live in the eschatological tension between the now and the not yet, it is understood that on the road of holiness we still have to deal with sin and its effects in the world. Liberation from the bondage of sin is the beginning of our striving for justice: we are free; we are forgiven; we are the recipients of God's grace. We are free to change and change the world. There are many examples of how Christianity has been an agent of change by supporting the revision of some "traditional" practices. For instance, when the Christian missionaries went to China in the late 1800s, they came face to face with the horrible practice of foot binding. Between the ages of four and nine, young girls' feet were bound with bandages, the toes curled under and the arch forced to collapse against the heel. As a result, the girls had tiny feet so that once grown up they could only walk with great difficulty with a swaying gait and mincing steps. The missionaries called for a stop to this practice and later Chinese Christian women added their voices for a ban to foot binding which was finally officially banned in the early 1900s. Such submissive practices continue to exist also today. The LWF Office for Women in Church and Society has been supporting projects in Kenya, Tanzania and Ethiopia that raise awareness of female genital mutilation (FGM) and try to put an end to this practice. Efforts to change a communion are most effective when they come from within the communion. For example, William Wilberforce (1759–1833) championed the abolition of slavery and the slave trade in the British Empire. His Christian belief was the main driving force behind his fight against the slave trade. The slavers in the British Empire were themselves also nominally Christians, as were the members of the British parliament who sanctioned the slave trade. Wilberforce finally succeeded to convince parliament of the inhumane character of the slave trade and succeeded in his fight against it.

There is always a need for people within communions prophetically to speak out against unjust practices. Within our LWF communion of churches, we also need people who out of their faith and out of the understanding

[9] Ibid., 24.

that they are liberated by God's grace, speak out against exclusiveness within their contexts.

My colleague is a Murut. She is an evangelist, trained to lead a church congregation and to teach the Word of God. She is very competent and her family supports her wish to serve God in the church ministry. Due to ill health she cannot work on the farm in her hometown. She therefore felt sent by God to the city and to this ministry. If God's liberating grace had not reformed and changed her people, the Muruts, she might not have been able to serve God as a leader in God's church, accepted and acknowledged by both male and female members of the congregation. However, her extended family still considers it to be most important that she be "a good wife" and although happy about her having a son who will carry on the family line, her in-laws are unhappy that her health does not allow her to have another child. She and her husband have found a way of sharing responsibilities at home and work without overburdening one of them. In this case, whereas the reform of "traditional roles in the family" has already taken place within the immediate family, the extended one still has a way to go.

> The member churches of the LWF are to
>
> - Recognize the policy
> - Engage in a participatory self-assessment of the assets for and challenges to the churches as they strive toward achieving gender justice.
> - Analyze the participation of women and men in the life of the church...at decision-making levels, access to theological education...to address possible inequalities in these areas.
> - Encourage women and men...[to move] beyond the traditional culturally assigned tasks in the life of the church and society...
> - Encourage church leadership to discuss and reflect on the interpretation of sacred texts that cast a different light on the meaning of the text...new interpretations when referring to women and men's roles and responsibilities.[10]

All these steps are important in order for reformation to take place. There will always be sin in our lives. There will always be the division between God and us, but is it not wonderful that we have been shown a better way; that sin does not have power over us anymore because of God's grace, because of our being justified by faith? Let us then make the effort and consider how God's liberating grace might free us to carry out gender justice and inclusiveness in each and every member church of the LWF.

---

[10] Ibid., 9.

Questions

How are women and men overburdened in church and society in your context? Provide examples.

How far does God's liberating grace extend in church and society in your context and does your church see justice as part of God's liberating grace?

How can gender injustice and exclusiveness be overcome in your context? Provide practical examples from your context that you can implement.

Education and the Reformation

Elżbieta Byrtek

The Reformation changed the world by beginning a new chapter in the history of Christianity and significantly impacting various areas of life such as education, the economy, politics and culture. It made use of such new fields of knowledge as geography and astronomy, combining them with philosophy, classical languages (Latin and Greek) and new inventions, such as the printing press. It played a crucial role in education, changed social life and greatly influenced the way in which children were brought up.

Being an educated and mature believer

Martin Luther believed that the Scriptures should be accessible and understandable for everyone. This meant that everyone should be able to read and write, which was one of the goals of public education. During the Reformation, many monasteries that provided education at the time were closed down because parents preferred their children to go to work and earn money. In light of this situation, Luther repeatedly insisted on the necessity and importance of education, stressing it in his sermons and writings (e.g., "To the Councilmen of All Cities in Germany that they Establish and Maintain Christian Schools, 1524" [1] and "Sermon on Keeping Children in School, 1530"). [2] Luther not only emphasized the value of both

[1] Martin Luther, "To the Councilmen of All Cities in Germany That They Establish and Maintain Christian Schools, 1524," in Helmut T. Lehmann (ed.), *Luther's Works*, vol. 45 (Philadelphia: Muhlenberg Press, 1952), 347–78.
[2] Martin Luther, "A Sermon on Keeping Children in School, 1530," in Helmut T. Lehmann (ed.), *Luther's Works*, vol. 46 (Philadelphia: Fortress Press, 1967), 213–58.

skills, reading and writing, but also underlined the fact that, in a changing world, the parents' knowledge and experience were not enough to help their children to understand the world around them. Luther added that the ability to make their own choices and maturity were also important and that knowledge was required in order to be able to express oneself. Education was no longer an issue for the church alone but became a public challenge. Martin Luther also openly declared that the access to education should not be determined by gender. Already in his "Treatise to the Christian Nobility," he specifically pleaded that "every town had a girls' school as well, where the girls would be taught the gospel for an hour every day either in German or in Latin."[3] He underlined that schools should not only be a place for teaching, singing, praying, reading and memorizing (as it was in the Middle Ages) but as "Christian schools" they should concentrate on explaining (lat. *explicatio*).

Philipp Melanchthon, Martin Luther's close associate and author of many seminal religious books, Bible commentaries, philosophical writings and someone who played an important role in the compilation of the *Confessio Augustana*, the basic Lutheran confessional writing, also contributed to the translation of the Bible. Furthermore, he was a great scholar and educator, founding schools, organizing school life and reforming colleges and universities, e.g., the universities in Wittenberg, Tübingen, Leipzig and Copenhagen. He initiated many changes, not only in the field of education, and encouraged others to carry the reforms further. He intensively worked on founding new schools and prepared a draft of the list of activities for the Humanist Gymnasium in Nuremberg (a secondary school with an emphasis on Greek and Latin), a model for the next fifty schools. He underlined that every child should be educated at the elementary level, regardless of their origin and stressed the fact that since all people are equal before God, education should be available to everyone. At the time, such claims were revolutionary. Already in late medieval times, the humanists had advocated for more education, but never for the general education of all. With its focus on empowering people to be mature Christians and citizens, actively participating in social life and church services, the Reformation gradually contributed to implementing the vision of education for all.

Questions related to reforms in the field of education and laying the foundations for public education were of great importance to Melanchthon. Many of his writings dealt with these issues and he underlined the importance of reconciling faith with education and training. He considered

[3] Martin Luther, "To the Christian Nobility of the German Nation Concerning the Reform of the Christian Estate, 1520," in Helmut T. Lehmann (ed.), *Luther's Works*, vol. 44 (Philadelphia: Fortress Press, 1966), 206.

education to be the foundation of the development in all spheres of life. Melanchthon believed that training and education resulted from piety and claimed that education, which strengthens communities, was the key to its maturity. He once said that no fortification will make the city stronger. This can only be achieved through educated, wise and talented people.

Melanchthon was a very popular teacher and his lectures were attended by an audience of up to six hundred people. He was convinced that boredom was the enemy of science and believed in the joy of learning.

The creation of universal education can be traced back to Melanchthon. He believed it to be the task of every Lutheran parish to organize a school and to hire a teacher. Melanchthon was called Praeceptor Germaniae (teacher of Germany) and was regarded as one of the greatest educational reformers in German history. Next to him, also Johannes Bugenhagen (1485–1558) needs to be mentioned as he played a crucial role in developing of a new system of elementary, secondary and higher education. In several parts of Europe, the Protestant communities used those new standards when establishing their own educational system, adjusting the new proposals to their contextual realities.

In addition, as a result of the Protestant activities in the field of education, a competition developed between Jesuits and Protestants in the organization of education and work on the translation of the Bible. While Melanchthon, Bugenhagen and other Reformers took care of educational reforms among Protestant Christians, the Jesuits influenced the formation of Roman Catholic schools. The latter also tried to improve the level of education among regular Roman Catholic priests. Piotr Skarga (1536–1612), a Polish Jesuit, preacher, hagiographer, polemicist, and leading figure of the Counter-Reformation in the Polish-Lithuanian Commonwealth, describes the sad condition of many priests' education during the Reformation. According to his descriptions, it was mainly scholars who used the translations; the books and the "rusty Bibles" were often laid aside unused.

The importance of vernacular Bible translations and catechisms

The Reformers understood that it was important to make the language of the Bible easily accessible as they wanted to encourage everyone to engage with it. This insight impacted the development of public education. Those wanting to understand the faith and its principles have to know how comprehensively to talk about it and learn how correctly to name symbols and experiences of faith. Therefore Martin Luther emphasized that it was crucial for people to have access to the Bible in their own language. Luther recognized the importance of the Bible and what its translation means to believers. In order to spread the Word of God in the language understood by everyone, the Reformation gave people a chance to have direct access to the Bible. While some translations of the complete Bible, or some of parts of it, had been made available already before the Reformation, they were not accessible to regular church folk and to many priests.

Martin Luther also made use of the late medieval genre of catechism, a collection of certain basic explanations of Christian teaching. The catechisms became very popular among lay people as they provided a simple, yet comprehensive, explanation of the Christian faith; they encouraged theological reflection and freedom rather than uniformity in the practice of the church. Luther's "Small Catechism" or catechisms compiled according to this example were translated into several languages already during the times of the Reformation (e.g., Finnish, Polish, Estonian, Slovenian, etc.). Those catechisms became the first printed books in many of those languages and were a milestone in the development of respective literary languages.

Also in Poland the translations of the Bible and catechisms played an important role in the development of literary language. The first publication of the complete Bible in Polish dates back to 1563 and was initiated by the Reformation. Stanisław Sarnicki (1530–1594), a Polish historian, testifies that before there were only three places in Poland where the Bible could be found: the king had one, the second one belonged to the archbishop and the third one was owned by the Protestant Ostroróg family. Before the publication of the complete Bible in Polish several parts of it, for example a few Psalters, had already been translated. New translations of the Psalms, published during and after the Reformation, helped to deepen the love for the Psalms. In 1545 Mikolaj Rej's Psalter was published, and other Polish translations followed.

The first Polish translation of the New Testament (1551/1552) was prepared by Stanisław Murzynowski (1527/8–1553), a Polish writer, translator and Lutheran activist during the Reformation. Murzynowski met Luther and Melanchthon during his studies in Wittenberg. His translation was published in several editions in Królewiec/Königsberg, today's Kaliningrad, and was even used by Roman Catholics who did not have their own translation. It was described as being more significant and precious to the Polish nation than the king joining new lands to the Polish kingdom. The translation was finalized at the height of the Reformation in Poland despite a number of difficulties, the most significant of which was the lack of terminology as a result of which many words and sentences were translated literally. There were many Protestant parishes in Poland at the time and their number was constantly growing as did the longing to have the complete Bible, not only the New Testament, available in Polish.

Prince Mikołaj Krzysztof Radziwiłł, "the Black" Radziwiłł (1549–1616), covered the costs of publishing the complete Bible translation (3000 ducats). The Brest Bible (Polish: Biblia Brzeska) was the first complete Protestant Bible translation into Polish, published in 1563 in Brest and dedicated to King Sigismund II Augustus. The dedication shows the strength of the evangelical faith. The translators had benefitted from the work of many scholars as well as from the translations of the Bible done by other communities. The Brest Bible is the result of a collaboration between academics from different disciplines–scientists, linguists and theologians.

Based on best foreign models (including the French Lefevre d'Etaples Bible) and not referring to the older Polish Catholic translation of the Vulgate, the Brest Bible is in fact the first Polish translation of the Bible from the original languages, perfectly combining the principle of fidelity to the original with the beauty of language. It reminds one of Luther's claims that a person who wishes to translate something, must know plenty of synonyms. A translator should listen attentively to the mother in her home, children on the street, and simple people at the market, and should translate in such a manner that they can understand the translated text. The Brest Bible contains a note on the usefulness of the Scriptures and the translation as such, a short note on the content of the Bible, the order according to which biblical books were translated and, finally, instructions for reading the Bible throughout the year. It was printed in a large gothic font, annotated and included beautiful woodcuts on the title page and throughout the Old Testament. Translators talk about their work in the preface, sharing information about the fidelity of the translation to the original languages, Hebrew and Greek. It is the creation of Protestant theologians who lived in the most beautiful period of the Reformation in Poland. The power and majesty of the Scriptures correspond to the strength of the Reformation movement in those days.

Sunday schools and the preparation for confirmation

Sunday schools date back to the late eighteenth century. Because many children were working very hard during the whole week, literacy was the main aim of Sunday classes. The Bible was an important teaching aid and the main source of the Christian faith. In the nineteenth century, Sunday schools were also called "Bible classes." Later these turned into church services for children. These activities were led by pastors as well as by educated lay people.

The history of confirmation work reveals that this field also played a significant role in elementary education. From an educational perspective, confirmation was preceded by intense preparations. Students took part in confirmation classes and each Lutheran child/teenager had to learn almost the whole text of Luther's "Small Catechism" by heart. For them it was a real textbook that helped them to develop their literacy skills.

In the Nordic countries, confirmation work and confirmation had a special meaning. In Denmark for instance it was not only an ecclesiastical matter, but also connected to civil rights and duties. In Norway, the law on confirmation passed in 1736 described confirmation training as one of the first forms of public education. It significantly contributed to the development of schooling. Confirmation training included some regular elements—baptismal education, catechization, which meant a public demonstration of the knowledge acquired during the period of baptismal education, a public confession of the creed and the first participation in Holy Communion. Additionally, in the eighteenth and nineteenth centuries, some civil rights such as marriage or even the creation of a bank account depended on the act of confirmation. In Sweden, catechization as such was initiated by the Lutheran church. It was written into church law in 1668 that the church is responsible for the process of teaching literacy skills. The most important subject was "Christendom," which prepared pupils for confirmation. The church worked closely together with the school and frequently one of the local pastors was the chairperson of the school. This close connection between school and church persisted for a long time but, over time, it became increasingly weak. Due to the new education regulations of 1919, Luther's catechisms were replaced by various text books and schools became non-confessional institutions. In Finland, a state church system was created during the period of Lutheran Orthodoxy, which since 1686 has formally been part of the Church Act. The Finnish Lutheran church was responsible for the entire national education system and confirmation classes were prepared in a way that supported the education of the citizens. In order to get married one had to have received Holy Communion and know Luther's "Small Catechism," which required that one was literate.

Next to the importance of Sunday schools and confirmation work, one also needs to mention new initiatives that combined educational, diaconal and missionary tasks and occurred especially in the nineteenth century in urban areas. One prominent example that served as a model for many similar diaconal initiatives was the foundation of the Inner Mission (German: *Innere Mission*, also translated as Home Mission). This was a movement of German evangelists, set up by Johann Hinrich Wichern (1808–1881) in Hamburg in 1848 (Wichern had partly been inspired by the City Mission in London and Glasgow). The Inner Mission worked for the deprived people and opened new perspectives to many young people who came from socially difficult conditions.

Church education of Lutheran youth

Reformation impulses had a remarkable influence on the development of education and pedagogical thinking. They contributed to the spreading of the interest in education beyond the church walls. Members of the city council were called to found elementary and modern classical grammar schools. The idea of training based on autonomy, freedom, maturity, rationality and responsibility proliferated. One of the reasons why Protestant churches were so successful in the field of education in the eighteenth and nineteenth centuries was the fact that they kept up the dialogue with the ideas of the Enlightenment. This dialogue was often not an easy one, yet it triggered many fruitful discussions within the churches.

To this day, one of the main areas of the church's work is taking care of the education of young people. The Reformation movement played a vital role by developing its own teaching systems and taking into consideration human needs and expectations. It is said that achieving the highest educational standards and professional qualifications is considered as one of the most important aspects of Protestant identity. In the diaspora, it has had an impact on the development of a positive image of the Protestant ethos.

In the Polish context, from the very beginnings of the history of Lutheranism, there are many examples of where a school was founded immediately after establishing a congregation. A school building was often even built before the church building. Just to give an example from the early days of Lutheranism in Poland: around 1550, Martin Glossa, professor at the Jagiellonian University of Cracow, arrived in Pisz, Masuria, and assumed the office of Lutheran pastor there. Founding a school, he became one of the precursors of the Polish education system.

Although numerous difficulties arose during the times of the Counter-Reformation, Polish Protestants remained very much aware of their religious identity and recognized the importance of education in building this identity. When Lutherans were forbidden to build churches with towers, they decided to build church towers with schools because those buildings belonged to them. They continued to teach the importance of education and remained clearly visible also in the eighteenth and nineteenth centuries. Wherever Protestants settled, their life in a new place started with the construction of a building that served as a school as well as a house of prayer. In central Poland, Lutherans and Reformed, coming mostly from Germany, Switzerland or the Netherlands, focused their religious life around the school. A school was not only a place of teaching but also the seat of the cantor who led the church services.

Lutheranism (as well as other mainstream Protestant movements) played a crucial role in the development of public education in Poland in general—a commitment that is still visible: today public schools are often housed in the buildings of former Protestant schools, such as Mikołaj Rej Secondary School in Warsaw. After the political changes in Poland in 1989, Protestant educational associations started to reestablish Protestant schools and kindergartens. Today, several schools are officially called "evangelical" and these institutions have a special place in local communities. These institutions are not created for Lutherans only and their educational goals, based on ideas deriving from Lutheranism such as tolerance, openness and a Protestant ethos, apply to all believers.

Reformation through education is a key Lutheran concept; reforming education is key to the fulfilled life of society in general and individuals in particular. However, questions regarding teaching remain valid. Evangelical schools are expected to provide high quality education and to propose innovative solutions to the existing educational crisis. Polish Lutherans appreciate and cherish their history, in particular their contribution to education. On the way towards the Reformation Anniversary in 2017, the Evangelical Church of the Augsburg Confession in Poland has embarked on an open discussion on youth education.

Religious educators have repeatedly referred to the Lutheran tradition and emphasize the importance of the church's educational responsibility within the religious community, in society and at school. Religious education is not merely about communicating a doctrine to all students, but also about being a responsible church and a responsible citizen in society. It shapes each student holistically and helps to improve the quality of life. This view of religious education in Poland was developed in 1990 when religious education was reintroduced at schools.

Education and the gospel

Religious renewal during the Reformation underlined that the justification of every human being is solely based on faith (*sola fide*) and that faith is something given solely by grace (*sola gratia*). "So faith comes from what is heard, and what is heard comes through the word of Christ" (Rom 10:17). Martin Luther insisted that the human being is justified by grace through faith and that every human being should look for a gracious God. For this purpose they need a Bible, the ability to read and write and a well-managed educational process.

If human beings have the opportunity to discover something about God and to reflect on religion and faith, they start to pose questions, seek answers and voice their concerns and doubts. This is very helpful for the process of understanding the message of the gospel: Christ's redeeming death, the liberation from sin and the power of God's grace. Faith that is not afraid of posing questions, seeking answers and staying in dialogue with those who do not share one's own opinion, is a living faith, one that will be able to survive in today's multilateral and complex world. A world where "right" answers given by external authorities do not necessarily speak to people but where Christians, liberated by God's grace, have a responsibility to talk about this grace to others and to be ready to engage in difficult dialogues. Our Reformation tradition has never been afraid of being in dialogue with prevalent philosophical and social paradigms which have often been mutually beneficial, even if frequently controversial.

Well-educated, mature and responsible Christians and citizens have been empowered through education to understand in depth, differentiate between primary and secondary questions and to be creative, open minded and responsive to the needs of others.

Questions

What has been the most important contribution of your church to education? How is it linked to the ideas emerging from the Reformation?

Does church dogma create limits for the educational process as such?

In your opinion, what kind of educational responsibilities and challenges emerge from the understanding that human beings are liberated by God´s grace?

Freed by God's Love to Change the World: A Youth Perspective

Monica M. Villarreal

Youth are leaders: Youth are church

I have served as an ordained pastor of the Evangelical Lutheran Church in America (ELCA) for over three years. My youthfulness shocks many when I answer the church door and greet people as the pastor. I have entered hospital rooms for visitation, only to be greeted by people exclaiming, "Are you old enough to be a pastor?" And as a woman serving in a community where few women are clergy the shock is twofold. But, I have to admit, as a young female pastor, challenging people's stereotypes of what or who a pastor looks like is one of my joys of faith.

In an aging church, I will be a "young" church leader for another twenty years. Sometimes it is difficult and tiresome feeling the constant need to justify my position as a church leader. As I talk with other young pastors many feel the same way. The same is true for many young people who do not feel called into professional church leadership but desire a voice and place in congregations to serve and make a difference in their community and world. Youth are not always given the support, encouragement, or invitation to lead the church. And sometimes youth are given the opportunity to lead as long as what is said and done is exactly what has been said and done for the last several years. The church will be in a grave leadership crisis if youth are viewed as a category of church. We are church together–young and old.

I have been asked many times why I became a pastor in the church. In North America, mainline Protestant denominations are experiencing a decline in membership and the church does not hold the same power or place in society as it did years ago. It seems like a fading and insecure profession to enter.

I did not grow up in the church like many others who enter the professional church leadership. I was baptized at the age of six alongside my mother who was baptized as an adult. I do not come from a particularly religious or church-going family and I did not often attend Sunday School (faith classes) as a youngster. As a teenager, faith and church made most sense when what was said in worship or Bible class was lived out in the world. For me, helping to build a house for a homeless family helped make sense of faith. Attending youth gatherings or Bible camp offered the opportunity to be a part of intentional Christian community that felt more authentic and real. Having space to ask questions about life and faith taught me that faith is not easy. Faith includes doubt. And I learned that questions are okay. The disciples asked Jesus many questions.

I became a pastor because during all of the really hard times in my life the church was a safe haven for me. Worship gave me a sense of peace and encouragement. The youth group offered opportunities for me to learn, to grow in faith and eventually have a leadership role teaching Bible/faith classes to other youth. The church accepted me, just as I am—a child of God. Through the church I came to know the love of God and my calling to proclaim the love of God in Christ Jesus that transcends all of the world's brokenness.

FREED BY GOD'S LOVE

> A Christian is a perfectly free lord of all, subject to none.
> A Christian is a perfectly dutiful servant of all, subject to all.[1]

In "The Freedom of a Christian," Martin Luther emphasizes the power of faith as believing in God's promise of a new life. When we believe in God's saving grace as a gift freely given and an expression of God's love then we are freed from the worry about our place before God or about being a "good enough" person to be loved by God. When Christ died on the cross for the injustice, violence and sins of the world he said to his followers, "And I, when I am lifted up from the earth, will draw all people to myself" (Jn 12:32).

Contrary to popular cultural values of Americans in the USA, the freedom that Luther speaks of is not freedom to do and say whatever one wants to, or to buy and sell just anything. Luther is not speaking about freedom of religion or freedom of speech or the many other "freedoms" that are the mantras of our culture today. Rather, Luther connects faith and freedom. Faith and freedom are relational. Without faith we cannot know the freedom

[1] Martin Luther, "The Freedom of a Christian, 1520" in Harold J. Grimm, Helmut T. Lehmann (ed.), *Luther's Works*, vol. 31 (Philadelphia: Muhlenberg Press, 1957), 344.

that we have in Christ. And because we have freedom in Christ, our faith in God's saving grace, which was poured out upon the whole world, Jews and Gentiles alike, we are drawn to share this love with others. Freed by God's love we are inescapably bound to one another in Christian community both near and far. We are both "freed from" and "freed for."

Freed from—Freed to

The Global Young Reformers Network[2] invites youth to think more deeply about what it means to be Lutheran and what it means to be Christian. Connecting through video chat, youth are encouraged to join the Young Reformers by sharing a personal story of being "Freed from" and "Freed to." For example:

> **Freed from: Perfection**—Children and teenagers in Singapore are expected to meet high standards in the pursuit of excellence. As a young person, I struggled with various issues of fear and self-worth. The breakthrough came when the Lord spoke to me through Psalm 139, where the psalmist spoke of how God created his inmost being, and knit him together in his mother's womb. Knowing that God valued me and had a plan for me even at conception, I knew I had no reason to fear. As the psalmist writes, I praise God because "I am fearfully and wonderfully made"!
>
> **Freed to: Service**—Knowing the grace that is in Christ Jesus, I now share that message of hope and redemption with people so that we might all come to treasure the precious gifts and talents that God has given. I actively serve in my church's youth ministry as well as other ministries. One verse that I keep in mind at all times is the Apostle Paul's exhortation in 1 Corinthians 10:31, "So, whether you eat or drink, or whatever you do, do everything for the glory of God."
>
> Lee "Darius" Zhen Ying (Lutheran Church in Singapore, for Asia)

[2] The Global Young Reformers Network is a program of the Lutheran World Federation, created by youth, for youth. Utilizing social media we seek to create a global network of youth to build relationships and dialogue among communion churches about what it means to be Lutheran and Christian in a religiously pluralistic context. We desire to give voice to young people as leaders in their churches and in the world. We are not forming a new Lutheran church, rather we aim to strengthen existing youth ministries across the communion and accompany churches in creating new youth ministries through the work of the LWF Youth Desk. In observance of the 500th Anniversary of the Reformation the Global Young Reformer's theme is "Freed by God's Love to Change the World." Creating a network of young reformers all over the world, we want to show what this means: ecclesia semper reformanda—a church in ongoing reformation.

Freed from: Immovable pews—When I first walked into the church that I now attend every Sunday I was surprised by the way in which the worship space was arranged. The altar is at the center and all the pews were moved so that they form a circle. What I experienced there, and I still experience every Sunday, is a shared, communal liturgy in which everyone can experience the gospel. We all have active roles during the service: saying the prayer of the day, playing musical instruments or reading the gospel. Being able to worship in the round creates an awareness of each other's presence and also places us at the same level. We are equal; there is no hierarchy in a circle.

Freed to: Creating new space—As Lutherans we believe that while traditions are not necessary for salvation, they are sometimes good for order, tranquility and common practice. But when they do not serve their purpose, when people are uncomfortable and the church is no longer inviting and God's message does not reach everyone, then we may need to consider reorganizing the pews.

Carolina Huth (United Evangelical Lutheran Church, Argentina, for Latin America and the Caribbean)

Freed from: Church walls—"[T]hose who do not love a brother or sister whom they have seen, cannot love God whom they have not seen" (1 Jn 4:20).

Who is your neighbor? Your brother and sister? Too often church buildings become a place of walls. There are those who are "in" and those who are "out." Our identity and belonging can easily be assigned to what church we attend. The early church wrestled with belonging. Some argued, "I belong to Apollos" or "I belong to "Paul" (1 Cor 1:12). We all belong to Christ. I have been freed from church walls to see the face of Christ in the unexpected. I have been freed from church walls to discover that God is at work in the community all around me. I have been freed from church walls to join in God's work.

Freed to: Rebuilding community—Although I live in the USA, the streets are not made of gold and I have yet to discover the land of milk and honey. Where I live and serve as a pastor, God calls us to rise up for justice, restore hope, and rebuild community. Significant poverty, unemployment, lack of transportation, vacant homes and violence shape people's daily lives. Empowered by the Holy Spirit and vision of Isaiah 58:6–12, I have been freed by the love of Christ for the purpose of rebuilding community.

Rev. Monica Villarreal (Evangelical Lutheran Church in America, for North America)

Many other stories are available at, **http://youngreformers.lutheranworld.org/updates**

Freed to change the world

God's love is power for transformation. In the waters of holy baptism we are transformed by God's love, claimed as children of God, gathered around God's Word and sent for the sake of the world. Having faith to believe in God's promise of new life the Holy Spirit empowers us to create new ways of being the church (the body of Christ) together. Our faithful response to God's love cannot settle for the status quo which so often supports ways of injustice and oppression. The gospel proclaimed must compel people of faith actively to engage in the redeeming work of Christ who is already at work in the world.

Martin Luther never intended to create a new church or to change the world. He had hoped the church leadership would heed the message of faith and freedom and be compelled to have mercy on the poor and oppressed. Luther sought to realign the church with the teachings of Scripture to address abuses of power and leadership. The Protestant Reformation became a religious and social movement that took on various perspectives and contexts throughout Europe in the years during and after Luther.

It is always good to examine our personal faith, communal faith and the faith of the whole church. Our first disposition toward God is confession that we have fallen short of the glory of God and are in need of forgiveness. The continued division among people, communities, religious groups and even among Christians is cause enough for self-reflection.

Youth at Concordia College in Moorhead, Minnesota, were asked what they hoped would be changed in our world in the next five years? Many expressed concern for public health care pertaining to the current national debate. Many expressed a desire for greater gender equality and less discrimination of people. Students would like to see more sustainable and renewable energy options in the future, and there was a deep desire for more peaceable relationships between peoples and countries. Sharing and proclaiming the love of Christ was identified as being vital for changing the world and church.

Grounded in Scripture and in the tradition of the Reformation we live according to the principle *ecclesia semper reformanda*—a church in ongoing reformation. Reformation is not our work but God's creative work of renewal.

> For God so loved the world that he gave his only Son, so that everyone who believes in him may not perish but may have eternal life. Indeed, God did not send the Son into the world to condemn the world, but in order that the world might be saved through him (Jn 3:16-17).

God's love transforms.

> Go therefore and make disciples of all nations, baptizing them in the name of the Father and of the Son and of the Holy Spirit, and teaching them to obey everything that I have commanded you. And remember, I am with you always, to the end of the age (Mt 28:19-20).

In Christ, we have been freed by God's love to change the world.

Questions

What have you been freed from and what are you freed for?

What change in the world do you wish to see? How can you as a person of faith help make that change?

What does being Lutheran mean to you?

Liberated by God's Grace: Grace and Peace. An Anglican Perspective

Timothy J. Harris

Martin Luther's experiences that gave rise to his very public protest at Wittenberg were at once both profoundly personal and ultimately global. It was nothing less than the rediscovery and reclaiming of the gospel itself, grounded in the grace of God and appropriated by faith in Christ. The gospel message proclaimed on the authority of the church by Johann Tetzel was a selective and skewed proclamation of the gospel.

Since the time of Christ, the gospel message has been entrusted to each generation, with gospel ministry seeking to do more than simply inform a belief system, but to reform and transform people from any and every culture and nation as they accept the invitation to follow Christ. Everyone has a "theology" of sorts, some perception of "god," even if it is some notion of "god" that is rejected by atheists. The evangelistic task for each generation is to shape and inform such perceptions of God in and through the person of Christ. This may be evangelistic in the sense of introducing people to God as revealed in Christ and bringing people to faith, but no less evangelistic in continuing to reform believers' understanding of God by entering ever-deeper into the enormity of God, barely glimpsed in and through the gospel traditions centered on Christ.

A humble thesis

I have but one thesis to offer in this chapter, a thesis offered in the spirit of ongoing reformation and transformation: **our gospel is too small.** Whether it be the gospel we embrace personally and seek to live out, or the gospel we proclaim and commend to others, our gospel is too small.

This is not a matter of dogmatic formulation, but a broader reality of (inevitable) limitations in the scope and depth of our gospel imagination. There is an inherent dynamic influencing and shaping every generation by which we domesticate the gospel to our own needs and preferences, and reduce it to terms shaped in significant ways by our culture (whether to accommodate, challenge, subvert or transform). The gospel cannot be "owned" by any one culture over against another, and every culture has unique capacities to give expression to gospel truths in ways often overlooked or unrecognized in other cultures and times.

To say "our gospel is too small" is not in itself a criticism, but a truth statement. Our understanding of the gospel will invariably be too small, shaped in part by our limitation in imagination and understanding, but also because of our inevitable cultural blinkers and blind spots. The eyes through which we perceive the gospel are calibrated and orientated around our own experiences, values and "norms" of life. What is "normal" to us and our expectations of life are very different to the experiences and expectations of others.

If my thesis above is in anyway true, then our response should be one of an increased appetite, a hunger for a bigger, richer, deeper understanding of the gospel. I am not seeking to instill a sense of guilt, much less a claim to a greater or truer understanding of the gospel over against others. It is rightly said that at the moment our reading of the teaching and example of Jesus ceases to confront, confound and challenge us that is the moment we have stopped hearing and engaging as disciples. It is no less true with the gospel. We cannot—and must not—reduce it to neatly packaged formulations and explanations and leave it at that. As many have expressed, the gospel of Christ is a wild gospel, a dangerous gospel, and a gospel that exceeds our capacity to comprehend and express.

The apostle Paul struggled to find adequate words to give expression to this gospel. In praying that the Ephesian church (and wider network) may know the riches of the Father's glory, strengthened through the power of God's Spirit, and experienced through the dwelling of Christ in their hearts, Paul prayed that "rooted and grounded in love" they may be granted "the power to comprehend, with all the saints, what is the breadth and length and height and depth, and to know the love of Christ that surpasses knowledge [...] filled with all the fullness of God" (Eph. 3:17-19).

At this point (Eph 3:20) Paul struggled with the inadequacy of language, and drew on a cluster of terms to invite the hearer to think bigger, to recognize a gospel "abundance" that exceeds our comprehension and imagination. The phrase, "able to accomplish abundantly," perhaps might be conveyed as "able to do infinitely, greatly, 'abundantly—and more' above all." It is a cluster of terms that appeal to the highest notion of comparison imaginable—and exceeds it.

In what ways do we diminish the gospel? First, we need to distinguish between the "how" of the gospel, from the "what" of the gospel. As Luther so robustly asserted and protested, we cannot—and must not—add anything to the "how" of the gospel. The gospel as the "power of God for salvation to everyone who has faith" (Rom 1:16) is established entirely in God's grace and in and through the saving work of Christ alone.

It is one thing to affirm that nothing can be added to the "how" of the gospel, but quite another thing when it comes to describing what this salvation looks like. Our gospel proclamation must include both the "how" and the "what." Our concern to underscore the "by grace alone" dimension tends to focus on the "how" side of things, while speaking of what that grace looks like, what it achieves, is too often given less attention. It is at precisely this point that we invariably diminish the "what" of the gospel.

In what ways then may we say our gospel is too small? Any answer to this will of course need to be varied, and recognize that the gospel is given a wide range of expression in differing contexts and through a variety of church and theological traditions. My thoughts below reflect my own context—essentially Western articulations of the gospel, and especially those associated with Reformed and Protestant traditions. Given this caveat, I suggest that our gospel is:

- **Selective:** Our reading of Scripture with reference to what we recognize as the "gospel" is invariably selective. Reformed traditions tend to privilege Pauline expressions of the gospel, and more often than not are oriented primarily around Romans and Galatians. Yet there is more to Paul's Gospel than addressed in Romans and Galatians, and there is more to the New Testament articulation of the gospel than identified with Paul. Where does the proclamation of Christ and the gospel traditions expressed in the Synoptic Gospels fit within our understanding of the gospel? How do we give expression to Johannine expressions of the gospel, or Lucan gospel theology, and that of the writer to the Hebrews and the "catholic" epistles? There is a profound unity of confession in the Lordship of Christ, but many distinctive streams make up this gospel tradition, and it is dangerous to privilege one over another. A more faithful approach is to draw widely on the rich gospel tapestry reflected in Scripture.

- **Reductionist**: Our desire for clarity and simplicity of message very often results in gospel summaries and schemas. While these may be effective in introducing gospel truths, they must never replace the richness and vastness of the gospel as reflected in Scripture, any more than a cartoon might replace a great work of art. Yet the danger of reductionism is deeper than gospel summaries and schemas. It is all too easy to reduce the gospel in ways that reflect our personal preferences in discerning truth and making sense of life. For some, it will be reducing the gospel to a series of propositional statements or affirmations. All may be true and well founded, but the gospel is also expressed evocatively and with an appeal to the imagination in Scripture. For others, it will be to focus on the experiential and the language of the heart and devotion. Again, this may be very true and faithful, but not at the cost of setting aside gospel affirmations found in Scripture. Either way, there is a very real danger of reductionism.

- **Individualist:** The moment we say "our Father" we automatically have brothers and sisters in the family of Christ. There is a great confusion in our Western thinking between "personal" and "individual." Salvation always has a profoundly personal character. We are known to God by name, a knowledge that started before we were created, and continues into eternity where our place within the kingdom of God is no less in personal terms. However, our personal relationship with God is not to be confused with an individual relationship with God. We are never individuals in the sense that we stand alone and apart from all other relationships. This is just not possible in our relationship with God, where we are required to recognize our brothers and sisters, our neighbors, and those who are otherwise pushed to the margins of society. We are never individuals in that sense. Yet, a proclamation of the gospel is often expressed in very individual terms, and runs a very real risk of reflecting our very individualistic Western culture, where (so media frequently tells us) life is "all about me." Expressed in such terms, our message can sound as though the gospel is similarly "all about me," and my need for the assurance that I'm alright with God. If this is the sum total of the gospel message, then it neglects a profound dimension of the great commandment, where our relationship with our neighbor is no less important than our relationship with God. Redemption certainly involves personal forgiveness and reconciliation, our sins washed away through the blood of Jesus. Our gospel should be no less personal, but so much more than addressing our personal needs alone.

- **Dualist***:* The separation of the spiritual from the material and physical realms is a Greek way of thinking that is not reflected in Scripture. The flesh and blood realities of life as God has created it is no less a dimension of life within the kingdom than the spiritual realm. Again, the gospel may be presented in terms that imply that all that truly matters is "spiritual" salvation and the entry of our "soul" into the heavenly realm, while the material is ultimately insignificant. Salvation is presented as a spiritual reality over against material or physical realities. However, Scripture never separates the spiritual from the material, and indeed has a fear of being stripped "naked" in the sense of being without a body (2 Cor 5:3). When Paul speaks of the "spiritual"' over against the "physical" (1 Cor 15:44) he is not speaking in material terms, but in terms of what it is that animates or drives us. How we were shaped and energized by the Spirit, over against being driven by the "flesh" (understood as our human rebellious nature). The proclamation of the gospel and God's work of salvation is in and through creation in its fullness, and we dishonor the gospel when we separate or strip away the physical and material world as being of no significance to the gospel message. This world does matter, and God's creative purposes have not been set aside. Our gospel becomes too small when we separate salvation from creation, and God's ongoing mission in bringing creation to be all that it was created to be and to become. More on this later.

- **Stripped of the great scriptural narrative***:* Salvation comes to us in Scripture as part of a much bigger narrative. The gospel is in a very profound sense God's story, from the creation of this world, the drama of a disobedient humanity, and a fall from grace that impacts on all the world, the integrated storylines of redemption, the gathering of people of God, called and chosen by God to be a blessing to all nations, all of which prepares for and culminates in the story of Christ–the gospel cannot be separated from this greater narrative without becoming less than the gospel as revealed in Scripture. We will never fully comprehend the extent of this narrative that reaches back before the creation of this world, and will reach its ultimate expression when the kingdom reign of God comes in its fullness.

- **In need of perpetual reformation***:* The gospel is bigger than any and every culture, and no ethnic grouping, nation or culture can claim any supremacy in their particular expression of the gospel. In cultural terms, the gospel needs to be continually "translated" into the many and varied expressions of gospel articulation, proclamation and lived realities that are part and parcel of human life. Whether the gospel challenges, confronts, accommodates or transforms, the evangelistic outcome sought is the same in each case–a better, richer and healthier version of that culture and society, not the imposition of another culture from elsewhere. There is no default "gospel culture," except as translated into and given expression in and through the social and

> cultural diversity across this planet, and across the ages. And just as culture is dynamic and continually being reinterpreted and given new expression, so too the gospel needs to be perpetually reforming as it spreads, grows and extends in making disciples of all nations (Mt 28:19).

The realization that our gospel is invariably too small should not only instill in us a hunger to go deeper and to expand our horizons. It should help us to see a richness in our received gospel traditions that may be all-too-easily overlooked in our familiarity with time-honored gospel terminology.

At this point, however, we need to ask a more fundamental question. Just what did the word "gospel" mean to the average person in the world of the early church? The word "gospel" simply means "good news," and just what the message of "good news" indicated depends on who is making the pronouncement. In the Graeco-Roman world of the New Testament, the public announcement of "good news" frequently orientated around the emperor, with associated assurances of benefaction (grace) and peace at the hands of the emperor, reinforcing claims of lordship, dedication and loyalty.

Grace and peace

Within Scripture, two terms that are frequently paired together function as icons of the gospel: grace and peace. Grace speaks of the character of God, and all that flows from this quality and attribute of God's being: God is a God of grace, the ultimate Giver. The existence of all things cannot be explained or valued without reference to the grace of God. This is given profound expression at the end of Romans 11 (verses 33–36) as Paul brings his extended treatment and statement of the gospel as "the power of God for salvation" in Romans 1 to 11 to completion. The passage merits repeating in full:

> O the depth of the riches and wisdom and knowledge of God! How unsearchable are God's judgments and how inscrutable God's ways! "For who has known the mind of the Lord? Or who has been his counselor?" "Or who has given a gift to him, to receive a gift in return?" For from him and through him and to him are all things. To him be the glory forever. Amen

God the Giver

God is the ultimate Giver. There is not a single person in all the world, nor in all history, to whom God is in any way indebted. Who is in any position to give God anything, to offer God advice, or claim to know the mind of

God? The grace of God is as extensive as the phrase "all things," and in the context of Paul's argument reflects Romans 1:18 through to the reference to the gifts and calling of God to Israel (Rom 11:29), now extended to all those identified "in Christ." The threefold "from him and through him and to him" probably reflects the threefold graces of creation, redemption and final salvation.

The grace of God is revealed in the mission of God, God in action. From the first words of Scripture, God is at work. God creates, moves, speaks, forms, brings order, shares God's dwelling place. God provides, brings forth fruitfulness and growth, and invites, enables and expects humanity to share in the outworking of God's grace.

Peace and the gifts of God

Our appreciation of the grace of God is given profound liturgical expression in a classic Anglican prayer of thanksgiving (this version based on *An Australian Prayer Book*):

> Almighty God and merciful Father,
> we give you humble and hearty thanks
> for all your goodness and loving kindness
> to us and to all people.
> We praise you for creating and sustaining us
> and for all the blessings of this life;
> but above all for your amazing love
> in redeeming the world by our Lord Jesus Christ,
> giving us grace and the hope of glory.
> Give us such a sense of all your goodness,
> that we may be truly thankful and may praise you
> not only with our lips, but in our lives,
> by serving you in holy and righteous ways;
> through Jesus Christ our Lord,
> to whom, with you and the Holy Spirit,
> be all honour and glory, now and for ever.
> Amen.[1]

Within the wider biblical narrative, the evocative imagery of the Garden of Eden as a place of safety and flourishing, of sanctuary as being drawn into the residence of God and of Sabbath rest as the goal (*telos*) of creation

[1] *A Prayer Book for Australia* (Mulgrave Vic: Broughton Publishing, 1995), 16.

are revisited time and again. Like a semantic basket, the rich Hebrew term shalom gathers up such notions and provides another expression of the gospel as the "peace of God," a peace that is at once profoundly personal, yet extended to all creation (Romans 8) and ultimately cosmic.

The notion of shalom is effectively summed up in a quote from Cornelius Plantinga:

> The webbing together of God, humans, and all creation in justice, fulfillment, and delight is what the Hebrew prophets call shalom. We call it peace but it means far more than mere peace of mind or a cease-fire between enemies. In the Bible, shalom means *universal flourishing, wholeness and delight*—a rich state of affairs in which natural needs are satisfied and natural gifts fruitfully employed, a state of affairs that inspires joyful wonder as its Creator and Savior opens doors and welcomes the creatures in whom he delights. Shalom, in other words, is the way things ought to be.[2]

The "promised land," the goal of the journey out of slavery (the "exodus") and through the wilderness, the realization of the land promised to Abraham and Sarah and their descendants, is expressed in terms of being a "sanctuary" (Ex 15:17). The well-known priestly blessing drawn from Numbers 6:24–26 sets the blessing from God in parallel to the quality of shalom received from God. In Deuteronomy, the land about to be entered is similarly described in Edenic-type terms (Deut 7:7-9), and the prophets use shalom as descriptive of redemptive hope: e.g., Isaiah 32:17; 48:18; 53:5; 60:17.

By the time of the New Testament, shalom had become the primary Jewish form of greeting (welcome and farewell). This is specifically picked up in Paul's variation in his greetings "grace and peace," which become his short hand for the gospel itself. The "peace" here (*eirenē*) is very much an expression of the shalom motif.

The language of salvation/being saved (*soteria/sōzō*) also has significant overlap with shalom (conceptually and theologically), and in the Synoptic Gospels includes social, mental, psychological and spiritual healing—very much in a holistic sense (avoiding a body/soul dualism). About one third of the content of the Synoptic Gospels details the outworking of *soteria* in the form of healings (understood in a wide semantic range)—this is what shalom looks like as a foretaste of the fullness of the kingdom.

The work of the cross and resurrection also relates to the work of God in Christ establishing "peace": "Therefore, since we are justified by faith, we have peace with God through our Lord Jesus Christ, through whom we

---

[2] Cornelius Plantinga, *Not the Way It's Supposed to Be: A Breviary of Sin* (Grand Rapids: Eerdmans, 1995), 10.

have obtained access to this grace in which we stand [...]" (Rom 5:1–2a). Similarly, understanding the "first fruits" of the resurrection as expressed in the New Testament as an all-encompassing reality—all creation is redeemed to become all it was and is intended to be. The "new creation" motif here is similarly tied to the prophetic vision of shalom being realized through the kingdom of God.

In the Gospel of John the motif of "life" is similarly tied to a quality of life now breaking into the present order through Jesus (Jn 10:10: "I came that they may have life, and have it abundantly"), and is also expressed through the language of "peace"—for example, John 20:19–26—"Peace be with you"; compare the commission in Luke 10:5 "Peace to this house." Paul also uses similar language in "proclaiming peace" (Eph 2:17) to both Jews and Gentiles, and in doing so "In him the whole structure is joined together and grows into a holy temple in the Lord" (Eph 2:21). In short, "preaching peace" is the realization of shalom through Christ and the Spirit, now manifest in the community of the church.

Similar connections can be made with references to God's provision of "rest" (Mt 11:28), and the movement of the people of God towards a state of "rest" (as the fulfillment of the promised land); see Hebrews 4.

Returning to Paul, the quality of shalom-peace is a distinctive attribute of experiencing the mind of Christ. The notion of "mind" is much wider than our narrow post-enlightenment limitation of mind to rational capacities. In the world of St Paul such "thinking" conveys a much deeper sense of intellect, desires, emotions, ambitions and will, combining to produce an "attitude of mind."

It is in this sense that Paul highlights in Philippians 4 what it means to be drawn into the "mindset" of Jesus. The path to true joy and the absence of anxiety is found in thinking as Christ does. Shalom, heart and mind and the gospel converge:

> And the peace of God, which surpasses all understanding, will guard your hearts and your minds in Christ Jesus. Finally, beloved, whatever is true, whatever is honorable, whatever is just, whatever is pure, whatever is pleasing, whatever is commendable, if there is any excellence and if there is anything worthy of praise, think about these things. Keep on doing the things that you have learned and received and heard and seen in me, and the God of peace will be with you (Phil 4:7–9).

Grace, peace and liberation

When the breadth of the gospel is understood in such terms, a variety of dimensions of liberation may be identified, the outworking of the gospel of grace that speaks as profoundly to today's contexts as it did in the world of the early church.

Liberated from pressures of self-sufficiency

Questions of how to live the "good life" featured as much in the ancient world as they do today. For some in the ancient world, the answer was to live entirely in the present: this is as good as it gets, so you may as well "eat, drink and be merry," for future prospects are bleak. This was essentially a nihilist outlook on life, devoid of greater purpose or any ground for future expectation. It was life without any deeper reason for hope. For others, the safest option was to withdraw into oneself. Where could someone go to find things which no one else can impact or control? The answer was to look within, and the capacity to respond to external matters (or people) that the individual alone was able to make. Such ancient approaches to the "good life" have popular counterparts in our world today.

It is true that to withdraw into that space in which we alone may respond holds anything or anyone who may threaten us at arm's length. It is true that a certain freedom may come in discounting any enduring or profound value in things that are external and transitory. However, the cost of such inner protection from anything that may disturb us is that it leaves us in a very lonely place. It has little space for sympathy or compassion (sharing in the joys or pains of others), and resembles Paul Simon's classic song "I am a rock":

> I've built walls,
> A fortress deep and mighty,
> That none may penetrate.
> I have no need of friendship; friendship causes pain.
> It's laughter and it's loving I disdain.
> I am a rock,
> I am an island.[3]

In another direction, the desire for self-sufficiency is the ambition to depend on no one, and to be in no person's debt. It is an approach to life that minimizes the need for faith or trust in others, for we control as much as possible. We are "masters and mistresses" of our own destinies. An inverse version of this approach to life is reflected in the rhetoric that "you can do whatever you want," if you have sufficient resolve and determination.

---

[3] At **www.azlyrics.com/lyrics/simongarfunkel/iamarock.html**

While it may be commended for encouraging people to have a go and not to be constrained by fears or an undue powerless identity, this approach only takes us so far, and nagging questions arise of "what if I cannot control everything?" or "what if I fail or my capacities are diminished in some way?" The end result is very frequently used to increase stress and anxiety levels. To be lord over our own lives results in making much depend on our own capacity to deliver our hopes, dreams and ambitions. And deep down, that can be a profoundly anxious place to be.

The gospel of liberation, whether articulated by Jesus (e.g., Mt 6:24–25) or Paul (e.g., Rom 6:19–20), locates true freedom not in self-sufficiency, but in being devoted to the most trustworthy and grace-filled of "masters," the Lord Jesus Christ. The language of becoming "enslaved" to God is the language of devotion to one who is worthy of our dedication, and through whom we are given life now and into eternity:

> But now that you have been freed from sin and enslaved to God, the advantage you get is sanctification. The end is eternal life. For the wages of sin is death, but the free gift of God is eternal life in Christ Jesus our Lord (Rom 6:22–23).

In the words of another classic Anglican prayer, the "Collect for Peace," addressed to "God the author of peace," continues with the memorable affirmation "whose service is perfect freedom." The God of grace and peace provides in the gospel the ultimate foundation for true liberation, at once both personal yet extended to all creation, inaugurating a realm where heaven and earth is in a process of becoming one reality.

Postscript

I offer three brief reflections in conclusion.

First, any reconsideration of the breadth and extent of the gospel must be shaped by the breadth and extent of the overarching biblical narrative. The Scriptural account of God revealed in action, from Genesis 1 through to Revelation 22, is a story that develops in the purposes of God from creation, through redemption in and through Christ, towards the fulfillment of God's missional purposes in the new creation, all that creation was intended to be and to become.

Secondly, locating the gospel in such terms also affirms that our service in the "here and now" matters. In the grace of God we are drawn into the mission of God. Our endeavors undertaken as we seek "excelling in the work of the Lord" will not prove in vain (1 Cor 15:58). In the greater biblical narrative there is continuity extending from the present realm into the fullness of the kingdom. Having said that, we live in anticipation of the "not yet," the confidence, hope and assurance that the best is yet to come.

Finally, a deepening of our understanding of the greatness of the gospel will result in a rediscovery of our awe and joy in God's purposes. In God's grace, we are part of the ongoing drama of creation and redemption. We are part of something so much bigger than ourselves. As in every generation, the challenge of our times is to rediscover our confidence in the gospel, to see God at work no less in our own time and experiences. The mission of God is seen in the sending of God of God's Son, who has promised to be with us always, even to the end of the age. The sending of God is seen in the sending of the Spirit, the ultimate "game changer" in sanctifying and transforming the people of God. This spirit of adoption extends to both the children of God (Rom 8:16) and to all creation as it waits redemption from the present travails, together drawn into the "freedom of the glory of the children of God" (Rom 8:21).

Martin Luther's discovery of the grace of God not only addressed his own need for personal assurance from his spiritual angst, it sparked a movement of ongoing reform, the heart of which must always be shaped by and draw us back to a deeper appreciation of the great gospel message of grace and peace. To God be the glory!

Questions

If someone outside the church approached you and asked, "What is a Christian?" (rather than "How do you become a Christian?"), how might you answer?

This chapter argues that the gospel is personal, but never individual (in the sense that it is just a matter between us and God). Do you agree, and what are the relational implications of the gospel?

The Christian message is often perceived by people outside the church to be quite a negative one (about things you have to stop doing): how might the church convey a more positive witness to the gospel understood as "grace and peace/shalom" in both word and action?

Bible Study: Isaiah 55:1-2

Zephania Kameeta

> Ho, everyone who thirsts, come to the waters; and you that have no money, come, buy and eat! Come, buy wine and milk without money and without price. Why do you spend your money for that which is not bread, and your labor for that which does not satisfy? Listen carefully to me, and eat what is good, and delight yourselves in rich food (Isa 55:1-2).

Introduction

To each and every Namibian, young and old, this divine invitation in the prophecy of Isaiah is indeed Good News to their ears and fills their hearts with great joy. The invitation is amazing and exciting.

> [C]ome to the waters; and you that have no money, come, buy and eat! Come, buy wine and milk without money and without price.

This is unbelievable! Not only those who are privileged, but all those who are thirsty are invited. No one is left behind. The invitation is also talking of "waters" and not just water. This means that there is plenty of water the supply of which will never be exhausted and each and everyone will have more than enough—not just for a few days, but for a whole lifetime.

Similarities in climate between Namibia and Israel/Palestine

The Mediterranean climate of Israel/Palestine is characterized by long, hot, dry summers. Rainfall is unevenly distributed, decreasing sharply as one moves southward. In the extreme south, rainfall averages less than 100mm annually. Rainfall varies from season to season and from year to year, particularly in the Negev Desert.

In the same way, Namibia's climate is hot and dry with erratic rainfall. Within Africa its climate is second only to the Sahara in its aridity. The average annual rainfall varies from less than 50mm along the coast to 350mm in the central interior and 700mm in the northeast. As in Israel/ Palestine, rainfall varies from season to season and from year to year.

According to the Joint Monitoring Programme for Water Supply and Sanitation, Namibia spends about three percent of its Gross Domestic Product (GNP) on the operation of its water utilities. This is by far the highest percentage of all Sub-Saharan countries. Per capita, Namibia spends about 80 USD annually on water supply and sanitation, while other countries in the region spend between 1 and 10 USD. In Namibia, providing direct access to water costs approximately 4,000 USD per capita on average.

Despite the shortage of water, the peoples of Israel/Palestine and Namibia, regard their countries as "a land flowing with milk and honey" (Ex 3:8)—and I am not excluded.

Therefore, when we hear the Isaiah's metaphor of water in God's invitation we in Namibia exactly understand this means.

Not for sale—sola gratia (verse 1)

The Reformation takes us back to the roots of Scripture. While the world is shouting at the poor, "Go away"—especially you the masses with no money or collateral, you who are not known or have no connection with those on top of the power structures—the Word of God is calling all who thirst for justice and peace. Here God's grace is at play versus the harsh and merciless capital which chases millions away to the rubbish dumps of this world, while the very few are filling their pockets with the wealth derived from the resources of all. Come and do not go away! This calling overrules the rejection by this world. The "go away" pronounced by those with capital power against the poor, lead to death; God's call to all of us to come leads to life in all its fullness.

While the world is dividing us into classes, God is calling each and every one of us—all. This is how we know God. When God sent Moses to Pharaoh, God did not say, Let some of my people go. God simply said, Let my people go. God loved the world and not only some in the world, and gave God's one and only Son. God's grace does not select some or divide into classes but it includes all who admit that they are thirsty.

Our commemoration of the 500 years of Reformation must address practically and meaningfully the thirst of millions of our people in our different countries. They thirst for justice and peace in their countries. We are thinking here about the thousands and millions who had to flee their homes and countries because of religious intolerance; those who on a daily basis are facing the ultra-barbarism of our times and are killed mercilessly; the millions who are thirsty for the eradication of the growing gap between the rich and the poor; women and men who are thirsty for gender justice and equality; the young people who are thirsty for employment; and those who are working but whose salaries are almost entirely eaten up by the high costs of rents for apartments—all of them thirst for a dwelling place of their own.

All the things that cause so much suffering in our world today are pointing to spiritual emptiness. Therefore, there is no excuse for churches born out of the Reformation not to take the lead in addressing these ailments haunting our generation and those to come, in a decisive and urgent way. We have spent a lot of time talking, what is now needed is action.

We are invited to come and to buy without money and without cost. If there is no money and no cost involved, why are we buying then? Why not "just come and take it?" What we are being offered is not cheap but expensive, not in the value of the world, but in God's value. Therefore this cannot be bought with money or any other riches of this world. No one in this world is able to pay for or buy that which is offered by God except God—and God already did that by giving God's Son to die for us so that we can be saved and live in his death and resurrection. We buy what is offered by God, not with our earthly possessions but with what God has already paid for. And this kind of divine transaction is what is called: The grace of God.

> For by grace you have been saved through faith, and this is not your own doing; it is the gift of God—not the result of works, so that no one may boast (Eph 2:8-9).

The root of the sores haunting humanity (verse 2)

"Why do you spend your money for that which is not bread, and your labor for that which does not satisfy?" This question points to sores from which we are suffering today: The European Union Bail Out of its member countries as a way of addressing the Euro zone crisis; the alarmingly growing gap between rich and poor; abject poverty; maternal mortality; malnutrition as an underlying cause of the death of infants and young children; corruption and theft of national resources from countries that lack the know-how of adding value to what is taken in big quantities from their lands; terrorism; refugees; untold suffering and the death of thousands of people who are not directly involved in the current wars to name but some.

If we only listened to this wake-up call and spend what is valuable for real bread and labor on what does satisfy, our world would be different and a better place to live in. The basis on which we are building to change the world for the better is completely wrong and therefore it produced the above mentioned and will make it worse, leading to total destruction. The foundation is wrong because it is the insatiable love for wealth (Mammon). Anything or anyone in way of that beastly love is crushed and destroyed. Money is spent for what is not bread but for crushing, destroying and poisoning humanity; creation is destroyed for the benefit of a handful greedy people and millions of poor workers are exploited to labor for what does not satisfy them and humanity as a whole.

In his letter to the Romans, the Apostle Paul points to a right foundation for believers, but also to all humanity especially for the world today:

> Love must be sincere. Hate what is evil; cling to what is good. Be devoted to one another in brotherly love. Honor one another above yourselves. Never be lacking in zeal, but keep your spiritual fervor, serving the Lord. Be joyful in hope, patient in affliction, faithful in prayer. Share with God's people who are in need. Practice hospitality. [...] Live in harmony with one another. Do not be proud, but be willing to associate with people of low position. Do not be conceited. [...] If it is possible, as far as it depends on you, live at peace with everyone (Romans 12:9-13, 16, 18)

The way in which we deal with our earthly possessions and with people around us must not be detached or separated from these divine values expressed so eloquently by the Apostle. Sincere love, the hate of evil and love of what is good; the loving devotion to each other and to humanity; respect for each other, humanity and the creation; joy and hope for the well-being of all; sharing and hospitality; harmony among one another, the nations and creation; humility and embracing those people of low positions and the radiation of peace wherever you are, should be the inspiration and basis of how one deals with one's money and earthly possessions. Equally, this is also what should happen within and between churches, governments and nations. This kind of Bail Out will yield more desirable fruits for all of humanity and the entire creation.

Governments and nations are deliberately blind to this simple but very powerful message of the prophets and apostles, therefore the churches commemorating 500 years of Reformation are challenged to put these prophetic and apostolic values into a reforming action. This indeed should be at the core of the commemoration of the 500th Anniversary of the Reformation. This will give relevance to the sub-themes of the Anniversary: Salvation not for sale; Human beings not for sale; Creation not for sale.

What this invitation means to us here in Namibia

"And you that have no money, come, buy and eat"—this is of great relevance to us today and is indeed good. In the twenty-five years after independence there have been many serious attempts to address and fulfill the Millennium Development Goals (MDG), but there still remain many challenges that need urgent and further serious consideration and action.

It is general knowledge that in this twenty-first century over 3 million children around the world still die every year of hunger, and Namibia is no exception. It is not for fun that children are scouring the rubbish dumps of our towns and villages around the country—they are trying to find something there which might fill their stomachs. Primary education in Namibia is now free of charge, but going to school on an empty stomach is a painful exercise and therefore, as a result of hunger, many children drop out of school and are exposed to all sorts of dangers and vices. When you see them you would not immediately notice that they are hungry, but after talking to them and knowing them closely, you realize that they have not eaten for a week or more.

As Ramadhani Abdallah Noor, a Tanzanian doctor and research associate at the Harvard School of Public Health and New Voices Fellow at the Aspen Institute wrote in September 2014,

> As an African doctor, I know that the ravages of serious malnutrition and hunger are not always visible. They are not always as manifest as they are in the protruding ribs of ghostly children hooked up to feeding tubes, like those I used to see in hospital wards in Tanzania. Chronic malnutrition, or "hidden hunger," shows itself in other ways—but it can be just as devastating and deadly. And while deaths from many other diseases, including acute malnutrition, have declined, hidden hunger remains pervasive.[1]

Not only young children are suffering from hunger, but also students. Those who do not stay in a hostel, but come from outside, survive the whole day at the university on a meager or no meal; and this adversely impacts their studies. As Noor notes,

> In Africa, hunger remains the leading cause of death in children, accounting for half of all deaths of children under the age of five and killing more than AIDS, TB, and malaria combined.

[1] At **www.project-syndicate.org/commentary/ramadhani-a--noor-laments-the-scourge-of-malnutrition-ravaging-the-continent-s-children**

Furthermore

> Addressing this ongoing crisis requires money—**an estimated $10 billion per year**—and new and better strategies to bring life-saving solutions to the mothers and children who most need them.
>
> But the cost looks far less daunting when one considers the cost of hunger. UNICEF estimates that the cost of Africa's child malnutrition is **$25 billion a year**. And this is not the whole story. Malnutrition costs an estimated **$3.5 trillion every year** to the global economy, owing to loss of productivity and higher health-care costs.[2]

I firmly believe that one of the new and better strategies to implement life-saving solutions for those who are ravaged by abject poverty and hunger is a national Basic Income Grant (BIG), which proved itself at Otjivero, and will drastically reduce poverty and unemployment, increase economic activities and improve educational outcomes and the health condition of the majority of the people of Namibia. As one aspect of redistribution the BIG needs to be accompanied by other measures to achieve transformative structural changes.

It is a false notion that giving money to the poor is like putting water in a bottomless pit. BIG will stimulate and inspire economic activity, growth and prosperity, not only for the poor, but for the country at large. It will furthermore uplift and bring life to the rural areas and this, in turn, will gradually remove the burden of supplying water and electricity to the urban areas, because as a result of economic activities in the rural areas, people will be attracted to move back there.

This happened on a smaller scale when people moved back from Windhoek and other places to Otjivero, because of the economic activities and life there. Therefore BIG will not only lift up and benefit the poor, but benefit the country and set us firmly on the course of a developed country in which the gap between rich and poor is narrowed and redistribution takes place, toward prosperity for all.

This is not an unrealistic dream or utopia, but an attainable reality for which many have suffered and sacrificed their lives. What we need to achieve now is the political will of unselfish leaders who carry the needs of the poor and of the whole country in their hearts. We equally need courageous and committed women and men who, walking in the footsteps of the prophets and apostles, confront the gods of capital and greed and challenge them with the good news of liberation, justice and peace for the poor.

---

[2] Ibid.

This should have happened the day before yesterday and not today. For Namibia it should have been twenty-five years ago. The poor and the hungry are tired of words, they want to see actions of redemption! The text of this Bible study does not say, Come so that you can be counted or registered or so that research can be done why you are thirsty; but just simply, come and drink. This is what is needed in this hour of need. Those in need want help now before they perish. Now is your hour and your moment. Budgets and money are not the question: come, eat and drink, so that you can live.

I want to conclude this article with my contextual translation of Isaiah 55:1-2:

You are free!
The Lord says,
Come, everyone who thinks
he is still a slave –
liberation is at hand!
Come, you who believe
you are nobody,
come out and be somebody!
Come! Buy justice and integrity—
it will cost you nothing!
Why continue living like nobody
while I am making you somebody again?
Why continue living like a slave
while liberation is a reality?
Listen to me and act on what I say,
and you will enjoy life in its fullness.

List of Contributors

Brakemeier, Gottfried, Rev. Dr, President of the Lutheran World Federation, 1990–1997, Brazil

Burghardt, Anne, Rev., Secretary for Ecumenical Relations, Lutheran World Federation, Geneva, Switzerland

Byrtek, Elżbieta, mag.theol., Assistant for Religious Education, Christian Theological Academy in Warsaw, Poland

Grosshans, Hans-Peter, Prof. Dr, Professor of Systematic and Ecumenical Theology, Faculty of Protestant Theology, University of Munster, Germany

Harris, Timothy J., Dr, Assistant Bishop, Anglican Diocese of Adelaide, Vice-Principal, St Barnabas Theological College, Adelaide, member of the Anglican-Lutheran International Coordinating Committee, Australia

Junge, Martin, Rev., General Secretary, Lutheran World Federation, Geneva, Switzerland

Kameeta, Zephania, Rev. Dr, Bishop Emeritus, Evangelical Lutheran Church in Namibia, Minister of Poverty Eradication and Social Welfare, Republic of Namibia

Ngui Au Sze, Rev., The Basel Christian Church of Malaysia, LWF WICAS-SEALUC Women Theologians Coordinator, Malaysia

Nordstokke, Kjell, Rev. Dr, Prof. Emeritus, Diakonhjemmet University College, Oslo, Norway

Villarreal, Monica, Rev., Evangelical Lutheran Church in America, member of the LWF Global Young Reformers Network's Steering Committee, USA

Creation—Not For Sale

Edited by
Anne Burghardt

Bibliographic information published by the German National Library

The *Deutsche Nationalbibliothek* lists this publication in the *Deutsche Nationalbibliografie;* detailed bibliographic data are available on the internet at http://dnd.dnd.de

Printed in Germany · H 7924

This book was printed on FSC-certified paper

Editorial assistance:	Department for Theology and Public Witness
Layout:	Department for Theology and Public Witness
Design:	LWF-Office for Communication Services
Printing and Binding:	Druckhaus Köthen GmbH & Co. KG

Published by Evangelische Verlangsanstalt GmbH, Leipzig, Germany, under the auspices of
The Lutheran World Federation
150, rte de Ferney, PO Box 2100
CH-1211 Geneva 2, Switzerland

Parallel editions in German and Spanish

ISBN 978-3-374-04160-2

Contents

Introduction

Anne Burghardt

This booklet is part of a small collection published by the Lutheran World Federation on the occasion of the 500th Anniversary of the Reformation in 2017. "Creation—Not For Sale" is one of the three sub-themes of the Anniversary's main theme, "Liberated by God's Grace." The popular essays in this booklet were written by authors from all regions of the Lutheran World Federation; the ecumenical voice is here represented by a Greek Orthodox theologian.

In light of today's massive exploitation of natural resources, it is crucial that we pay attention to God's entire creation. We read in Genesis that God considered creation to be "good" and entrusted creation into human care. The notion of "dominion" in Genesis 1:26 has often been misused and it has all too frequently been overlooked that God declares all creation to be "good," quite apart from its usefulness to humans. The renewed relationship between God and human beings therefore also has implications on how humans relate to the rest of the creation, since creation primarily belongs to God and is only entrusted into our hands. The essays in this booklet explore different aspects of the theme "Creation—Not For Sale," ranging from subject as varied as genetic engineering and raising the question of "whose" rather than "who" we are to issues of climate change and climate justice, land grabbing, etc. The list of topics addressed in the essays is far from exhaustive. Nonetheless, we hope to offer some initial impulses for theologically informed discussions on the understanding of being created by God and on the integrity of creation.

And God Saw that it was Good: Reflections on Theology of Creation

Barbara R. Rossing

The sacredness and goodness of creation is a conviction affirmed in Scripture and in core Lutheran theological principles.

The poetic refrain "God saw that it was good" anchors the creation story in Genesis 1. Repeated six times, with variation, the refrain culminates in the declaration of "very good" on the sixth day (Gen 1:31). The Hebrew conjunction *ki* can also be translated adverbially as "how": "God saw *how* (*ki*) good it was" (Common English Bible). "How good" evokes God's delight in discovering each element of the world as good. God finds joy in creation.

"Good" is the key word–the goodness of all, as God looks at each aspect of the world. *Tov* in Hebrew expresses joy and relationship, as well as beauty. One rabbinic commentary translates *tov* as "beautiful."[1]

Genesis 1 is liturgical poetry, showing us the beauty of each element of creation. Sun, earth, atmosphere ("firmament"), oceans and all biological organisms, including humans and all species of plants and animals: each has its own ecological niche, and each is declared beautiful and good in the eyes of God.

Seeing the earth

God's first response–seeing–can also serve as a starting point for us today. Genesis 1 situates humans within the enormity of the whole cosmos. Thanks to photos of the earth from space, we are now able to see the earth as never

[1] Ellen Bernstein, "Creation Theology: A Jewish Perspective," in *The Green Bible* (New York: HarperCollins, 2008), 1–53.

before. The 1972 iconic image of the earth taken by the crew of the US Apollo spacecraft, the most widely distributed photograph of all times, reveals the beauty of the earth as a blue marbled planet, with living oceans and continents. We can see what the astronauts saw: the earth's sheer beauty, its vulnerability, as well as a new sense of humanity's place on the planet, all suffused with an overwhelming sense of awe. Astronaut Michael Collins describes it:

> I remember so vividly what I saw when I looked back at my fragile home—a glistening, inviting beacon, delicate blue and white, a tiny outpost suspended in the black infinity. Earth is to be treasured and nurtured, something precious that *must* endure.[2]

As astronaut Bill Anders said about circumnavigating the moon in 1968, "We came all this way to explore the moon, and the most important thing is that we discovered the earth."

Seeing the earth today means opening our eyes to see its beauty and also its vulnerability—the devastation humans are causing to God's good creation. Astronauts record their shock in seeing changes to the earth such as the diminution of the polar ice cap. Commander Ellen Collins, the first woman to lead a US space shuttle mission, told how she saw the island of Madagascar: "We saw deforestation [...}. The rivers and streams that normally would be a bluish-gray color are now brown from the erosion of soil flowing into the ocean."[3]

The thinness and vulnerability of the earth's atmosphere relative to the rest of the planet is also something astronauts see. From space, the earth's atmosphere looks like a "thin blue line"—thinner than the peel of an apple relative to the apple. Genesis describes this protective layer as a "firmament."

Carbon dioxide itself is colorless, so the build-up of carbon dioxide and other greenhouse gases in the atmosphere cannot be seen directly from space. What can be seen are the effects of increasing concentrations of carbon dioxide on the planet—the drying up of large lakes such as Lake Chad in Africa; catastrophic flooding in Asia; deforestation in the Amazon and Congo River basins; shrinking glaciers in the world's mountain ranges; smoke from unprecedented wildfires; and dustbowls caused by drought. Too much heat from greenhouse gases (primarily carbon dioxide) is killing ecological systems humans need for our survival.

---

[2] Michael Collins, "Foreword," in Roy A. Gallant, *Our Universe* (Washington, D.C.: National Geographic Society, 1980), 6.

[3] Cited in Wangari Maathai, *Replenishing the Earth: Spiritual Values for Healing Ourselves and the World* (New York: Doubleday, 2010), 57.

Good, very good

God sees each creature as "good." By calling each creature good, God initiates an ongoing relationship of love with the earth and with each of its creatures. God "is *affected* by what is seen."[4] As Norman Habel notes, a similar exclamation of "good" is used to describe the response of Moses' mother when the child is born. Moses' mother "sees he is good" (Ex 2:1). Similarly, in Genesis 1, "God beholds Earth emerge from the waters below and 'sees it is good'."[5] Earth is God's living child.

For God, earth's ongoing creative ability—the process evolutionary biologists describe as its capacity for bringing forth new species—is "good." With amazing scientific insight, Genesis describes earth as a partner with God in creating more life forms. Written before our scientific worldview, Genesis differs from our modern cosmology. Still, its appreciation of earth's ongoing creativity coheres with our understanding of the biological processes of evolution and speciation. Beginning with the creation of plants on the third day, the earth itself becomes a cocreator with God, bringing forth creatures of its own—"The earth brought forth vegetation" (Gen 1:12). This is repeated on the sixth day with the emergence of animals, "Let the earth bring forth living creatures of every kind" (Gen 1:24). Creation is a process from below, in which creatures also become cocreators, bringing forth more and more creatures of their own in the bounty of life and creation. God calls this entire process good.

What does the goodness or beauty of creation mean for us today? It can mean a number of things. The creatures are good as food for people to eat, as Martin Luther emphasizes in his commentary on Genesis. God's feeding of hungry people with the good gifts of creation becomes increasingly important in an age of hunger.

Utility for humans is not the primary meaning of "good," however. "Good for humans" is not what God says. This is important because stripping the earth's resources through extractive mining, drilling, agriculture and industry has been justified on the grounds that God gave humans "dominion" over creation in Genesis 1:26. But if we look closely at each day's creation, we see that God declares the creatures as good for their own sake, quite apart from any usefulness to humans. This is a perspective shared by God's speech from the whirlwind in Job 38–41.

---

[4] Terrence Fretheim, *God and World in the Old Testament: A Relational Theology of Creation* (Nashville: Abingdon Press, 2005), 40.

[5] Norman Habel, *The Birth, the Curse and the Greening of Earth An Ecological Reading of Genesis 1-11* (Sheffield Phoenix Press, 2011), 42.

Perhaps most importantly, goodness also means interconnectedness, an ecological principle. God declares the entirety of creation to be "very good" (*tov ma'ov*, Gen 1:31). This superlative on the sixth day is not reserved for humans alone, as some anthropocentric interpretations have claimed. Rather, it is when God saw everything, and how the whole creation works together as an interconnected living ecological system, that God declares everything to be very, very good.

Good as common good

The goodness or "good" of creation poses ethical questions for us today.

A "good" can become a noun, indicating one's own private property or possessions—"my goods," in English, similar to the Greek *ta agatha*. Jesus' story about the man who builds bigger barns in order to hold all his "goods" (Lk 12:18, 19) contains an urgent warning about the perils of hoarding goods for one's own exclusive gain. In his warped vision, the man thinks he himself has produced his own goods. He fails to realize that it is the earth that brought forth his abundant crops. The man loses his soul. Martin Luther labels this hoarder "Mammon."[6]

If "good" is understood primarily in terms of private gain, without considering the consequences for our neighbor, for future generations or for ecosystems, we are all imperiled. God calls us to see the goodness of creation by valuing inter-relationships most of all.

The 500th Anniversary of the Reformation in 2017 comes at an urgent moment for creation. It is time for a new reformation, ethicist Larry Rasmussen and other theologians argue: What we need is an ecological reformation that turns the church towards earth-healing and the common good.[7] In laying out the contours of what an eco-Reformation might look like, Rasmussen underscores the need for an economy that fosters the common good, so that "the primary goods of the commons—earth, air, fire, water, light—are cared-for requisites of a shared good, a good for both present and future generations of humankind and otherkind."[8]

We live at a moment when goods are commodified, but nature and the atmosphere are still too often treated as a sewer or as a resource with no

---

[6] Margot Kassmann, "Covenant, Praise and Justice in Creation: Five Bible Studies," in David G. Hallman (ed.), *Ecotheology: Voices from South and North* (Geneva/Maryknoll: WCC/Orbis, 1994), 42.

[7] Larry Rasmussen, "Waiting for the Lutherans," in *Currents in Theology and Mission* 37 (2010), 86–98.

[8] Ibid., 78

value or price. Most countries of the world have not yet put a price on carbon dioxide pollution. Industries are allowed to burn fossil fuels without paying for the consequences of their pollution. Poor people's livelihood is threatened by unsustainable development. The Bible teaches a political economy of "enough for all," based on sharing of what is given for the common good of all (Ex 16). Love for neighbor, including future generations as our neighbor, is at the heart of both the Bible and Lutheran theology.

Luther's theology of creation and the cross

God's grace is not for sale, Martin Luther insisted five hundred years ago. Luther's bold economic critique called for reform not only in the church but also in the debt structure of society that was impoverishing people.[9] Today, we can extend Luther's reformation insight about the pricelessness of grace and life itself into other realms, including creation itself. Creation and future generations are my neighbor, whom I am commanded to love. They are not for sale.

We can draw on incarnational and sacramental theology that discerns God in all of life. In his writings on the Lord's Supper against the Calvinists, Luther insisted that the finite can really hold the infinite: *finitum capax infiniti*. "Deep incarnation" is a phrase coined by the Danish Lutheran Nils Gregerson to express the idea of the radical incarnation of God in all matter. Incarnational and sacramental theology insists that God is present, as Luther says, "in every little seed, whole and entire [...] Christ is present in all creatures, and I might find [Christ] in stone, in fire, in water, or even in a rope, for [Christ] is there."[10] Rasmussen and others call this Luther's "joyous panentheism." Today, even as creation is degraded, we can embrace Luther's joyous insistence that God is present

> in every single creature in its innermost and outermost being, on all sides, through and through, below and above, before and behind, so that nothing can be more truly present and within all creatures than God himself with his power.[11]

---

[9] Guillermo Hansen, "Money, Religion, and Tyranny: God and the Demonic in Luther's Antifragile Theology," in Wanda Deifelt (ed.), *Market and Margins: Lutheran Perspectives* (Minneapolis: Lutheran University Press, 2014), 31–68.

[10] Cited by Larry Rasmussen, op. cit. (note 7).

[11] Martin Luther, "That These Words of Christ, 'This Is My Body,' etc., Still Stand Firm Against the Fanatics, 1527," in Helmut T. Lehmann (ed.), *Luther's Works*, vol. 37 (Philadelphia: Muhlenberg Press, 1961), 58.

The Lutheran theology of the cross—the insistence that God is present also and even most of all in brokenness and pain—can also help us to face the sin of ecological devastation, the injustice of the effects of climate change on the poorest of the poor—and to formulate an analysis of both sin and redemption capable of addressing the ecological crisis.[12]

Indigenous communities' spiritual perspectives can also help us to recover an emphasis on the goodness of creation. Sami Lutheran theologian Tore Johnson underscores the communal nature of creation, in which all living beings are seen as interrelated in a circle of life. "Sami tradition reflects the idea that creation has a voice that should be listened to." [13] Johnson calls for an eco-theological starting point that begins with creation, doing "theology from the circle of life."[14]

Are fossil fuels "good"? Energy and the common good

In order theologically to address the climate crisis we must also address the question of the goodness and risks of fossil fuels, as part of God's creation. Energy poses a problem of competing goods. God's first act of creation in Genesis 1 is light, the energy that powers our life. The sun's light provides energy in abundance to sustain everything on earth. Each hour of every day the sun delivers more energy to earth than humans consume in an entire year.[15] Humans have recently discovered how to tap into ancient sunlight—by burning solar energy banked deep within the earth in the form of coal, oil, and natural gas, buried for millions of years beneath the earth's surface.

Energy is essential for human flourishing. But how do we balance the need for the development of cheap fossil fuels with the risks of carbon dioxide pollution? Climate scientists note that we need to leave three-fourths of known petroleum resources in the ground, in order to stave off dangerous changes to the planet. Commitment to the common good, to future generations, necessitates transitioning away from fossil fuels towards renewable energy.

---

[12] Wanda Deifelt, "From Cross to Tree of Life: Creation as God's Mask," in Karla Bombach and Shauna Hannan (eds), *Eco-Lutheranism: Lutheran Perspectives on Ecology* (Minneapolis: Lutheran University Press, 2013), 169–76.

[13] Tore Johnson, "Listen to the Voice of Nature: Indigenous Perspectives," in Karen Bloomquist (ed.), *God, Creation and Climate Change: Spiritual and Ethical Perspectives,* LWF Studies 02/09 (Minneapolis/Geneva: Lutheran University Press/The Lutheran World Federation, 2009), 101.

[14] Ibid., 106

[15] James B. Martin-Schramm, *Climate Justice. Ethics, Energy, and Public Policy* (Minneapolis: Fortress Press, 2010), 3.

Bishop Mark Narum of North Dakota, suggests that Luther's catechism question, What does this mean? is a question we might ask also about energy policy. Many residents of the Western North Dakota Synod of the Evangelical Lutheran Church in America (ELCA), where Bishop Narum serves, have benefited from an enormous oil shale boom, made possible by the development of hydraulic fracturing and horizontal drilling technology. Bishop Narum underscores the good that oil has brought to land owners and to the region's employment. Oil poses complex pastoral issues in congregations, requiring listening to diverse views. Narum asks, "If God is creator of all and God says, 'It is good,' what about petroleum?"[16]

As part of God's good creation, petroleum is certainly "good." But does that mean we should extract and burn it all as fossil fuel? Or today, might petroleum perform an even greater "good" when left in the ground? Perhaps God has safely sequestered carbon in the sedimentary rock layers, over millions of years, in order to keep the earth's atmosphere's temperature at the ideal level for life. Whereas in the nineteenth and twentieth centuries the "good" of oil-rich rock formations was seen as the energy they provided humans to fuel our economic growth, they may now have an even greater good as a storehouse for sequestered carbon in the ground.

God's love for creation in Genesis 1 invites us to explore complex ethical questions, to listen to one another, and to take bold, prophetic action to care for the whole of creation as our neighbor. Creation is endangered by human sin, as the astronauts are seeing. "How good!" expresses God's love for each element of creation. That love that sees the earth in all its brokenness and beauty is the same love that compels us to act today. Luther's vision of deep incarnation calls us to care for the earth and all its communities of life.

Questions

What does it mean to say that God's creation is "good, very good" in an age when everything is for sale? Is anything priceless?

What steps of eco-Reformation might be needed and are possible in your church context?

Do we need to put a price on the creation, on ecosystems, in order to value them?

---

[16] Mark Narum, "Prairie, Petroleum, Pondering: What Does this Mean?" in Bombach and Hannan, op. cit. (note 12), 150.

Responding to the Word of God and Creation. Ethical Reflections on Genetic Engineering and Responsive Science

Ulrik Becker Nissen

As the 500th Anniversary of the Reformation is commemorated, two significant and immediate lessons emerge. We are awed by wondrous conditions that do not change. There is, on the one hand, the central Reformation insight that salvation is by faith alone and that righteousness is granted to us solely by God's grace. This has not changed over the last 500 years and of this we still need to be reminded today. On the other, when we read the writings of Martin Luther and the other Reformers, we are immediately struck by the enormous shift in some of the challenges that we need to address. Whereas certain societal and ethical issues bear resemblance to those of the seventeenth century, we are today dealing with radically new matters such as genetic engineering for instance, where we can search in vain for concrete reflections in Luther's writings. Even if such subjects raise new moral questions, we need to draw on the resources of our living traditions when dealing with these concerns. For the Lutheran tradition to remain alive and vibrant, we need to go back to our sources. In this way the Reformation lives on in the midst of new challenges, where we have to reflect on what our Lutheran heritage implies with regard to new political, ideological, cultural and scientific matters. In this essay I shall focus on the following questions: In light of the Lutheran Reformation, what does the theology of creation imply for contemporary Lutheran theology? We will consider this question in view of central insights in Luther's theology of creation and what it means that the world is created by the Word of God. Second, what does a Lutheran theology of creation imply for the understanding of "whose" we are? When we examine topics such as genetic engineering, is the most crucial question "who" we are, or, rather, "whose" we are? Third, we will conclude our reflections by focusing on genetic engineering. In light of the two previous sections, how are we to assess genetic engineering? What would it imply if we were to think of science as a responsive concept?

The Lutheran theology of creation and the Word of God

When we consider contemporary concerns such as genetic engineering for instance, we face a challenge that is no different from the other fundamental questions that theology has always been confronted with. Where, then, do we turn when we seek answers to these difficult issues? One approach is to turn to the natural sciences or to take a broader philosophical approach. We can certainly learn a lot from this, but does it lead us to a proper theological understanding? In order for it to be theology in any ordinary sense of this term, we must emphasize genuine theological resources. We need to situate the starting point of our reflections within a hermeneutic shaped and informed by church and Scripture. This does not neglect other resources but maintains a proper awareness of where theology comes from. Theology is a view from somewhere.

Reflections on the foundation of theology are particularly pertinent considering Luther's emphasis on the centrality of Scripture for the Christian faith and theology. *Sola scriptura* implies that a Lutheran theology can never ignore the normative role of Scripture. If a Lutheran church forgets the normative role of Scripture, it gives up being church in the Protestant sense of the term. When we take this Lutheran insight as our starting point, then the obvious place to go is Luther's "Lectures on Genesis" in order to reflect on how we are to understand creation today. In these lectures we are immediately reminded of two things: (1) creation is called into being by the Word of God; and (2) creation in its origin is an expression of God's beneficence.

In his comments on the first verses of Genesis, Luther emphasizes that God creates heaven and earth through the Word. "The Father creates heaven and earth out of nothing through the Son, whom Moses calls the Word."[1] The world is created by the Word of God, which is Christ himself.

[1] Martin Luther, "Lectures on Genesis Chapter 1–5," in Jarolsav Pelikan (ed.), *Luther's Works*, vol. 1 (St Louis: Concordia Publishing House, 1958), 9.

For Luther, Christ is present and at work in God's creative work from the very beginning. He follows up on this in his exegesis of Genesis 1:3, where the Word is emphasized as the means and instrument of God's creative work and how this points forward to the Johannine understanding (Jn 1:1) of Christ as the Word of God.[2] The intimate link between creation by the Word of God and Christ as this very Word is significant for the theological meaning of creation. God calls the world into being by God's Word, draws the human being into a responding and living relationship, and spiritually nurtures the human being by God's Word. Therefore Oswald Bayer can say that for Luther creation is fundamentally about the establishment and preservation of community.[3] Creation points forward to justification by faith, and just as the justified sinner responds with gratitude, Luther understands creation as an expression of God's beneficence, pointing forward to the ultimate good, justification by faith in Christ.

The other central motif in Luther's theology of creation is its expression of God's solicitude and benevolence. We find this view in Luther's reflections on the first time it is said that God finds the creation good (Gen 1:10). Luther points out that the meaning of this verse is that God has created a good dwelling place for the human being (even if still not created) and wishes the human being to respond with gratitude.[4] The same reading is continued with regard to the following verses of Genesis 1:11, where Luther argues that when human beings are created, they will find an already fully equipped and marvelous place to live in. God takes care of human beings and gives them all they need. It is significant to note that also here Luther draws a parallel to God's beneficence with respect to the spiritual gifts, where God also gives us all that we need. This is the "[...] concern, care, generosity, and benevolence of God" that we already find in these first pages of Genesis and that we are to consider the significant lesson of these verses.[5]

Therefore, when we attempt to identify some theological key points in Luther's theology of creation, we can safely say that for Luther creation is not just about the origin of matter. Rather, it is about the relationship to and community with God and our fellow creatures. Luther's emphasis on the Word and God's beneficence is an expression of God's calling creation into a living and responsive fellowship. It is from this perspective that we can concur with Dietrich Bonhoeffer, who says that the meaning of creation can only be known from the perspective of the church. We can never reflect on

---

[2] Ibid., 16f.

[3] Oswald Bayer, *Martin Luthers Theologie: Eine Vergegenwärtigung* (Tübingen: Mohr Siebeck, 2003), 88ff.

[4] *LW*, op. cit. (note 1), 35.

[5] Ibid., 39.

the meaning of creation from a neutral point, but can only contemplate the meaning of creation from the particular place, there where we have encountered God's beneficence. Therefore, Bonhoeffer argues that it is hopeless to hypothesize about the origins without an awareness of where we come from. We can only know about the origins as those who live from Christ.

> The attempt—with the origin and nature of humankind in mind—to take a gigantic leap back into the world of the lost beginning, to seek to know for ourselves what humankind was like in its original state and to identify our own ideal of humanity with what God actually created is hopeless [...]. Only in the middle, as those who live from Christ, do we know about the beginning.[6]

Whose are we? Responding to creation and the will of God

The emphasis in both Luther and Bonhoeffer on the Word of God and the response to this Word moves the focus in the understanding of the human being away from "**who** we are" to "**whose** we are." We are not on our own. Rather, we stand in a living and responsive community with the Triune God as our Creator, Redeemer and Sanctifier. It is this living community with God that we are called to respond to and to obey the Word and will of God.

The responsivity as a defining feature of what it means to be a human being also implies that we are not on our own. It is not sufficient to pursue a modernistic account of the individual as an autonomous being. Rather, we have to maintain that we have the center of our being beyond ourselves and in that sense we are "eccentric beings." We live our lives on "borrowed breath," we are not our own creators. David Kelsey makes an extensive argument for this in his theological anthropology, where he contends that the human being is rightly understood as created, consummated and reconciled. As created beings we are living on "borrowed breath," as consummated we are living on "borrowed time" in anticipation of the eschatological hope, as reconciled we are living by Christ's death.[7] Kelsey's argument is comprehensive, but the central idea in his work is the understanding that a Christian theological anthropology must be understood in light of the Christian traditions in order to provide a substantial contribution within

---

[6] Dietrich Bonhoeffer, "Creation and Fall: A Theological Exposition of Genesis 1-3," in Martin Rüter, Ilse Tödt, and John W. De Gruchy (eds), *Dietrich Bonhoeffer Works*, vol. 3, transl. Douglas Stephen Bax (Minneapolis, MN: Fortress Press, 1997), 62.
[7] David H. Kelsey, *Eccentric Existence: A Theological Anthropology*, vols 1 and 2 (Louisville, Ky.: Westminster John Knox Press, 2009).

this context. This rootedness in a particular community does not preclude the discussion with other approaches, but it identifies more clearly how to understand these issues from a Christian theological perspective.

If we understand the human being as fundamentally an eccentric being, we move the focus from ourselves to seeking and realizing the will of God. When Bonhoeffer reminds us that we cannot understand creation as separate from Christ, he is at the same time reminding us of the reality of our lives. There is no reality apart from Christ and therefore the true understanding of reality is revealed only in Christ. For the Christian this means that we are called to live our lives in discipleship. We are not called to be the masters or mistresses of our own or other people's lives, but to live our lives following Christ and seeking the will of God in all that we do. When we focus our attention on **whose** we are, we are at the same time asserting that we are servants. We are living our lives with a calling according to which we are to respond with faithfulness. As Christians we have a lord, and we are called to be obedient to God's will. Bonhoeffer formulates it succinctly when he states that the Christian is called to be obedient, but at the same time it is an obedience intimately related to responsibility as a responsive concept that binds together obedience and freedom.

> Obedience without freedom is slavery, freedom without obedience is arbitrariness. Obedience binds freedom, freedom ennobles obedience. Obedience binds the creature to the Creator, freedom places the creature, made in God's image, face-to-face with the Creator [...] In responsibility both obedience and freedom become real [realisieren sich].[8]

The obedience to the will of God grows out of the response in faith and gratitude to God. As Luther so excellently shows, this is a response that is an integral part of living as a created being, surrounded by all the good things God has provided for us with creation and with the spiritual gifts bestowed upon us in Christ. So when we approach an issue such as genetic engineering, we are not simply engaging with this issue from the perspective of how far we can go. Rather, the Christian approach should be to ask what the responsible (understood as a responsive concept) approach is to this technology. The responsible approach reminds us that ultimately we are not on our own. Ultimately, we are called to live our lives in responsive community with God and with our fellow creatures. This is a responsivity

[8] Dietrich Bonhoeffer, "Ethics," in Clifford J. Green (ed.), *Dietrich Bonhoeffer Works*, vol. 5, transl. Reinhard Krauss, Charles C. West and Douglas W. Stott (Minneapolis: Fortress Press, 2005), 287f.

which reminds us of our creatureliness, just as it cautions us to live our lives seeking the will of our Lord and the best for our fellow creatures.

Genetic engineering in light of responsive science

The concept of the human being as a responsive being carries with it a reservation concerning the concept of co-creation. In Philip Hefner's *The Human Factor,* [9] the human being is understood as "[...] created co-creators whose purpose it is to be the agency, acting in freedom, to birth the future that is most wholesome for the nature that has birthed us."[10] Hefner supports this thesis by pointing to three basic elements: (1) The human being as created by God to be a cocreator; (2) the evolutionary process as a conditioning matrix; and (3) freedom as key to God's intention. Balancing these three elements, Hefner seeks to maintain an understanding of God as Creator and the human being as created—understood in light of contemporary scientific and evolutionary insights.[11]

Hefner's position has been widely debated. One of the critiques raised is that he goes too far with his concept of the human being as "cocreator" and instead to employ the term "creative creatures." Hefner rejects this proposal due to its insufficient framing of the dual nature of the human being—"[...] a creature who has been brought into existence by nature's processes, and who has been given by that nature the role of free cocreator within those same processes."[12] Admittedly, the dual nature of the human being as both conditioned and free is a view shared by most theologians and philosophers, as we can affirm this both from tradition and from our experiences. The more substantial problem with Hefner's proposal lies with his understanding of God, the human being and the relation between the two. In order to argue for his position, he tones down its implications for the concept of God,[13] limits the role of tradition in the construction of his proposal,[14] and situates his theory in a methodology taken from the natural sciences.[15]

Even if the concept of the human being as created cocreator can be said to express part of the scientific responsibility we have as human be-

---

[9] Philip Hefner, *The Human Factor: Evolution, Culture, and Religion* (Minneapolis, MN: Fortress Press, 1993).

[10] Ibid., 27.

[11] Ibid., 31ff.

[12] Ibid., 39.

[13] Ibid., 32ff.

[14] Ibid., 17ff.

[15] Ibid., 23ff.

ings for the continuous development of the sciences and the possibilities of new scientific technologies, the fundamental problem with the concept is that it presumes too much with regard to the human being. It tends to move the center of human life to the human being itself and thereby to eradicate the responsive dimension of the human condition. This danger is particularly pertinent when we approach the question of genetic engineering, particularly when it takes the form of manipulation with or genetic enhancement of human beings.

When we address the question of genetic engineering, we have to be aware that this is a very broad concept covering many different scientific potentials and ethical issues. Basically, genetic engineering is the attempt to replace a piece of DNA in the cell of a living organism with the intention of producing a new trait or characteristic. This can be used for medical purposes such as in the treatment of genetic disorders with gene therapy; animals can be modified for the purpose of research; crops can be enhanced either for the purpose of growth or to improve the conditions of children suffering from malnutrition, etc. There are many good and noble reasons for genetic engineering—not to do so in some cases would be ethically questionable. When genetic engineering is used to construct T cells for treating cancer there is a moral argument for endorsing the development of this new technique. When we can use genetic engineering to advance treatment possibilities for various kinds of diseases, it would be morally wrong to argue against this, if we do not have very good reasons for doing so. However, at the same time, there are certain uses of genetic engineering, where we have to be very cautious and probably warn against the use of this technology in these contexts. This is particularly the case, when genetic engineering is claimed to be a technology we can use for designing or enhancing certain hereditary traits in human beings. Generally, we have to be extremely careful when we use such a radical technology to make permanent changes in the genetic profile of a given organism. With regard to plants, this has given rise to concern about genetically modified crops and how inherited new genes in the seeds of a plant may spread in unpredictable ways to wild plants. With regard to human beings there has been a strong concern about hereditary changes and research on gametes that lead to permanent changes in the human genome. Again, the concern is whether we can foresee the future implications of the deep and fundamental changes we make.

Instead of seeing the human being as created cocreator, I contend that we should understand the human being as a responsive being. The concept of responsivity lies deeply within the Lutheran tradition, and emphasizes the human being as living in responsive community with God and fellow creatures. As created beings we are not semi-Gods, but created creatures living our lives in light of God's will. But, at the same time, we have a responsibility and calling. We are called to do our very best in developing new kinds of biotechnology and improving on current approaches to science and medicine. Our task is to find the path between Scylla and Charybdis—the Scylla of an overestimation of our role as created beings, and the Charybdis of a subservience to the forces of depravation at play within creation. It is here that we can aim at having both a positive view of biotechnology, and at the same time maintain that we are finite beings living our lives on borrowed breath.

Questions

What role can 500-year-old Lutheran texts play in the contemporary assessment of current scientific and technological challenges?

Does the concept of the human being as a "responsive being" carry more weight theologically than the alternative "created cocreator"?

What kinds of genetic engineering can we endorse theologically, and where should we be cautious?

Natural Disasters and God's Good Creation

Naoki Asano

God's nature

Who is God? What is God? Where is God? Numerous questions arise when one starts to think about God. The answers differ depending on one's faith and culture, and even among people of the same faith one will hear different views. Human beings tend to "create" God in their own image. While it is true that people have their own opinion about God, they generally share a common view about God's nature, namely that God is good. God is what is good. Everything good is from God. God is the source of goodness. Even though in terms of etymology there is no clear link between God and good, in theological terms we can state that everything good is from God.

God's creation

Creation set in when God pronounced, "Let there be light" (Gen 1:3), "and God saw that the light was good" (Gen 1:4). God created the sky, water and land. God saw them and commented, "It was good." God created the plants, stars and living creatures, saying, "It was good." And, finally, God created humankind. Then "God saw everything that he had made, and indeed, it was very good" (Gen 1:31). Creation completed.

Humankind was created with special attention and care. "God created humankind in his image; in the image of God he created them" (Gen 1:27). And "God blessed them" (Gen 1:28). Human beings are unique because of the imbedded image of God and the blessings bestowed upon them that God did not impart on other creatures. It is no wonder that in reference to human beings God said, "Indeed, it was very good" (Gen 1:31). God was pleased with God's own work of creation.

It should be noted that God made human beings unique for a particular reason: God wanted to create a partner for Godself. God told the man and woman, "Be fruitful and multiply, and fill the earth and subdue it; and have dominion over the fish of the sea and over the birds of the air and over every living thing that moves upon the earth" (Gen 1:28). God commissioned them to care for life on the planet. Human beings were ordered to control all creatures and nature so that they would have life in abundance. In light of having been created in the image of God and with special blessings bestowed upon them, human beings could have observed God's ordinance and grown plants and bred animals while safeguarding their natural environment on earth, under the sea and in the air. Unfortunately, this is not how it turned out 4.6 billion years later. What went wrong? In view of the planet's increasingly serious environmental deterioration, what are the implications of the original sin committed by Adam and Eve by eating the fruit of a tree of knowledge of good and evil?

Two key terms in Genesis, "subdue" and "have dominion," describe more precisely what God expected of human beings. In human terms, both terms can easily be misconstrued since they imply having powerful authority over something or somebody. When discussing issues such as the destruction of nature and the exploitation of natural resources, non-Christian environmentalists sometimes accuse Christians of the biblical interpretation of creation, according to which God let human beings "subdue" and "have dominion" over the creation. Is such a Christian faith to blame for our global problems? If not, is it the Bible that leads to such deterioration? Or, ultimately, is God to blame for letting it happen—God who ordered God's blessed creatures to "subdue" and "have dominion" over nature? Taking into account that God is eternally good, it would make no sense to blame God for this. Nothing evil comes from the source of goodness.

Before and after the Fall

In the following, I shall look at the creation story from a wider perspective. God saw that creation was very good. Creation proved to be perfect. Everything went well. "Subdue" and "have dominion," the two annoying terms used by God while "handing over" the creation to Adam and Eve, might sound different when we acknowledge that under God's sovereignty, even subduing and dominion can have a sound connotation. According to the biblical narrative, the Fall of the ancestors of humankind did not only affect their own lives, but also those of the whole of creation, since creation had been totally committed into their hands. The Fall changed the whole scenario of God's ongoing creation. Human beings changed the meaning of the two terms and the way in which they were implemented. God's reign and dominion are thus different from human ones which are always in danger of being corrupted by power.

God freely chose to create the world and let human beings control it. Human beings are also blessed with the freedom to choose. We try to choose what we believe is right using our God-given free will, but unfortunately we very often fail. Human will, even though it is a gift from God, is in bondage to sin as Luther expounded in "On the Bondage of the Will."[1]

Natural disasters

Natural disaster is one of the most challenging theological issues. It is difficult to deal with because when it actually takes place we cannot help asking why God let the tragedy happen. There is no satisfactory answer to this dilemma and thus to the question of theodicy.

The Book of Job is very often referred to in relationship to questions of theodicy. Job's friends tried to explain to him why Job had to suffer such calamity in spite of his faithfulness to and righteousness before God. Eliphaz told him, "You have sinned" (Job 35:6); Bildad advised him to repent; and Zophar warned Job that his guilt deserved punishment. No one could comfort his sorrow and agony. Job could not figure out why he had to suffer loss and pain in spite of his faithful life before God. Finally God speaks to him out of the whirlwind, "Where were you when I laid the foundation of the earth? Tell me, if you have understanding" (Job 38:4). The Word of God overwhelmed him with the supreme authority of the Creator and sovereignty of the Almighty. Job answered the Lord, "I am of small account; what shall I answer you? I lay my hand on my mouth" (Job 40:4). Job saw God as the ultimate being, before whom he has nothing to say, no need to find reasons why he had to suffer. God was there as ultimate goodness. God's goodness cannot be measured by human reasoning. Suffering should not be an indicator for how much a human being has merited or sinned. Retributive justice, a conventional view of God's judgment that regards human suffering as punishment, is denied.

Earthquakes and tsunamis, floods, hurricanes and tornadoes regularly involve people and cause casualties. We call them natural disasters. They are the workings of nature of which we are a part.

---

[1] Martin Luther, "The Bondage of the Will, 1525," in Helmut T. Lehmann (ed.), *Luther's Works*, vol. 33 (Philadelphia: Fortress Press, 1972), 3–295.

Job's experience shows us ways to look at the calamities and sufferings caused by natural disasters. First and foremost it is not retributive justice that God enforces to punish evil people. They befall anyone at any time, regardless of who we are. Jesus made this very clear when he met the man who was blind from birth and his disciples asked him who had sinned so that this man was born blind. Jesus said, "Neither this man nor his parents sinned; he was born blind so that God's works might be revealed in him" (Jn 9:3). Let us remember what we have learned from the Book of Job. God revealed Godself and God's works when Job severely suffered. This blind man is another Job in the New Testament. Retributive justice is by no means biblical.

11 March 2011, 2:46 pm

A massive earthquake measuring 9.0 on the Richter scale jolted East Japan. It triggered powerful *tsunami* waves that reached heights of up to 40.5 meters and hit the coastal areas of Tohoku (northeastern), Japan. This was the moment that changed the history of Japan. In Tokyo, three hundred kilometers away from the epicenter, big shocks triggered explosions of gas tanks and soil liquefaction, plunging the city into chaos. On 12 and 14 March, two nuclear reactors at Fukushima nuclear power plant exploded and spread radioactive substances over large areas of eastern Japan. The largest earthquake ever to be recorded in Japan left behind numerous casualties and killed 18,000 people.

"My God, My God, why have you forsaken me?" Takashi Yoshida, a pastor of a Reformed church serving in the affected area, reported that Jesus' cry resonated among the Christian communities of Tohoku district. They could not help but ask, Why Tohoku? Takashi Yoshida had heard people saying that this was God punishing the greedy Japanese people. His own reply to this was the following: "I thought at this very moment that this is not the punishment to those who were killed, but this is God punishing me since I took the easy cozy life with the economic prosperity that was built upon the hard work of many victims for granted." His response reminds me of Job, when, at the very end, he said to the Lord, "I had heard of you by the hearing of the ear, but now my eye sees you; therefore I despise myself, and repent in dust and ashes" (Job 42:5-6). Having said above that theologically retributive justice does not help us to understand the tragedy and ease the pain of the victims, it still happens that people who have suffered under major (natural) catastrophes, tend to interpret their sufferings this way.

It was Friday when the earthquake occurred, two days after Ash Wednesday in 2011. The following day, there was deadly ash from radiation fallout. When the nuclear power plant exploded and the radioactive substance leaked into the air of Fukushima, pastor Yoshida thought that this world had changed completely, from the beautiful creation of God's land to the place of sorrow and pain, where no human beings or any living creatures ought to live. The earthquake needs to be examined from another perspective. The earthquake and tsunami are indeed natural, but we must never forget the fact that the explosion of a nuclear power plant is a human-made disaster. This human-made monster irrevocably damaged the land, left it contaminated and barren, and robbed the local people of their houses and property.

God created us in God's own image and we hold this image inside ourselves in various ways. One of the facets of such a blessed image of God is human creativity that produces creative works in the fields of the arts, design, music, manufacturing, buildings, cooking and so on. Such human creativity enriches life and makes it joyful. After the Fall of Adam and Eve, however, such human creativity has not always successfully revealed the Creator's image. It began to "walk" on its own, without knowing where to go, often turning its back on God. Nuclear energy was a product of human creativity, primarily to win World War II.

Immediately after the earthquake, the four Lutheran churches in Japan together set up a rescue program. Japan Evangelical Lutheran Relief (JLER) sent a group of people to carry out relief work. Its ministry is closely related to the victims of the disaster who have suffered spiritual, psychological and physical damage and its mission includes listening and deeply caring for the victims and providing the necessary support so that they may find a future life of hope and joy. In March 2014, the JLER's three-year program came to an end. Although the program itself has ended, the JELC decided to continue the work, as much as possible focusing on the victims of the Fukushima radioactive emissions and accompanying them by listening to their stories and supporting their daily needs. We know this is not a "once for all" support, but a continuous, long-term support over several decades. In the future, to serve as the church for our suffering neighbors will be another missional challenge. This ministry has become another mission that God has entrusted to us as a part of God's continuing creative activity.

The Australian theologian Frank Rees experienced the earthquake and tsunami that hit the southern part of Western Samoa on 29 September 2009. Later he wrote a theological reflection on the catastrophe, in which he quoted two historic theologians, Jürgen Moltmann and Dietrich Bonhoeffer. Both have a common theological understanding of God working in the suffering world. Moltmann writes of "the accompanying activity of God"[2]

[2] Jürgen Moltmann, *God in Creation: An Ecological Doctrine of Creation. The Gifford Lectures, 1984-1985* (London: SCM Press, 1985).

who also suffers the painful reality of the modern world with the suffering people. God is not only the one who created the whole universe, but also the one who continuously accompanies the suffering people through the new creation.

Dietrich Bonhoeffer wrote from prison, "only the suffering God can help." By quoting from Bonhoeffer, Rees asserts that only God who is actively and lovingly engaged with the suffering world can help us,

> God is a full participant in the life of the world. To suffer, here, means to be subject to the choices of others. To suffer means to be able to receive and to accept what others decide, as well as to have one's own capacity and wishes and purposes.[3]

These two theological statements about God are encouraging and inspiring as we continue to carry out our Christian mission to serve people in need and in pain. Both theologians affirm a suffering God who accompanies people in pain. God accompanies those who strive to serve as well as those who suffer. At the same time, we should note that suffering and pain are not something cursed or that God denies. God accepts and willingly suffers such hardships with us while continuing to create new life despite confusion and darkness, sometimes caused by human creativity. This ministry of connecting and staying close to the affected people is our participation in the *missio Dei*.

The image of prayer

"God created humankind in his image; in the image of God he created them" (Gen 1:28). According to Genesis, being created in the image of God is something that is only granted to human beings. It presupposes our ability to think about, to remember and to believe in our Creator. This gives human beings the ability to respond to God's call and to create a relationship with God. The response to God's call may express itself in witness and prayer. Prayer can thus be seen as indication that human beings are created in God's image. This image was only granted to human beings. Prayer as the tool for us to communicate and engage with God is consequently something that makes us distinctively human. No other creature is gifted with prayer. We know that some other capabilities characterize human nature such as speaking languages or using tools. But apes are known to be intelligent

[3] Frank Rees, "God of the tsunami: A theological reflection on the experience of disaster and some implications for how we live in the world," at **www.ttgst.ac.kr/upload/ttgst_resources13/20124-270.pdf**

enough to understand some simple words and to communicate with their breeders. They know how to use sticks to pick bananas from the tree. Speaking languages and using tools do not prove that human beings are exceptionally gifted with God's image.

Prayer can also mean lamentation; in the Old Testament Psalms we often encounter expressions of lament (Ps 22:1: "My God, my God, why have you forsaken me?"–the words Christ cried out on the cross according to Mark 15:34), desperate questions asking God, Why does this happen to me? Most often there are no straightforward and quick answers to these questions, yet bringing them before God may be the beginning of a healing process. And one day we might even receive a response to our lamentation.

Sometimes it might be difficult to bring those questions and laments before God on one's own. In the aftermath of the horrendous tsunami, some non-Christian families came to visit churches, seeking help. In most cases they came because they had lost someone in their family. One day a pastor received a phone call from a mother who asked him, Where is my son now? Why did it have to be my son? Is it because he did something bad? Tell me pastor, where is he now, heaven or hell? The pastor could not answer anything at first. The conversation lasted for about an hour and towards the end he said to her, "I can pray to God and this is the best I can do for you now. If you don't mind, may I pray for you and your son?" The request to allow him to pray calmed down her troubled mind. She replied in tears, "Yes, please do. Please pray for us." It is nothing special that a pastor prays for others. But the pastor later remembered this conversation and said,

> I never thought before that prayer was such an effective pastoral caring method. I thought my primary calling for ministry would be to preach and teach the Bible to the congregation. But now I know intercessory pastoral prayer is so powerful for spiritual healing.

Intercessory prayer is not only for pastors who are professionally trained and theologically equipped for such grief counseling. It should not be confined only to pastors–it should be practiced by every Christian whenever people are grieving among us. We are all privileged with the gift of prayer and commissioned to use it for our neighbors. It is God who created God's image in us. This image was created so that we can connect with our Creator who wants us to use this image through prayer for God's purpose, for God's mission.

Questions

Do you think the conventional understanding of theodicy (explanation of why a perfectly good, almighty and all-knowing God permits evil) is meaningful in witnessing God in today's world? If yes, why and how?

Besides prayer, are there other ways in which the image of God in human beings is being expressed?

Why is important for us as citizens of the earth to maintain God's good creation?

Responsible Stewards of God's Creation: Advocating for Climate Justice

Martin Kopp[1]

Take a deep breath—I mean, really, do so before reading any further. You have felt air fill your lungs and then being expelled back into the atmosphere. There is maybe no other experience that is more common than this one. Breathing is so normal that one generally does not even think about it. One actually forgets that one breathes—it is so perfectly normal.

Yet, one minute ago, something exceptional happened. You may not be aware of it, but you belong to the first generation of human beings ever to inhale 400 parts per million (ppm) of CO_2 with each breath you take. That means that 400 of one million molecules that entered your lungs were CO_2 molecules. It is a first in human history. Indeed, since the first *homo sapiens* was born, the concentration of CO_2 has oscillated between 180 and 280 ppm.

This is not the kind of firsts to celebrate. The latest Intergovernmental Panel on Climate Change's (IPCC) report underlines that the reality of climate change is "unequivocal." It states that there is a 95–100 percent probability that, since the mid-twentieth century, human activity is the main driver of climate change due to the exponential increase of greenhouse gases (GHG) emissions. Human societies emit GHG mainly by burning fossil fuels that are, or used to be, carbon stocked in the ground until human beings put it into cars, power plants, planes... and released it back into the atmosphere.

This is not trivial. The rise in GHG levels in the atmosphere increases the greenhouse gas effect. It is true that this effect is normally very posi-

[1] Martin Kopp is the LWF's delegate to the UN climate conferences.

tive: it allows life on earth as we know it. It can be compared to a blanket put over the planet and without it the mean surface temperature would be -18°C instead of +15°C. The problem is we are making the blanket bigger. The atmosphere has already warmed by 0.85°C and if we fail to shift toward low-carbon societies by the middle of this century, surface temperatures may well increase by between 4°C to 8°C.

This is not harmless. Such increases would have tremendous consequences, including an increase in the intensity and frequency of extreme weather events (heat waves, floods, droughts, hurricanes and typhoons, wild fires); rising sea levels; the acidification of the oceans; changes in rain patters; the loss of biodiversity. In other words, a complete upheaval in our ecosystems, which would provoke the destruction of livelihoods (houses, fields, livestock); famines; water shortages; serious economic crises and costs; thousands if not millions of deaths; massive migration and social as well as international conflicts. Climate change may be the most serious threat confronting human societies today.

That having being said, why exactly is climate a matter of "justice"? And, why should Christians feel concerned? Is there a strong theological grounding for action by believers and churches? If so, how can they advocate for climate justice?

Climate change: an issue of justice

Climate change constitutes an issue of justice in a threefold way: it is a matter of international, intergenerational and social justice. Let us explore those three angles.

International justice

The second part of the IPCC's report is dedicated to the impact of climate change on human societies, the adaptation they demand and the vulnerability they expose. The latest IPCC report underlines the fact that while **all** countries will be affected by climate change, the maximum harm will probably be done in the so-called "developing" countries as well as in the so-called "least developed" countries.

Historically, it is developed countries that have emitted the most GHG. This is why climate change is a matter of international justice: the countries that have emitted the least carbon will be the most affected. This poses obvious questions of distributive and restorative justice between nations, i.e., not only ecological but also economic justice. One should not forget for instance that some countries may disappear completely under water. The

President of the Maldives, Mohamed Nasheed, is already looking to buy land for the population of his country.

But it needs to be pointed out that the levels of GHG emitted by the global South since 1850 is about to reach the levels emitted by the global North.[2] In 2010, the global South was responsible for 48 percent of all emissions and this figure is expected to reach 51 percent by around 2020. China, for example, has become the first worldwide emitter.

This raises the question of whether this solves the question of international justice. I do not think so because, first, in the global South many countries that have low emissions are among the main victims of climate change. Second, and more importantly, the countries of the global North consume a considerable portion of what the South produces—polluting industries have merely been relocated. It appears that the question will soon have to be reformulated: it will no longer be "developed" as opposed to "developing" countries, or the global North as opposed to global South, but rather emitters versus victims.

Intergenerational justice

Here the data is crystal clear: Previous and today's generations have emitted significant amounts of GHG and it is the coming generations who will suffer the most. Although models and scenarios for the future generally stop in 2100, Andrew Dessler states that "many scenarios have significant emissions and warming that extend into the twenty-second century and well beyond."[3] If our generation fails to cut emissions in time, human-induced climate change will last for centuries and affect the lives of many generations to come. Our current use of fossil fuels and land poses serious questions of intergenerational justice.

Social justice

Climate change raises issues of social justice: those who suffer first and foremost are the poor and most vulnerable among us, for instance the unemployed, migrants, women, children, elderly and disabled. Most of the time, they have not even had access to the activities that cause most of the GHG emissions.

---

[2] Den Elzen, Olivier, Höhne and Janssens Maenhout, "Countries' Contributions to Climate Change: Effect of Accounting for all Greenhouse Gases, Recent Trends, Basic Needs and Technological Progress," in *Climatic Change* 121/2 (2013).

[3] See Andrew Dessler, *Introduction to Modern Climate Change* (Cambridge: Cambridge University Press, 2011), 123.

Two reasons explain this. As has been pointed out, on the one hand it is the "developing" and "least developed" countries that are located in geographical areas that will be exposed to the most severe consequences of climate change. On the other, it is easily understandable that poor countries and populations are less able to face the challenges brought about by climate change. For instance, the Netherlands is wealthy enough to try to protect the coast against rising sea levels. The same does not apply to Bangladesh where rising sea levels will displace millions of people who will become "climate refugees."

Whereas this is blatantly obvious in the global South, it applies universally. When hurricanes Rita and Katrina struck New Orleans, that is to say a city in one of the wealthiest countries in the world, it was the poorest who suffered the most. Wealthy people did not live in neighborhoods that can easily be flooded, had enough money to flee the disaster and the resources necessary to start over elsewhere. Poor people saw their houses destroyed and had to stay in a deserted city, unable to pay for a new house. I worked in New Orleans with the Evangelical Lutheran Church in America's Lutheran Disaster Response. It took our twenty-five-person French youth group two weeks to clean three houses. I remember very clearly that the family we helped had been living for months in a small caravan, parked in the garden beside the rotting house. This experience will remain imprinted in my mind as proof of the vulnerability of countries we generally judge "too wealthy to fail." We must not forget the inequalities among their populations.

Today, one can no longer separate the fields of social and ecological justice. It was very appropriate that on the occasion of the twentieth anniversary of the IPCC, UN General Secretary, Ban Ki-Moon, identified climate change as a serious threat to reaching the Millennium Development Goals.

Green and just: a theological grounding to address climate change

At the theological level, the relationship with creation and the utmost importance attributed to justice are the two legs of a Christian stance on climate change. Both perspectives can be included in a broader spiritual climate of recognition, grace and love.

A renewed understanding of the theology of creation

Over the last few decades, academic research has reworked the most famous biblical texts and founded a renewed theology of creation. Also, theologians have rediscovered the richness of the Reformers' theology and the underestimated tradition of dialogue between faith and the natural sciences.

The world is God's creation (Gen 1:1-2:25). The first article of the Apostles' Creed confesses, "I believe in God, the Father Almighty, Creator of heaven and earth."[4] All forms of life are confessed to be creatures. We are no gods. We cannot ground our relationship with the rest of creation as if we were the owners of it. God is the true owner of creation. And this creation is confessed to be "very good" (Gen 1: 31).

We are responsible for God's creation. Our relationship vis-à-vis the other creatures is indeed defined by four verbs in Genesis 1 and 2: "to subdue" and "to have dominion" (Gen 1:28); "to cultivate" and "to keep" (Gn 2:15). The first two verbs have been misinterpreted as constituting a command to exploit nature. For instance, the French philosopher, René Descartes, famously spoke of the human being as the master and owner of nature. In his article "The Historical Roots of Our Ecological Crisis,"[5] American historian Lynn White Jr. has even identified the Western Judeo-Christian tradition as one of the main roots of the current ecological crisis. What is often forgotten is that at the end of his article he also identified resources in this tradition that would help to overcome the pattern of domination.

As for the verbs used in Genesis to illustrate our relationship to other creatures, today we recognize that those terms actually express our responsibility when it comes to the fate of creation. In particular, the verb "to subdue" is used in Hebrew to describe the relationship of a king toward his subjects, and the Old Testament perspective is one of responsible care. As for the two other verbs, they express clearly the fact that we are to be good stewards of God's creation.

Hence, the Bible offers an anthropocentrism éclairé and limited by the dignity of other creatures. It does not open a space for total liberty, but one of responsibility.

The theology of justice

Justice irrigates the entire Scriptures, from the very heart of the Law to the essence of the gospel. It is of utmost importance in the eyes of God. Guillermo Kerber quotes a few relevant verses in his article *La justice climatique*.[6] In the Old Testament world, the widow, the orphan and the stranger exemplify the figure of the vulnerable person and they are the object of God's special love and care: "The Lord watches over the strangers; he upholds the orphan and the widow, but the way of the wicked he

[4] Robert Kolb and Timothy Wengert (eds), *The Book of Concord. The Confessions of the Evangelical Lutheran Church* (Minneapolis: Fortress Press, 2000), 21.
[5] *Science* 3767, vol. 155 (1967).
[6] Guillermo Kerber, "La justice climatique," in *Sources* (Janvier/Février 2011).

brings to ruin" (Ps 146:9). There can be true and sustainable peace only through justice:

> Faithfulness will spring up from the ground, and righteousness will look down from the sky. The Lord will give what is good, and our land will yield its increase. Righteousness will go before him, and will make a path for his steps (Ps 85:11–13).

In the New Testament, Jesus Christ's ministry is understood as an accomplishment of justice. In the Gospel of Matthew, Jesus states at the beginning of his sermon on the mount: "Blessed are those who hunger and thirst for righteousness, for they will be filled" (Mt 5:6). At the end of his ministry, Jesus shares a parable that is a call to act on behalf of the vulnerable in this world (Mt 25:31-46).

From recognition to grace and love

In the face of climate change, these theological considerations determine a clear ethical stance. Climate change is the result of a corrupt relationship with the whole of creation, including one's fellow human beings. By regarding creation as a stock of resources to be extracted, exploited and burnt until the last remaining accessible molecule, whatever the price in human and creational terms, a minority has put itself in a situation of sin. To take Martin Luther's metaphor, big emitters have turned inward on themselves (*incurvatus in se*). Anyone who has tried to walk in a city while looking at their own belly button knows, being turned or curved inward on oneself inevitably leads to bumping into another person: we cannot see others and the environment around us, who and which we fatally harm. The former president of the LWF, Mark S. Hanson, used strong words when he identified this general situation as spiritual blasphemy.

This anthropological position is dangerous, if not lethal. Many sisters and brothers have already died due to extreme weather conditions and the future of everyday life is threatened. This is also true for many animal and plant species. The loss of biodiversity is steadily increasing and as Robert Barbault points out,[7] it is estimated that we are on the verge of the sixth great extinction of the species, in which climate change plays a significant role.

As Christians we know how vital it is to be able to recognize our sin and to repent. This will help us to be committed: God forgives, and as we are liberated by God's grace, we can turn to the world and start on a path

[7] See Robert Barbault, "Loss of Biodiversity. Overview," in *Encyclopedia of Biodiversity* (Amsterdam: Elsevier, 2013), 656–66.

of courageous action. We are at the heart of Luther's view regarding the Christian commitment. This still applies today and our deeds flourish out of the reconciliation and peace brought about by God's gracious mercy.

However, I am afraid that this will not suffice to bring high-carbon societies and ways of life onto a sustainable path. Those of us living in the so-called developed countries need to change how we look at the world, and those living elsewhere should be cautious not to adopt a Western social imaginary.[8] We should learn to pause, contemplate, be grateful for what is given to us and love. Yes, we should love creation, including our neighbors. We protect that which we love, but neglect that to which we are indifferent. If creation is reduced to videos on a flat screen or figures in a WWF report, there can be no true conversion and, consequently, no effective personal practices and public policies. But love requires time. I believe that there would be significant progress if we were to spend more time outside, in direct contact with and in awe of God's good creation—this is all the more relevant as humankind increasingly lives in urban areas. We need to be in actual relationship to creation. This shift is the precondition for a shift in our economic paradigm toward a frugal and hopefully just society. Here we reach the very core of the issue: with regard to climate change, it is our values and views of the world that are at stake.

Creation—not for sale?

Unfortunately, the dominant social imaginary only recognizes value through price. Incentives to fight climate change that seem to work best are economic ones. Nowadays, money is the true good. Proof of the fact is that one of the main political tools to tackle climate change is to put a price on carbon emissions through a cap-and-trade strategy. And a sign of the hegemony of the economy is the fact that civil society is currently shifting its advocacy narrative. Indeed, up to now it had insisted on the moral obligations of the emitters toward those who suffer from the consequences of their emissions. This strategy has failed. The trend is to change the discourse and to tell states and companies that tackling climate change is in their own economic interest, a strategy known at the level of individuals. For instance, people seem much more willing to insulate their houses

[8] The term "imaginary" comes from the philosopher Cornelius Castoriadis. Theories of the social imaginary seek to explain the way imagination, not simply reason, figures in the construction of central social institutions, representations, and practices.

because it will reduce the heating bill rather than because it will prevent the displacement of somebody living far away and in the future.

So, creation—not for sale? But what if the best way to save creation from severe climate change and its impacts were to underline the financial advantages of taking bold action on this issue? Should we, as Christians, use an economic argument in order for people and governments to make the morally right choice? Would this be true to our identity as a communion of churches? This is a tough question. At the time of writing these lines the issue has not been debated within the LWF, and I myself have not yet made up my own mind. Nonetheless, as civil society is changing its narrative the question will have to be discussed and the LWF will have to come up with its own position.

Personally I realize on the one hand that the timing is extremely short: the new treaty is awaited in 2015 and the world's emissions are expected to peak in 2020 before beginning a decline that would cut the world's emission by 80-95 percent in 2050. This is a very ambitious target. Both the urgency of the need for action and the well-known catastrophic consequences of runaway climate change could speak for the efficiency argument: we do not have time to overthrow the social imaginary and make it more sensitive to moral rather than economic arguments- provided this were even possible. This is why we should use what currently moves the targeted audience.

On the other hand, I clearly see that a Christian advocacy based on financial incentives could be seen as contradictory: are we not using as a tool the exact same element that has created the crisis we are in? Can a communion of churches rely on the economy, when Jesus himself had a harsh discourse on wealth and was an example of a frugal way of life? Can the communion use the egoist trigger, when its mission is to be the voice of the voiceless, the poor and vulnerable?

In this section, we have clearly moved from the why we should address climate change to the how we should advocate for action, raising a challenging overarching question. One of the current advocacy initiatives is the fast for the climate,[9] to which the LWF is fully committed. Since the UN climate conference COP19 that was held in Warsaw, Poland, thousands of people around the world fast on the first day of every month, both in solidarity with the victims of climate change and to put pressure on governments toward an ambitious treaty to be signed in Paris, France, in late 2015.

Fasting has changed the way I look at the world. Living in a "developed" country, I had never gone to bed hungry; now I do so once a month. I realize that this is the daily experience of hundreds of millions, some of them because of extreme weather events, others because of the decade-to-decade

[9] See **www.fastfortheclimate.org**

shift in climate patterns. Fasting made climate change real for me, opened my eyes and brought me closer to my neighbors. This is one of the reasons why fasting once a month is interesting: climate change appears to us in the global North as a distant reality, both in space and in time. Through the concrete feeling of hunger, the distance between me and the victims is cancelled. My empty stomach makes me think of them all day long and experience actual compassion.

But also, coming back to the economic question and the angle of our advocacy, fasting sets a symbolic gesture of moderation. In the so-called "developed" countries we live in societies that need growth to keep going, societies that are based on ever-increasing production and consumption. Through fasting we symbolically show that the path towards a sustainable and just future requires us to change the societal paradigm—"system change, not climate change!," says a famous slogan. In short, as Gandhi stated very truly: we need to learn to live more simply, so that others may simply live. There is enough on earth for everybody's need but not for everybody's greed.

Questions

Does your country already experience the consequences of climate change?

Is your church committed to the issue? How could it address climate change further?

What would be your position about the problem raised in the last section? Say you were to meet governments and businesses, would your Lutheran advocacy be based on economic or on moral arguments?

Creation not for Sale: How to Share Land—Problems around Land Ownership in Tanzania

Stephen I. Munga

Introduction

It is obvious that creation is not and will never be for sale. If it were for sale, then there would have to be a seller and a buyer. Who owns creation? Who would want to own and therefore to buy it? Creation is God's free gift to all. Creation includes the land on which most of the world's populations earn their livelihood. We are all aware that the majority of people, particularly in the global South, depend on the land for their very existence. We exist on the land and it is here that we feel that we belong to this world and are part of creation. We also know that there are those who want to own land, at least to possess a large part of it. This denies others a place where to exist and their means of earning their livelihood. God has entrusted creation to us all and the 148,940,000 sq. km. of land area on this earth is a place where all of us can exist.

The importance of land

In the biblical creation story we encounter God who entrusts humankind with the care of creation. God does so for the benefit of all human beings so that they may take care of creation while, at the same time, using it to sustain their lives. What we see here is the interdependence between humankind and creation—we are not owners of creation but simply stewards of it. God the Creator remains the author and owner of creation until the end of time. Our relationship to God with regard to creation is a covenantal one—an agreement between unequal parties. God the Creator will always have the upper hand and we are to take care of creation in accordance with God's commands.

Besides the creation story, another biblical text, Leviticus 25, refers to land related issues and speaks about the Sabbath year, the year of rest. The fiftieth sabbatical year is the year of jubilee. This chapter is highly relevant as the Lutheran World Federation (LWF) commemorates the 500th Anniversary of the Reformation in 2017. The LWF will commemorate this historical event with the declaration that we are "liberated by God's grace." The text from Leviticus gives us a taste not only of how jubilee is related to liberation but also how land stands at the heart of what is to be liberated in the jubilee year. Land is equal to being able to exist—this applies particularly to the poor. The land was given to them by the Creator and any land transaction has to be just so as to please God who is our justice. The year of jubilee is clearly marked by setting free people and property as well as the benchmark for determining prices or for regulating the selling and buying of land and property. The law made provisions that the land should not be sold, but only leased, until the year of jubilee when it was to be returned to the family that owned it or their heir.

> When you make a sale to your neighbor or buy from your neighbor, you shall not cheat one another. When you buy from your neighbor, you shall pay only for the number of years since the jubilee; the seller shall charge you only for the remaining crop years. If the years are more, you shall increase the price, and if the years are fewer, you shall diminish the price; for it is a certain number of harvests that are being sold to you. You shall not cheat one another, but you shall fear your God; for I am the Lord your God. All bargains ought to be made by this rule: You shall not oppress one another, not take advantage of one another's ignorance or necessity, but you shall fear your God (Lev 25:14-17).

In the year of jubilee, people return to their own property and it is thus the year of freedom and atonement when property, including land, is freed and the bonds of slavery and poverty are loosened. Property and owners are brought together again. This law enabled people to preserve their tribes and families, while waiting for the coming of the Messiah. The liberty every person was born to, whether sold or forfeited, should return during the year of jubilee. This was a typical analogy to the redemption by Christ from the slavery of sin and of being brought again to the liberty of the children of God. The declaration of liberation by the LWF fits well within the same parameters. It has to be so in order to be realized, otherwise the declaration of the LWF becomes an empty slogan.

Problems around land ownership in Tanzania

In a country, the backbone of whose economy is agriculture, land is central to the livelihoods of millions of people. Tanzania is among many African countries whose people are mainly small-scale farmers who are the main producers of both food and cash crops. More than eighty percent of Tanzania's population live in rural areas and depend solely on subsistence farming and pastoralism as their main sources of livelihood. Land, therefore, is the most important commodity. It should be remembered that land is the scarcest commodity of all. This is so because we cannot increase its size and are losing swathes of productive land due to various forms of destruction. This being the case means that land has to be distributed justly and used productively so as to sustain the lives of the people.

Land grabbing, *poraji ardhi* in Kiswahili, is a widespread practice in Tanzania. Whether alleged or true this is not a new phenomenon in Tanzania or in other parts of the global South. The exploitation of land and natural resources has had a profound impact on land tenure. During the nineteenth century, European colonizers went to Africa, partitioned the continent and plundered its land and natural resources. The colonizers' policies left a gruesome legacy in their wake, characterized by a series of land and resource conflicts, land litigation, loss of peoples' control over land and natural resources, exposure to alien land tenure systems and natural resources management. Ongoing land disputes in Tanzania have created and boosted a modern neocolonial system that enhances the power of a few wealthy people and companies as well as transnational corporations at the expense of smallholder peasants and indigenous communities who are displaced and dispossessed. The scale, magnitude and discourse around the current rush for land in Tanzania makes this moment unique and important in history and it calls for immediate action.

Among fast emerging deals in the world are the "land deals" that are considered good by some humanitarian scholars, clean by some politicians and profitable/beneficial by some economists and investors. Consequently, these land deals are considered good by the governments of the receiving countries while they deny poor citizens the customary rights that assured them of the protection of their natural heritage and survival. It is paradoxical that in a country such as Tanzania, land is the property of the state and people are given their share to hold and use according to the laws. If land is taken away from a person in the public interest, then that person has to be fairly compensated. Yet, this appears not to have been the practice so far.

There is considerable evidence based on empirical studies about international land deals and their positive and negative impact and the World Bank report 2008–2009 provides eye-opening information on the matter. Land deals worth about 60 million hectares were concluded worldwide, with two-thirds of the land acquired situated in Africa. In addition, there are some individual deals for very large areas. For example, Liberia recently signed a concession for 220,000 hectares, while by 2010 Tanzania is said to have finalized land deals amounting to more than 1.8 million hectares. This is a shocking amount of land to be given out by a single country. One of the questions that we need to ask is how transparent these deals are. How involved are the people who live in those areas where land is given away on a massive scale? How participatory is the whole process? Can members of the general public access the information about these land deals? These questions regarding issues of justice and transparency lead us to reviewing the legal provisions and the actual implementation of such.

In 1923, the British colonial state in Tanganyika passed the Land Tenure Ordinance in 1923 (later referred as Land Ordinance, 1923) according to which the whole territory, whether occupied or unoccupied on the date of the commencement of the ordinance, was declared public land. It was entrusted to the governor to be held for the benefit of the native communities. On the basis of the Land Ordinance, the independent nation of Tanzania passed its own land laws, which were rather more detailed than the colonial ones, and entrusted the whole land to the president of the country. It should be taken into consideration that here we are not only talking about the laws but also the institutions responsible for executing these laws. For example, the new land laws, introduced in 1999, intended to resolve the land conflicts and to deal with situations that had not been provided for under the old laws. It cannot be denied that the new land laws have made some significant changes with regard to addressing previous land problems. However, the question remains as to whether these new laws have really attended to the realities on the ground and have met the desired ends.

The importance of having good (e.g., just) laws cannot be disputed. Equally crucial is the need for good and efficient institutions that execute the laws. Why do we have the laws but more and more land conflicts? Are these conflicts new in the sense that they are not provided for under the current legislation? Are there really new situations or is something not working properly somewhere? Finally, how knowledgeable are the local communities about these laws? Thinking through these questions opens up debate which can lead to common solutions that guarantee justice and sustainable peace. This is the reason why the Evangelical Lutheran Church in Tanzania (ELCT), in collaboration with Sebastian Kolowa Memorial University, prepared a consultative consultation on land justice.

Apart from looking at the challenges from the perspective of the legal instruments there is a need to follow up on what has transpired on the ground, i.e., existential situations. Over the past years, there has been a growing discussion, both nationally and internationally, on various land related matters. The media and different land forums have alerted the world to the scale of land transactions in many different parts of the global South. Research on land use and land cover has been conducted and reports written on land grabbing, or land acquisition. The challenge related to the matter is the division between investors and communities. There is a marked difference in perception as to the positive and negative effects of the land transactions, now often regarded as land grabbing, and their outcomes. Areas targeted are the forest and other reserved areas as well as other areas on which villagers depend for food, artisanal mining and livestock grazing, all crucial sources of livelihood.

Although the Tanzania Village Land Act of 1999 requires that people are compensated for any land loss, the process for consulting on this and determining the level and manner of payment of compensation has been fraught with conflict. Much of the compensation is paid by the investor through the state authorities rather than directly to the local people. It also takes an inordinately long from the time when the valuation is completed to when the actual compensation is paid. Furthermore, compensations do not consider the dynamic future streams of income but only static values at the time of valuation. In case that the locals are not compensated properly, it causes frustration and can lead to abject poverty. Such complications arise primarily because of the lack of transparency in the deals. These problems are potential critical threats to sustainable peace which need urgent attention.

In this context, the Evangelical Lutheran Church in Tanzania (ELCT) commissioned Sebastian Kolowa Memorial University (SEKOMU), through the Institute of Justice and Peace (IJP), to organize and conduct a three-day conference on land justice for sustainable peace. This conference was held in Dar es Salaam, Tanzania, 10–13 September 2013. This international consultation engaged the government, Faith-Based Organizations (FBOs), civil society organizations (CSOs), the diplomatic community, international organizations, the business community, members of parliament, the academic and research communities and the media. The main objective of the consultation was to look into the matter by examining various research in this are and to suggest a way forward on how to deal with the situation.

With that objective in mind, the concept note of the conference took into account various points of departure, including the land laws in Tanzania and the conflicts facing the communities. There are a number of existing reports on legal instruments, some of which are based on empirical studies as there are a number of sources reporting on the conflicts. In the context of good governance both the laws and the institutions that execute them ought to indicate the positive benefits for society. In other words, the new laws are expected to be better in terms of distributing benefits and justice to societies than the ones that preceded them.

After three days of serious discussions the land conference gave birth to the Tanzania Land Forum as a platform for key stakeholders. The purpose here was that after recognizing the magnitude of the problem, those who were at the conference decided to deal with the situation in a strategic manner. Therefore, those who were at the conference are the founders of the forum. Much has been done to ensure that the forum takes off. This includes the organizational structure and key guidelines while at the same time attending to the most pressing issues on the ground through the Institute for Justice and Peace of the Sebastian Kolowa University.

Concluding remarks

The world has frequently fought against dehumanizing practices. During the time of apartheid in South Africa, many countries were in solidarity with the oppressed and told the oppressors that it is wrong to oppress another person on the basis of the color of their skin. Currently we hear the cries of many because of various forms of economic injustice, civil wars, terrorism, hunger, segregation, corruption and new forms of slavery in their countries and the world at large. In the context of these we ask ourselves: whence come such injustices? There are different ways in which people are victimized by their governments: There are those who have being displaced as a result of their land having been taken away from them in order to make way for—often foreign—investment. Others have had their environment destroyed and water sources polluted in the name of investment. We hear stories of people suffering from incurable diseases caused by poisonous chemicals in mining areas. Their cries of pain and agony fall on deaf ears because their governments and those in powers care more about their personal benefit than the lives of those who have put them into power. These people cry because of unjust treatment, because they have been subjected to losses—the loss of their property, their land, their lives, dignity and humanity. They are crying out because their freedom has been taken away and they have been subjected to slavery in their own lands. These are people waiting for the jubilee as the time for God (*kairos*) to set them free. Their cry is God's calling for their freedom and restoration of their property and dignity. Let their cry be God calling the LWF to attend to their pains and speak up for their freedom and restoration. If the LWF declares that we are "liberated" then it should as a communion of churches attend to those who are suffering. Let this be God's calling and sending to the special mission of jubilee—liberating those who are subjected to the pains of injustice.

Questions

Do you think that we have plenty of land in developing countries so that it can just be given away?

Do we need international legal instruments that transparently regulate the issuing of land globally, particularly in light of booming land investments?

Can the LWF play a role in the ongoing scramble for land in different parts of the world, particularly in developing countries?

Creation is not up for Sale, but what about our Theological Conscience?

Cibele Kuss

> O dry bones, hear the word of the Lord [...] I will cause breath to enter you, and you shall live. I will lay sinews on you, and will cause flesh to come upon you, and cover you with skin, and put breath in you, and you shall live [...] (Ezek 37:4–6).

I very much like the symbolism of the dry bones that have the hope of being changed. This dryness affects the whole of God's creation. According to the Christian vision of unity and diversity the whole of creation awaits the resurrection of the whole body, bringing abundant life and dignity for all creatures. We are part of the places and lands where we are born and live. I am writing this article in my *oikos* in Brazil. And here in Brazil, as in many other countries, we are witnessing the blatant destruction of forests and the spread of agribusiness and its devastating effects.

In light of our interdependence with the environment, destroying the bones of the forests in the form of increased greenhouse gas emissions triggering climatic changes such as serious floods, droughts and storms affecting the earth's cycles, contributes to violating our human rights. How are we to approach this? And in what way? The most strategic question is, What are we doing to confront this continuing dryness of the bones of creation? We cannot forget that there are bones that are not, and do not wish to be, indwelt by the Spirit of God, the breath of the divine *ruach*. Those are the bones indwelt by the dark sides of the spirit of capitalism, as represented by the arms industry, agribusiness and a society that is consumerist, misogynist, homophobic and predacious of all the good things of the earth.

In the context of five hundred years since the Reformation, what does theology say to us? The Brazilian feminist theologian, Nancy Cardoso, has asked a timely and provocative question concerning the role of theology:

> And what about theology? Well [...]. It is wavering between peace in the church, the comfort zone of the university and the unrest of the people in their struggles. It is high time to remember! And not to forget where we have come from and with whom we want to go forward. These are difficult times, and a theology that merely observes protests from afar, or which is living only with past struggles, which are still alive but are not today's struggles – such a church does not know the toughness and revolutionary passion of the twenty-first century.[1]

Looking on and observing do not really tell us much about who we are and with whom we want to journey. Obviously, it is not enough to say in our worship services that we must share land and bread, if all we are doing is observing the struggles of the people from afar. For a long time now, creation, Pacha Mama or Mother Earth has ceased to be sacred and has become a vast valley of dry bones, a creation that is being destroyed, fought over and sold, and far from being venerated and held in reverence for its immense diversity and loveliness.

In the capitalist system, God's creation has a price, an owner and a buyer. A minority of individuals and organized groups, who have lost in their bones the spirit of shared life, rule over and buy plots of land and water sources, that are essential for life on our planet, and fight over the fauna and flora in their diversity. The little creatures are not interesting. They are not even noticed.

Large-scale estate farming asses the land and calculates the profit of single crop farming of genetically modified soya or how many million head of cattle are going to be slaughtered and sold on the market, where people pay high prices for poor quality food. They do not see that the birds and the trees are important. They never say or understand the poetic words of the Brazilian poet Manoel de Barros, "I listen to the colors of the birdsong."[2] And they have never even heard of the Bible passage that reads, "If you come on a bird's nest, in any tree or on the ground, with fledglings or eggs, with the mother sitting on the fledglings or on the eggs, you shall not take the mother with the young" (Deut 22: 6). Millions of species and living organisms are being decimated by the poisonous pesticides that are being used by agribusinesses around the world.

In December 2014 it was thirty years since the explosion in the pesticides factory of Union Carbide, now Dow Chemicals, in the town of Bhopal, India, where over 16,000 died and at least 560,000 were seriously poisoned. These kinds of accidents tend to happen there where the workers' lives are

---

[1] At **https://www.facebook.com/notes/757117881043910/) 01.17.15**

[2] Manoel de Barros, *O livro das ignorãças*, 3ªed. (Rio de Janeiro: Civilização Brasileira, 1993).

deemed not to be worth much and a safe and healthy working environment is not one of the enterprise's priorities. The argument that food for feeding the population can only be produced by using poison had fatal consequences for large parts of the population in this particular case. In 2013, the pesticide market made a total profit of US$ 11.5 billion, divided between six huge international corporations: Monsanto, BASF, Syngenta, Dupont, Bayer (the company that produced the lethal gas used by the Nazis) and Dow Chemicals.

This sinful use of pesticides in Brazil is poisoning our people. It is in the rivers, the soil and the food. Every day we come into contact with these poisons. Most serious of all is the organization of agribusiness representatives in the field of Brazilian legislation, the so-called Bancada Ruralista (rural lobby), allied with the Bancada Evangélica (evangelical lobby), known as the 3B (Bala, Boi e Biblia–bullet, cattle and Bible). Their main aim is to protect agribusiness at all costs–slave labor, deforestation, confiscation of the land of indigenous peoples and former slaves. That group of dry bones is so well organized that in 2014 it succeeded in getting a law passed that allows pesticides to be used that had previously been prohibited in the country because of the high level of harm they were causing.

The Spirit of God breathes on the bones of organic farming

The women and men engaged in small-scale organic farming put ecologically clean food on our tables. Small-scale organic farming is a model of family farming that combines food production with the preservation and conservation of ecosystems and their natural biomes. Organic farming does not use pesticides, artificial fertilizers or genetically modified seeds.

There are groups and organizations in our churches that have not stood aside from the struggles of the people. One example here in Brazil is the Support Center for Small Farmers, or CAPA, founded over thirty years ago by the Evangelical Church of the Lutheran Confession in Brazil (IECLB). It has five branches in three of the country's states and receives institutional support from the Lutheran Diaconal Foundation.

In October 2014, representatives from eleven countries, members of the working group of the World Health Organization (WHO), while discussing Articles 17 and 18 of the Framework Convention on Tobacco Control,[3]

[3] The Framework Convention on Tobacco Control is an international treaty approved in 2003, bringing together around 180 countries in adopting measures to restrict consumption of tobacco and tobacco derived products. Brazil has been a signatory to the Convention since 2005.

devoted three working days to examining the work of the Support Center for Small Farmers and decided to present it as a possible alternative for adoption in other countries.

Brazil is a major world producer of tobacco. The largest part of the production of tobacco leaves (a total of 96.4 percent) is concentrated in the southern region of Brazil, where there are approximately 150,000 tobacco producers, 90,000 of whom are in Rio Grande do Sul.

The WHO group meeting took place in Pelotas, RS, in the far south of Brazil, 1–3 October 2014, organized by the Ministry of Foreign Relations, the Ministry of Health and the Ministry of Agricultural Development (MDA). The reason why this particular location was chosen was the result of the work of CAPA—regarded as excellent—in the National Program for Diversification in Tobacco Growing Areas.

The spirit of organic farming has breathed new life into the poisoned lives of so many individuals, who for decades had suffered the effects of the pesticides used in the single-crop production of tobacco. Bones, with flesh, tendons and healthy skin, have changed the life of God's creation in that territory. CAPA is confronting a giant called agribusiness. The spirit of God is breathing on the lives of small families engaged in organic farming. CAPA receives support from the German agency Bread for the World and is a partner of the Lutheran Diaconal Foundation (both of them IECLB organizations) and a member of ACT Alliance. It celebrated its thirty-fifth anniversary in 2013.

In these struggles we are witnessing the presence of the church inspired by the Reformation movement and we acknowledge it as an instrument of freedom and of love. That presence occurs in the diaconal activity of theology bringing about change. Diakonia understands that the economy, for example, can only be just if it founded on solidarity, justice and just gender relationships. In a just economy, all people have access to justice and a dignified life (Jn 10:10).

The aim is not the accumulation of goods, but a fair sharing for all (Mt 6:19–21) and the preservation of the environment. Living according to the principles of diakonia implies being committed to being merciful and to live differently. Furthermore, it suggests opposing the current economic system that can oppress and whose social costs are not acceptable to God. From a democratic, ecumenical, inclusive and environmental perspective, economic development must be accompanied by social justice and an improvement in the standard of living for all. Unfortunately, people are living according to the logic of how capitalism functions, with wealth and income accumulation and the destruction of creation.

Creation is not for sale and our theological consciences even less so. Our greatest challenge is to read the signs of the times. To struggle for life is to struggle for the whole of creation, for people's freedom and for the right to diversity, the right to be different, the right for the well-being of the earth and for the song of the birds. This means reaffirming the God of history, who is still insistently calling us into the future, so that we can continue to be involved in the struggles of the poor for change.

The women and men of CAPA in Brazil are an example of people who try not to sell their conscience and not to betray their faith in God the Creator. Together with so many various diaconal initiatives for change in the world, they represent a radical rediscovery of the gospel of Jesus Christ and God's grace and love for the whole creation. Creation is not merely a passive object and inanimate resource that we are free to use at will, but should be regarded as a living thing. We know from ecologists that in the earth's ecosystem all living things are interdependent. May we become more aware of the consequences of this interdependence and may the Spirit of grace and freedom breathe new life into our bones and into our testimony in this world in its diversity, so that we can experience in the depths of our being the toughness and revolutionary passion of the twenty-first century.

Questions

*What can you share from the territory/*oikos *where you are living regarding political, economic, environmental and cultural exploitation?*

How can transformative diakonia contribute to confronting the capitalist exploitation of natural resources?

What are the experiences of hope existing in our churches that concretely affirm that creation is not for sale and even less so, our theological consciousness?

A New Heaven and a New Earth: Orthodox Theology and an Ecological Worldview

John Chryssavgis

The world is a burning bush of God's energies.
– St Gregory Palamas (Fourteenth century)

The world is charged with the grandeur of God!
– Gerard Manley Hopkins (Nineteenth century)

Introduction

We have come to appreciate that the crisis that we are facing is not primarily ecological; indeed, it has less to do with the natural environment and more to do with the way in which we misunderstand or mistreat the world. Nonetheless, our concern for the environment is not a consequence of some superficial or sentimental romanticism. It essentially arises from our effort to honor and dignify God's creation. It is a way of paying attention to "the mourning of the land" (Hos 4:3) and "the groaning of creation" (Rom 8:22).

Tragically, however, we appear to be caught up in selfish lifestyles that repeatedly ignore the constraints of nature, which—we now know—are neither deniable nor negotiable. Unfortunately there will be some things that we learn about our planet's capacity for survival, which we will discover only when things are beyond the point of no return. This is why it would be fair to say that the hallmark of every human effort for environmental preservation should not be success, but humility.

It is the sense of modest realism that ultimately connects with creation. In its own distinctive way, the earth unites us all: beyond any individual or collective efforts, and beyond any doctrinal or racial differences. We may or may not share religious convictions or political principles. But we do share an experience of the environment: we share the air that we breathe, the water that we drink, and the ground that we tread—albeit neither always equally nor always fairly. But by some mysterious connection that we do not always understand (and sometimes choose to ignore), the earth itself reminds us of our interconnectedness.

This is surely the deeper connection between religion and environment. For, healing a broken environment is a matter of truthfulness to God, humanity and the created order. So religion clearly has a key role to play in this critical issue of global concern; indeed, a spirituality that remains uninvolved with outward creation is ultimately uninvolved with the inward mystery too. After all, the environment is not primarily a political, economic, or technological issue; it is a profoundly religious and spiritual issue.

Three ways of perceiving the world

How, then, do we reverse the process of defilement or pollution? How do we repent for the damage we have wrought upon our planet? How do we return to the vision presented in the Genesis account of creation? Orthodox theology and spirituality present us with three helpful ways[1] of restoring within ourselves a sense of wonder before God's creation:

- Icons (as the way in which we perceive creation)
- Liturgy (as the way in which we celebrate creation)
- Asceticism (as the way in which we respect creation).

The iconic vision of nature

A sense of the holy in nature implies that everything that breathes praises God (Ps 150:6). When our heart is sensitive to this reality, then "our eyes are opened to discern the beauty of created things" (Abba Isaac the Syrian). Seeing clearly is precisely what icons teach us to do. The world of the icon offers new insights; it reveals the eternal dimension in everything that we experience. Our generation, it may be said, is characterized by a sense of self-centeredness toward the natural world, by a lack of awareness of the beyond. We appear to

[1] This article draws upon John Chryssavgis, *Light Through Darkness: Orthodox Spirituality* (Maryknoll NY: Orbis Books, 2004).

be inexorably trapped within the confines of our individual concerns. We have broken the sacred covenant between ourselves and our world.

Well, the icon restores; it reconciles. The icon reminds us of another way of living and offers a corrective to the culture that we have created, which gives value only to the here and now. The icon reveals the inner vision of all, the world as created and as intended by God. For, by disconnecting this world from heaven, we have in fact desacralized both. The icon articulates with theological conviction our faith in the heavenly kingdom. It does away with any objective distance between material and spiritual, time and eternity, creation and divinity.

This is why the doctrine of the divine incarnation is at the very heart of iconography. For, in the icon of Jesus Christ, the uncreated God assumes a creaturely face, becoming "the most handsome of all" (Ps 45:2), a "beauty that can save the world" (Fyodor Dostoevsky). In this respect, the entire world is an icon; "nothing is a vacuum in the face of God," wrote St Irenaeus of Lyons in the second century. This is why, in icons, rivers have a human form; so, too, do the sun and the moon and the stars and the waters. All of them assume human faces; all of them acquire a personal dimension–just like people; just like God.

The liturgy of nature

What an icon does with matter, the liturgy does with time. If we are guilty of relentless waste in our world, it is perhaps because we have lost the spirit of worship. We are no longer respectful pilgrims on this earth; we have been reduced to mere tourists. Our original sin lies perhaps in our prideful refusal to receive the world as a sacrament of communion. The truth is that we respond to nature with the same sensitivity, the same tenderness, with which we respond to human beings. Moreover, the way in which we relate to other people on earth reflects the way we pray to "our Father in heaven." There is a profound connection between heaven and earth.

Liturgy, then, is precisely a commemoration of this innate connection between God and people and things. When we recognize this interdependence of all persons and all things–when we celebrate this "cosmic liturgy," as St Maximus the Confessor described it in the seventh century–then we can begin to resolve the environmental crisis. For, then we will have acquired, as St Isaac the Syrian noted in the same century,

> A merciful heart burning with love for all of creation–for humans, birds, beasts and demons–for all God's creatures.

The world in its entirety comprises an integral part of the liturgy. God is praised by trees and birds, glorified by the stars and moon (Ps 19:1), worshipped by sea and sand. There is a dimension of art and music in the world. This means, then, that whenever we reduce our spirituality to ourselves and our own interests, we forget that the liturgy implores God for the renewal of the whole polluted cosmos. And whenever we narrow life to our own concerns and desires, we neglect our vocation to raise creation into the kingdom.

The way of the ascetics

Of course, this world does not always feel or look like heaven; a quick glance at the suffering inflicted through war alone is sufficient to bring us to our senses. Still, St Paul writes:

> Through Christ, God was pleased to reconcile to himself all things, whether on earth or in heaven, by making peace through the blood of his cross (Col 1:20).

Reference here to "the blood of the cross" is a clear indication of the cost involved. There is a price to pay for our wasting. And this is the value of *ascesis*; for, genuine asceticism leads to a spirit of gratitude, to the rediscovery of wonder in our relationship with the world. The ascetic is one who is free, uncontrolled by abusive attitudes and habits, characterized by self-restraint, as well as by the ability to say "no" or "enough." Without asceticism, none of us is authentically human.

In his now classic article entitled "The Roots of our Ecological Crisis," Lynn White already suspected—although he did not elaborate on—the truth behind asceticism, noting that:

> The Greek saint contemplates; the Western saint acts. The Latins [...] felt that sin was moral evil, and that salvation was to be found in right conduct. [...] The implications of Christianity for the conquest of nature would emerge more easily in the Western atmosphere.[2]

It appears that the contemplative approach leaves a softer, gentler impact on creation. Paradoxically, then, ecological correction may in fact begin with environmental in-action. This is what the discipline of asceticism is all about: it is the way of silence, vigilance and detachment. It is the way of humility, of learning to tread more lightly on this planet.

Consider one example of asceticism, namely fasting. We Orthodox fast from dairy and meat products for half the year, almost as if to reconcile one half of the year with the other, secular time with the time of the kingdom. To fast is to learn not simply to give up but to give. It is not to deny but

[2] *Science* 155 (March 1967), 1203–07.

to offer; it is learning to share, to reconnect with human beings and the natural world. Fasting means breaking down barriers with my neighbor and my world; it is recognizing in others faces, icons; and in the earth the very face of God. Ultimately, to fast is to love; it is to move away from what I want to what the world needs. It is to be filled with a sense of goodness and God-liness, to see all things in God and God in all things.

Three models of caring for creation

Now, if our ecological prayer is to move from the distant periphery of abstract theology to the center stage of practical living, if our spirituality is to become "incarnate," then there are three complementary models that are proposed in the Orthodox tradition.

The biblical model

According to this model, the church is called to be in solidarity with the weakest parts of the body of Christ. It must stand for the most vulnerable, the helpless or voiceless elements of this world, which according to St Paul has been "groaning in labour pains, awaiting to obtain the freedom of the glory of the children of God" (Rom 8:21f.).

Furthermore, the earth is a member of our body, inseparable from our flesh and life. In the same way as the God of Israel once heard the cry of the poor and the oppressed (Ex 3 and Jn 4), God also hears the silent cry of the earth. This is the biblical covenant, God's promise to the people of Israel: that God listens to the world, God attends to the world, God tends to the smallest details of this earth.

The ascetic model

In the second model, we might think of the three Rs of spiritual life: renunciation, repentance and responsibility.

- **Renunciation** is an ancient response (even pre-Christian) as well as a universal response (even non-Christian). As we have already seen, renunciation is a way of learning to share. Therefore, it has social consequences; it reminds us to use material goods respectfully. Renunciation is about living simply and about simply living.

- **Repentance** is a return to a God-given life "according to nature," as the desert fathers and mothers would say. In repentance, we confess that we have sinned. Moreover, we confess that do not share, that we are self-centered, that we in fact abuse the resources of the earth. Through repentance, we recognize that we have fallen short of our vocation "to till and keep" the earth (Gen 2:15) which I like to interpret, in a manner more literal to the Greek translation, as "to serve and preserve."

- **Responsibility** is a challenge, a choice. Having renounced whatever clutters our mind and our life and, after repenting of our wastefulness, we can direct our lives toward creation and its Creator.

The sacramental model

Orthodox Christians achieve all this precisely through the sacraments. Unfortunately, in many church circles, the sacraments are often reduced to ritual observances. Yet, the sacramental life is much more than a way of pious inspiration or individual reward. It is crucial that we recall the sacramental dimension of the whole world, recognizing that nothing whatsoever is secular or profane. God is—and is within—the very constitution of our world. If God were withdrawn from the world, the world would collapse. Such is the depth of a sacramental worldview.

Orthodox Christians in fact prefer to speak of every moment and aspect of life as being sacramental—from birth through death. So the sacraments do not work in some magical manner; they function "mystically," silently permeating the hearts and lives of those who choose to be open to the possibility of encounter with God—much like the flow of blood in the human body, or the flow of water in rivers and oceans.

Conclusion

We normally call this crisis "ecological," which is accurate only in so far as its results are manifest in the ecological sphere. Yet, the crisis is not first of all about ecology. It is a crisis about us; it is a crisis about the way in which we envisage and imagine our world. It is a spiritual battle against—to quote an Eastern Christian mystic—"movements and powers within us, which are disordered, unnatural, and hostile to God's creation" (Maximus the Confessor in *To Thalassius*, chapter 51). We forget that we are less than human without God, less than human without each other, and less than human without creation.

Therefore, what we ultimately need is a discipline of humility. For, pride is a uniquely human attribute; it belongs to Adam. Whereas humility through simplicity can reconcile a world otherwise divided by pride; frugality and communion will preserve a planet otherwise exploited by greed. If we are guilty of relentless waste in our world, it may well be because we have lost the spirit of simplicity and the spirituality of compassion.

Ecological sin: The arrogance of domination

It is no wonder, then, that Ecumenical Patriarch Bartholomew surprised the theological and secular worlds alike when he identified carelessness or indifference to the natural environment as tantamount to sin. It is plainly wrong to regard sin only as the negative impact of our behavior on other people, whether individually or collectively, while disregarding the ecological and cosmological consequences of our behavior. As His All-Holiness remarked at Santa Barbara in 1997:

> For humans to cause species to become extinct and to destroy the biological diversity of God's creation, for humans to degrade the integrity of the earth by causing changes in its climate, stripping the earth of its natural forests, or destroying its wetlands [...] for humans to contaminate the earth's waters, its land, its air, and its life with poisonous substances—all these are sins.

The vocation and covenant to cherish and care for the creation is the principal reason for which God placed Adam and Eve in the garden of Eden (Gen 2:15), namely "to till it and keep it"—a phrase I like to translate (based more faithfully and literally on the Greek translation of the Septuagint) as "to serve and preserve it." It has not, of course, helped in the least that we have also misconstrued the biblical term "dominion" (Gen 1:28, Ps 8:5-8) as "domination" in an unashamedly self-centered and self-serving manner; after all, "dominion belongs to the Lord" (Ps 22:28). Anthropocentrism is an entrancing temptation to which we are all guilty of surrendering at one time or another, and which has detrimentally burdened our perspective and practice.

Responsibility: What can I do?

There are of course numerous practical ideas available and readily accessible today for parishes and people that would like to become aware of their ecological impact on the planet and on others. Indeed, some churches and congregations have already undertaken steps or even made considerable progress toward this goal. Moreover, parishes and parishioners can make a difference by becoming sensitive to what they use (energy efficient light bulbs and heating/cooling systems), what they can reuse (recycled paper, bags, ink cartridges, glassware and cutlery), what they waste (electricity, water, heat, energy, even cups and plates), and what they do (carpooling or support of local products).

Most importantly, however, we can all learn to do and live with less. In order to alter our self-image, what is required is nothing less than a radical reversal of our perspectives and practices. It is the only way that we can envision "a new heaven and a new earth" (Rev 21:1). The balance of the world has been shattered. The ecological crisis will not be solved with sentimental slogans or smiley stickers but by proposing self-denial as a solution to self-centeredness, by exercising self-control and self-restraint.

And here, I think, lies the heart of the problem. For we are unwilling—in fact, we violently resist any call—to adopt simpler lives. We have misplaced the spirituality of simplicity and frugality. The challenge before us is this: How do we live in such a way that promotes harmony, not division? How can we acknowledge daily that "the earth is the Lord's" (Ps 24:1)?

Accountability: Stewardship of God's creation

While there are numerous passages in the Old and New Testaments that provide insight into the principle and practice of environmental awareness and stewardship, it is a message that acquires increasing urgency in light of our ultimate accountability on Judgment Day. This is particularly evident in Christ's parable about the faithful and prudent steward in Luke 12, which concludes with the following warning: "From everyone to whom much has been given, much will be required; and from one to whom much has been entrusted, even more will be demanded" (Lk 12:48). This is a verse that might not meet with general agreement at a political level; yet it is a statement that deserves close attention at a spiritual level: "Blessed is that slave whom his master will find at work when he arrives" (Lk 12:43).

Like the servant in the parable, we, too, will be held accountable to the Master: "What is this that I hear about you? Give me an account of your management" (Lk 16:2). We will surely be judged for the abuse of the earth that has been entrusted to us "to preserve" as well as for the unjust distribution of its resources to human beings that we are called "to serve"—namely, for the devastation of God's creation by human beings unjustly usurping the right to control it and arrogantly presuming the right to manipulate it, as well as for the exploitation of the poor (and the poor nations) by the rich (and the rich nations).

Nevertheless, if we open ourselves—if we avail ourselves and become sensitive—to all people and to the whole creation, then we shall recognize our history as inextricably linked to the destiny of the whole world. We shall also begin to perceive the universe in its unfathomable interconnectedness. And we shall feel the spirit of God as a gentle breeze and hear the seal's heartbeat as the pulse of our own life.

Questions

What elements of your tradition do you share with the spiritual tradition of the Orthodox Church in experiencing and expressing the sacredness of God's creation?

What elements of your tradition are unique in perceiving our relationship with and responsibility toward our planet?

How can you/your congregation/your community change hardened habits related to your attitudes and practices toward the natural environment?

Bible Study: Romans 8:19-21

Elena Bondarenko

> For the creation waits with eager longing for the revealing of the children of God; for the creation was subjected to futility, not of its own will but by the will of the one who subjected it, in hope that the creation itself will be set free from its bondage to decay and will obtain the freedom of the glory of the children of God (Rom 8:19–21).

As we read this passage we return to the Old Testament story of the creation of the world and the sad consequences of Adam's Fall. At the beginning God created a wonderful creation that is called to bring forth other living creatures.

> And God said, "Let the waters bring forth swarms of living creatures [...]." (Gen 1:20).
> And God said, "Let the earth bring forth living creatures of every kind [...]." (Gen 1:24).

God created creation so that it could bring forth life on its own. In the end, God created human beings "in the image of God" (Gen 1:27)—a special creature called to take care of God's other creation and to be God's interlocutor. However, the story continues: the first human beings, Adam and Eve, fell; they were disobedient and became careless. Without thinking they virtually destroyed the tree "in the middle of the garden" (Gen 3:3), which was forbidden for them. The consequences of this carelessness and lack of thought affected not only guilty human beings, but also the other part of creation:

> And to the man [Adam] he [God] said, [...] "cursed is the ground because of you [...] (Gen 3:17)

The curse applied to both—human beings created in the image of God and the nature that surrounds them. It is in the massive exploitation of animals reared in terrifying conditions, the prodigious destruction of nature for economic benefit (e.g., tropical rainforests), the pollution of whole landscapes by the mindless exploitation of minerals, highly poisonous industries and frequently insufficient waste management that rational human beings can palpably feel the curse on creation. Attempts to point the finger at the problems are usually regarded as naïve and backward. Critics are always in danger of being made ridiculous and sometimes even have to fear for their lives. It seems as if the curse expresses itself in greed and the inability to differentiate between good and evil. It is not always the spoilers and sellers of creation who are ruthless. Frequently there appears to be no alternative or people lack the necessary education to consider the results of their actions. Nevertheless, as the Apostle Paul reassures us, not only the curse but also the gospel of salvation is addressed to both human beings and nature.

Paul writes that creation eagerly awaits revelation. The emptiness and futility of creation are the consequences of human sin. The corruption and decay of creation know no freedom and often serve sin, and just as servitude is related to corruption, freedom is one of the elements of glory. Just as corruption embraced the whole of creation, the gospel of liberation will embrace human beings and nature, as we see in our passage from Romans.

The Apostle Paul has his own understanding of the gospel, which differs from the concept of the gospel in the synoptic tradition. Paul understands the gospel not in the tradition of the coming reign of God (continuing the Old Testament tradition), but for him the gospel unfolds in a variety of ways:

- christologically: "the gospel concerning his Son, who was descended from David according to the flesh" (Rom 1:3);

- ecclesiologically: "[...] the word of faith that we proclaim" (Rom 10:8, the witness of the early church);

- soteriologically: "For I am not ashamed of the gospel; it is the power of God for salvation to everyone who has faith, to the Jew first and also to the Greek" (Rom 1:16).

Central to Paul's theological discussions on the gospel is the idea of God's reconciliation with human beings and creation through Jesus Christ alone. This reconciliation transforms human beings, bringing them to witness in work: the Word of the gospel becomes flesh in the sacraments of Baptism and Holy Communion (1 Cor 10:1-5, "sacraments" were mentioned here for the first time) and the witness of the Christian community is realized in life (2 Cor 6:4-10).

Thus, as Christians we are aware that we are responsible for our witness. We know that not only we, but the whole of creation, look forward to salvation from corruption. We know that creation does not belong to us simply because it surrounds us and we are strong enough to exploit it; creation belongs to God.

In our world we have become used to creation being for sale or, even worse, creation being used for destructive purposes. We have developed sophisticated weapons and dangerous technologies. Over the last 100–150 years, the progress in all scientific areas has been stunning when compared to the slow development over the previous thousands of years. The progressive development of certain technologies has often directly or implicitly included an increased ability to destroy the integrity of the environment. This is not to say that technological progress is bad as such, but one should always be aware of the possible misuse of certain technologies.

Creation was not meant for sale, just like human beings and their achievements. Creation was meant for life in honor of God. Human beings were destined for profound and divine life in dialogue with the Creator. A careless attitude to creation, particularly to the Creator, became the starting point of a path to destruction and greed.

"Why are you putting me to the test, you hypocrites?" (Mt 22:18). "Woe to you, scribes and Pharisees, hypocrites! For you tithe mint, dill, and cumin, and have neglected the weightier matters of the law: justice and mercy and faith. It is these you ought to have practiced without neglecting the others" (Mt 23:23). With these harsh words Jesus condemned the hypocrisy and commercialization of faith practiced by the religious leaders of his day.

The affirmation that creation is not for sale is closely linked to the nucleus of the Lutheran Reformation—justification by faith and the grace of God. This is particularly relevant since in today's consumer societies there is sometimes the perception, rather like during the Middle Ages, that blessings can be bought and sold. We need a renewed awareness of this core Reformation concept, especially in countries, such as Russia, where there was no Reformation movement per se but only a meeting of cultures, starting with the time of the Russian Empire and the Romanov royal family. Lutheran congregations existed in every major city and we still find traces of this influence in St Petersburg and to some extent in Moscow.

Unfortunately, throughout recent Russian history, reformation has always been considered to be a strange, Western concept, designed to enslave the Russian people to a Western way of thinking and life. For this reason, it was time and again attacked by the czarist authorities and later the Communist rulers. In general terms, no reformation movement as such took place in Russia and the concept of justification by faith and God's grace alone is still new and attractive. Despite powerful opposition, some people are happy to find support in the church for their protest against a culture where everything is for sale. Those who recognize that in the long term creation is not for sale may well discover the Lutheran heritage that sends out the powerful message about God's liberating grace. Within the framework of the 500th Anniversary of the Reformation the LWF sends out a compelling message: salvation, human beings and creation are not for sale. They are not commodities and must not be treated like this. They are God's good creation and must be treated accordingly.

Questions

In what way is the message that creation is not for sale relevant in your country and cultural context?

Is there a way to connect creation-not-for-sale with the development of social and diaconal institutions?

How can we implement the message that creation is not for sale in our lives? (give concrete examples)

List of contributors

Asano, Naoki, Rev., Pastor, Ichigaya Lutheran Church, Japan

Becker Nissen, Ulrik, PhD, Dr Theol., Associate Professor, Department of Theology, Aarhus University, Denmark

Bondarenko, Elena, Rev. Dr, Dean of Moscow Deanery, Evangelical Lutheran Church of European Russia, Russian Federation

Chryssavgis, John, Rev. Dr, Archdeacon of the Ecumenical Throne, Greek Orthodox Archdiocese of America, USA

Kopp, Martin, PhD student, University of Strasbourg, LWF Climate Justice Advocacy Officer, France

Kuss, Cibele, Rev., Executive Director, Lutheran Foundation of Diaconia, Brazil

Munga, Stephen, Bishop Dr, Evangelical Lutheran Church in Tanzania, Chancellor, Sebastian Kolowa Memorial University in Lushoto, Tanzania

Rossing, Barbara R., Rev. Prof. Dr, Professor of New Testament, Lutheran School of Theology at Chicago, USA

Human Beings—Not For Sale

Edited by
Anne Burghardt

Bibliographic information published by the German National Library

The *Deutsche Nationalbibliothek* lists this publication in the *Deutsche Nationalbibliografie;* detailed bibliographic data are available on the internet at http://dnd.dnd.de

Printed in Germany · H 7924

This book was printed on FSC-certified paper

Editorial assistance:	Department for Theology and Public Witness
Layout:	Department for Theology and Public Witness
Design:	LWF-Office for Communication Services
Printing and Binding:	Druckhaus Köthen GmbH & Co. KG

Published by Evangelische Verlangsanstalt GmbH, Leipzig, Germany, under the auspices of
The Lutheran World Federation
150, rte de Ferney, PO Box 2100
CH-1211 Geneva 2, Switzerland

Parallel editions in German and Spanish
ISBN 978-3-374-04160-2

Inhalt

Introduction

Anne Burghardt

This booklet is part of a small collection published by the Lutheran World Federation on the occasion of the 500th Anniversary of the Reformation in 2017. "Human Beings–Not For Sale" is one of the three sub-themes of the Anniversary's main theme, "Liberated by God's grace." The popular essays in this booklet were written by authors from all regions of the Lutheran World Federation; the ecumenical voice is here represented by a Reformed theologian.

The renewed relationship between God and the human being in Christ, expressed by the doctrine of justification, inevitably provides a deeper insight into the creation of human beings in God's image and the understanding that human beings will be renewed through God's Grace. Human beings can therefore not be regarded as commodities whose value can be measured in terms of profit only. This booklet explores different aspects of the theme "Human Beings–Not For Sale," ranging from an interpretation of Lutheran anthropology to human trafficking, migration and sustainable ways of living together. The list of topics addressed by the essays is far from exhaustive. Nonetheless we hope to offer some initial impulses for theologically informed discussions on the dignity of all human beings.

The Human Condition—A Lutheran Perspective

Friederike Nüssel

"Human beings—nor for sale." Why and in what sense can Lutherans endorse such a statement? In this paper I will consider some major points of Christian anthropology from a Lutheran perspective. Before going into detail, we shall briefly reflect on some significant changes during the sixteenth-century Reformation. The Reformers benefitted in various ways from the development of Renaissance humanism and the new attention to the achievements of human beings in the areas of philosophy, philology, architecture, the fine arts, engineering, etc. During this era of progress, the church in the West was unable to respond to the ever more pressing need for reform. Instead, the major concern of the Roman Church was to defend its political influence and to preserve and emphasize the role of ecclesial hierarchy in late medieval society, especially through the practices of penance and indulgences.

Luther's discovery: God's grace—not for sale

In this context, the young Martin Luther (1483–1546) had promised to devote his whole life to God and to become a monk. He sincerely strove for a pure monastic life, was constantly investigating God's will and trying to accumulate merits as satisfaction for his sins. While the practice of penance and indulgences offered ways to compensate for deficiencies, Luther, however, by constantly ransacking his conscience never felt that he had done enough on his part to love God so that he would deserve God's justification. His struggles with himself eventually led him to struggle with God and to ask "[w]hat kind of God would it be who summons humans by their own powers to love him above all things but clearly has not given them the capacity for it, and in the end elects the one and rejects the other?"[1] The more he asked this question the less he was able to love God with his whole heart. Luther ended up in a vicious circle and felt like a slave.

With the pastoral support of the superior in the order Augustinian Order, Johann of Staupitz, and through intense Bible study over the years, Luther learned to understand God's justice and righteousness in a new way. He saw that according to the Bible, God was not righteous by punishing trespasses and rewarding human obedience but, rather, by granting righteousness in and through the life, death and resurrection of God's Son Jesus Christ. In a biographical review in the preface to the edition of his Latin works (1545), Luther described the deep, personal effect of his theological discovery. While this late document is not a reliable resource for reconstructing Luther's development as a reformer and his original reformed insight, it still gives an impression of how Luther's discovery of God's real righteousness changed his life and attitude to God. Luther felt born anew. Now he could trust in God and love God for God's mercy and unconditional love. Hence, he no longer felt a slave to God's Law.

Moreover, he realized that the ecclesial practices of penance and indulgences did not do justice to God, because they neglected God's pure grace and unconditioned mercy realized in Jesus Christ and promised in the gospel. As a result, Luther criticized the ecclesial practice to picture God as a dealer who sells God's grace to those who prepare themselves by works. But, according to the Bible, God's grace is not for sale. God's justification is not to be earned by works. Rather, God grants justification by faith alone to those who trust in God's grace revealed in Jesus Christ.

The doctrine of justification by faith alone became the core idea in Luther's theology and the reformation movement in Wittenberg. In the "Smalcald Articles" of 1537 Luther says:

> Nothing in this article can be conceded or given up, even if heaven and earth or whatever is transitory passed away. As St. Peter says in Acts 4[:12]: "There is no other name [...] given among mortals by which we must be saved." "And by his bruises we are healed" (Isa. 53[5]).
>
> On this article stands all that we teach and practice against the pope, the devil, and the world. Therefore we must be quite certain and have no doubt about it. Otherwise everything is lost, and the pope and the devil and whatever opposes us will gain victory and be proved right.[2]

---

[1] Bernhard Lohse, *Martin Luther's Theology: Its Historical and Systematic Development* (Minneapolis: Fortress Press, 1999), 33.

[2] Cf. Martin Luther, "The Smalcald Articles, 1537," in Robert Kolb and Timothy Wengert (eds), *The Book of Concord. The Confessions of the Evangelical Lutheran Church* (Minneapolis: Fortress Press, 2000), 301.

Therefore, the article of justification was taken as the basic and chief article of faith by which the church stands or falls according to Lutheran teaching. It also shapes the Lutheran understanding of God's creation and the human condition.

Towards a realistic understanding of the human condition

Along with his discovery of God's true righteousness, Luther came fully to recognize the radical character of sin. Had human beings been able to turn away from sin and lead their lives in accordance with God's will, then it would not have been necessary for God to send God's Son for the salvation of humankind. At the same time, it is only God who could overcome the power of sin. God's almighty grace culminates in the fact that God creates the conditions for the regeneration of human beings and their reconciliation with God. Hence, God is not passive in receiving satisfaction through the meritorious death of Jesus Christ. Rather, through the incarnation, God is involved in the whole work of salvation. In Luther's view, Jesus Christ does not suffer pain and death only by his human nature, but God suffers with God's Son and through his resurrection overcomes the power of sin and death. In "On the Councils and the Church, 1539" he explains the intimate relation between Christology and soteriology:

> [...] Christ is God and man in one person because whatever is said of him as man must also be said of him as God, namely, Christ has died, and Christ is God; therefore, God died – not the separated God, but God united with humanity. [...] We should always rejoice in true faith, [...], and thank God the Father for such expressible mercy that he let his dear Son become like us, a man and our brother! [...] We Christians should know that if God is not in the scale to give it weight, we, on our side, sink to the ground. I mean it this way: if it cannot be said that God died for us, but only a man, we are lost; but if God's death and a dead God lie in the balance, his side goes down and ours goes up like a light and empty scale. Yet he can also readily go up again, or leap out of the scale! But he could not sit on the scale unless he has become a man like us, so that it could be called God's dying, God's martyrdom, God's blood, and God's death. For God in his own nature cannot die; but now that God and man are united in one person, it is called God's death when the man dies who is one substance or one person with God.[3]

[3] See the passage in Martin Luther, "On the Councils and the Church, 1539," in Helmut T. Lehmann (ed.), *Luther's Works*, vol. 41 (Philadelphia: Fortress Press, 1966), 103f.

In light of this revelation of God's grace human beings may learn to perceive their true situation with new eyes. While God's Law in the Ten Commandments allows recognizing individual sins, the life and death of Jesus Christ, God incarnate, allow us to recognize the radical character of human sin and forsakenness, which for Luther culminates in the attempt to achieve righteousness before God by works, because in this very attempt human beings ignore God's unconditional grace. By not fully trusting in God's benevolence and grace, human beings fail to fulfill God's first and basic commandment that, according to Luther's interpretation in the "Small Catechism," commands "to fear, love, and trust God above all things."[4] In the "Heidelberg Disputation, 1518" Luther states,

> The person who believes that he can obtain grace by doing what is in him adds sin to sin so that he becomes doubly guilty.[5]

While Luther's understanding of sin is based on his understanding of God's righteousness and salvation, it is also nourished by experience and psychological insight. From experience Luther could tell that the human being "constantly transgresses the First Commandment by not putting all his trust in God."[6] The reason for this lies in the very nature of sin, which, in line with Augustine, he found in a perversion of the will according to which human beings are self-centered. Without faith in God, human beings constantly seek their own advantage and honor, rather than God's and their neighbor's. They not only use the physical but also the spiritual gifts to their own advantage since they think that they can earn righteousness before God through their works. Luther does not regard it as wrong if human beings want to do good works and fulfill the Law. But as long as human works are done for the sake of self-justification, they cannot praise God as God's love and unconditional grace are ignored. Moreover, in the attempt to justify themselves, human beings misconceive the limitations of their intellectual and moral capacities and ignore their fundamental dependence on the power of God's Spirit.

Luther's doctrine of sin may appear to convey an extremely pessimistic idea of the human condition. In fact, almost no other Christian denomination has such a radical understanding of sin. While, for most Christian traditions, sin consists in a lack of faith and a corresponding self-centeredness according to which human beings tend to strive for their own recognition and tribute, rather than to concentrate on the needs of their neighbors in an altruistic manner, Lutheran theology sees the fatal character of sin in the fact that it entangles human beings

---

[4] Martin Luther, "The Small Catechism, 1529," in op. cit. (note 2), 351.

[5] Martin Luther, "Heidelberg Disputation, 1518," in Helmut T. Lehmann (ed.), *Luther's Works*, vol. 31 (Philadelphia: Muhlenberg Press, 1957), 50.

[6] Paul Althaus, *The Theology of Martin Luther* (Philadelphia: Fortress, 1996), 145f.

in a constant self-deception regarding their autonomy that results in manifold attempts of self-justification, not only toward God, but also in human relationships.

Obviously, in the context of modern secularization the theological notion of sin has become unpopular. As a result, the word "sin" in everyday language is used only in a trivial sense. While Lutherans might be tempted to say that in this development the deceptive character of sin has merely reached another level, it is more fruitful to reflect on the consequences that arise from a loss of the radical notion of sin in a theological sense. In Lutheran theology the insight into the radical character of sin corresponds to his insight into the overwhelming power of God's grace. Without exception all human beings depend on God's grace and providence in order to leave self-centeredness behind and turn to real trust in God and orientation toward the other. Hence, "so that no one might boast in the presence of God" (1 Cor 1:29). The doctrine of sin is unpopular precisely because it points to the negative side of the equality of human beings. Yet, to acknowledge sin in light of God's grace helps to be realistic about one's own capabilities and offers a compelling reason to be forgiving and generous with others.

Human beings—made to take responsibility

Luther's understanding of the *conditio humana* is realistic as it deconstructs illusions about the human ability perfectly to love God and to lead a perfect life before God. As a consequence, Lutheran theology has often been accused of undermining the role of ethics and human behavior and works. It even appeared defeatist. But Luther's perception of human incapacity in relation to God is only one side of his thought on the human condition. In light of his discovery of God's righteousness and pure grace he comes to appreciate God's good creation and providence. In the "Small Catechism" he teaches the believer to take from the first article of the Apostle's Creed.

> I believe that God has created me together will all that exists. God has given me and still preserves my body and soul: exes, ears, and all limbs and senses; reason and all mental faculties. In addition, God daily and abundantly provides shoes and clothing, food and drink, house and farm, spouse and children, fields, livestock, and all property—along with all the necessities and nourishment for this body and life. God protects me against all danger and shields and preserves me from all evil. And all this is done out of pure, fatherly and divine goodness and mercy, without any merit or worthiness of mine at all! For all of this I owe it to God to thank and praise, serve and obey him. This is most certainly true.[7]

[7] Martin Luther, "The Small Catechism, 1529," in op. cit. (note 2), 354–55.

Equipped and protected in this way, human beings are called to cooperate with God, who has made God's creatures, and in particular human beings, to serve God and constantly to fight evil.[8] It is the particular responsibility of human beings to work for the good in this world and to promote justice and peace. This is possible because human beings are created in the image of God (cf. Gen 1:26f.). While late medieval scholastic teaching explained the image of God in psychological categories, with a focus on rational capacities, Luther saw the essence of the *imago Dei* in the special relationship with God through which human beings are created to participate in God's justice, holiness and truth. This is what distinguishes human beings from all other creatures and endows them with a special human dignity that essentially includes the responsibility for one another as well as for other creatures.

But what is the effect of sin on the *imago Dei*? With regard to this question we can learn how in early Lutheran theology, philosophical terminology on the one hand, and philological exegesis on the other, came into conflict. According to patristic and medieval readings of Genesis 1:26, the image of God was the substance of human beings. Thus, sin could only destroy the similarity or Godlikeness, but not the divine image itself. Luther, however, discovered that, in philologicaln terms, the two terms "image" and "likeness" in Genesis 1:26 have the same meaning. He concluded that original sin must result in a loss of the *imago Dei*. Accordingly, Luther and Lutheran theology saw the scope of salvation in the restoration of the *imago Dei*. Yet, in Aristotelian terminology, the idea of a loss and restoration of the *imago Dei* is aporetic because a loss of the *imago Dei* would come down to a loss of human substance. Luther did not care too much about a philosophically coherent terminology. While he would affirm that human beings do not cease to be God's creatures, even if they turn away from God in sin, he would also insist that sin is a radical perversion of the will that by nature is irreversible without God's help. His theological successors attempted to reconcile theology and philosophical terminology by a number of distinctions, before philosophical enlightenment led to a general critique of Aristotelian philosophy. As a result, modern Lutheran theology interprets the Godlikeness of human beings no longer in ontological categories.

Rather, what Godlikeness means can only be understood by looking at Jesus Christ, whom the Apostle Paul describes as the second Adam. Jesus Christ was truly Godlike in fully devoting his life to the proclamation of God's gospel of the future kingdom. He would never act in his own interest, but in the interest of his fellow human beings, especially in the interest of those who were outsiders in the society of the time. He took responsibil-

[8] Cf. Luther's lecture on the book of Genesis, *WA* 42, 56, 30f.

ity for them, he suffered and died for them on the cross and in this way revealed what love can do. So, in him we can perceive the true character of the *imago Dei*. It is not an ontological quality that human beings own. Rather, it lies in the ability to develop a trusting relationship with God by which human beings will do justice to God and will be free to concentrate on the needs of their neighbors. Thus, faith in Jesus Christ helps to live out the human condition to which human beings are created.

Luther's perception of the human condition is realistic in the sense that he fully acknowledges the power of sin and the dependence on God's life-giving grace. It is neither pessimistic nor does it in any way nourish a defeatist attitude. Human beings are God's creatures and benefit from God's providence in all circumstances. They are created in the image of God and will be renewed through God's grace. God's grace is not for sale and, correspondingly, human beings are not for sale. They do not have a value that human beings could measure or compare—whether or not they believe in God. While sin by nature corrupts the adequate relationship with God and the right attitude toward God, it does in Luther's view not destroy the intellectual and emotional outfit of human beings and their capacity to promote civil encounter and social welfare. Human beings are capable of and responsible for contributing to communal life and peaceful encounter in a civil society in their own way with their individual calling and charisma. This is possible without faith in Jesus Christ as it is possible to acknowledge human dignity and human rights without being a religious person. Faith is not a necessary condition to realize that human beings are not for sale. Yet, with the insight into the character of God's grace we get the chance to be more realistic about the human condition. As we can be more honest about our own intentions, we may be more forgiving with others, and as we look at the selfless life and death of Jesus Christ, we may realize that true responsibility culminates in true love of and attention to the needs of others.

Questions

Nowadays, the notion of sin is unpopular. Even in Christian talk there is a tendency to play down the radical character of sin as a phenomenon that used to be crucial in the Lutheran tradition. How do you perceive this today? What is the responsibility in our talk about sin?

Lutheran theology is challenging as it combines a strong sense of sin with a strong sense of responsibility. In light of God's grace we may be more realistic and, at the same time, the gospel opens our sense for taking responsibility for the sake of the other. How can you relate to this in your context?

Human dignity is taken as a core idea in modern political, philosophical and theological discourse. It is not evident that Christianity has been a good advocate of human dignity and human rights throughout the centuries. What could or should be a particular Christian or Lutheran contribution to promote the idea of human dignity in today's world?

Human Trafficking

Ebise Dibisa Ayana

Article 3 of the *Protocol to Prevent, Suppress and Punish Trafficking in Persons Especially Women and Children, Supplementing the United Nations Convention against Transnational Organized Crime,* adopted and opened for signature, ratification and accession by General Assembly resolution 55/25 of 15 November 2000 of the Office of the High Commissioner for Human Rights, defines human trafficking as follows:

> the recruitment, transportation, transfer, harboring or receipt of persons, by means of the threat or use of force or other forms of coercion, of abduction, of fraud, of deception, of the abuse of power or of a position of vulnerability or of the giving or receiving of payments or benefits to achieve the consent of a person having control over another person, for the purpose of exploitation. Exploitation shall include, at a minimum, the exploitation of the prostitution of others or other forms of sexual exploitation, forced labor or services, slavery or practices similar to slavery, servitude or the removal of organs.[1]

This protocol entered into force on 29 September 2003[2] and many countries are using it to combat the trade in human beings. The purposes of this protocol are to prevent and combat trafficking in persons, paying particular attention to women and children; to protect and assist the victims of such trafficking, with full respect for their human rights; and to promote cooperation among state parties in order to meet those objectives.[3] The protocol

---

[1] At **www.ohchr.org/EN/ProfessionalInterest/Pages/ProtocolTraffickingInPersons.aspx**
[2] At **www.unodc.org/unodc/treaties/CTOC/**
[3] Ibid.

helps to enforce laws to combat human trafficking and to set principles for domestic law to address organized crime. It outlines all possible methods involved in the trafficking of human beings.

My intention here is to analyze the problem of the victims of trafficking and to deconstruct it on the basis of theological exploration. The aim of this study is to provide further reflections on the extent and nature of the trafficking of Ethiopian women and to enable churches and communities to gain insight into this reality in Ethiopia. The trafficking of women in Ethiopia is a growing reality, and one of the main questions for the churches and theologians is what theological response can be given to this reality and what actions could be taken in order to address the problem and help the victims.

THE SCOPE OF HUMAN TRAFFICKING

Throughout the world, human trafficking, especially the trafficking in women and children, is wide spread. It is a crime against humankind, involving the acts of recruiting, transporting, transferring, harboring or obtaining people for exploitation by use of force, deception or other means. Thousands of men, women and children fall into the hands of traffickers, in their own countries and abroad. Many countries in the world are affected by trafficking, whether as the country of origin, transit or destination of the victims.

The global report on trafficking (UNODC) shows that, globally, human trafficking is on the increase. According to the 2009 report covering the years 2003–2007, 155 countries are affected by human trafficking as source, transit and/or destination countries.[4] The majority of the victims, of whom ninety-eight percent are women and girls, are aged between eighteen and twenty-four.[5] According to the International Organization for Migration (IOM),

> Although the global scale of human trafficking is difficult to quantify, as many as 800,000 people may be trafficked across international borders annually, with many more trafficked within the borders of their own countries. Finland is both a transit and a destination country for tens or even hundreds of victims of trafficking every year.[6]

---

[4] **https://www.unodc.org/documents/human-trafficking/Global_Report_on_TIP.pdf**
[5] Ibid.
[6] At **www.iom.fi/index.php?option=com_content&view=article&id=93&Itemid=109**

This shows that it is not only a problem of poor and underdeveloped countries. For instance, my country, Ethiopia, is a country of origin for men, women and children who are trafficked primarily for the purpose of forced labor and, to a lesser extent, for sexual exploitation.

> Ethiopia is a source country for men, women, and children trafficked primarily for the purposes of forced labor and, to a lesser extent, for commercial sexual exploitation. Rural Ethiopian children are trafficked for domestic servitude and, less frequently, for commercial sexual exploitation and forced labor in agriculture, traditional weaving, gold mining, street vending, and begging. Young women from all parts of Ethiopia are trafficked for domestic servitude primarily to Lebanon, Saudi Arabia, and the UAE [...].[7]

Human trafficking has reached dimensions that are comparable with other illegal businesses such as drug trafficking. People are exploited in several ways, including sexual exploitation, forced labor, low wages and heavy workload. Worldwide, women and children are forced into abusive labor, prostitution and exploitation.

Articles 3, 4 and 5 of The Universal Declaration of Human Rights state:

> Article 3
> Everyone has the right to life, liberty and security of person.
> Article 4
> No one shall be held in slavery or servitude; slavery and the slave trade shall be prohibited in all their forms.
> Article 5
> No one shall be subjected to torture or to cruel, inhuman treatment or degrading treatment or punishment.[8]

While several countries have passed laws addressing the major forms of trafficking such as sexual exploitation and forced labor, many countries in Africa for instance do not have legislation on human trafficking, or they have laws that only criminalize some aspects of human trafficking such as child trafficking.[9] In some countries, the issue of trafficking is a very recent phenomenon.

---

[7] **www.state.gov/j/tip/rls/tiprpt/2009/123136.htm**
[8] At **www.ohchr.org/en/udhr/documents/udhr_translations/eng.pdf**
[9] Op. cit. (note 4).

The effects of trafficking on human beings

Human trafficking affects the well-being of human beings and has serious emotional, psychological, physical and social consequences.

> Common abuses experienced by trafficked persons include rape, torture, debt bondage, unlawful confinement, and threats against their family or other persons close to them as well as other forms of physical, sexual and psychological violence.[10]

These result in problems affecting the whole person and their self-perception. Trafficking does not lead to a life in freedom but to one of turmoil and, ultimately, death.

For the victims of trafficking, the dangerous conditions during the actual journey may lead to illness and injury. At the destination, women often suffer from health problems such as head and heart, liver and kidney problems.[11] Rates of injuries to Ethiopian women are the highest in the categories of broken bones, head trauma and bodily injuries that may finally lead to mortality.[12]

> The majority of injuries and illnesses reported by women were the result of physical and sexual abuse [...] women were beaten, raped, and deprived of sleep, food, and other basic necessities, leading to fatigue, weight loss, and vulnerability to infection.[13]

In the context of trafficking, risks to reproductive and sexual health generally result from sexual abuse and violence. Trafficked women who are used as commodities for sex frequently suffer from different sexually transmitted diseases, including HIV. Women who become pregnant as a result of rape or forced sex are susceptible to undergo unsafe abortions.

Due to the distortion of their dignity, the trafficked migrant women often develop self-hate, different phobias, abnormal feelings of shame, self-imposed isolation to the point of not leaving the house and sometimes losing consciousness.[14]

---

[10] At **www.iom.int/jahia/webdav/site/myjahiasite/shared/shared/mainsite/projects/documents/ct_brochure_en.pdf**

[11] Ibid.

[12] Ibid.

[13] Ibid.

[14] *The Health Risks and Consequences of Trafficking in Women and Adolescents. Findings from a European Study, Including: Human Rights Analysis of Health and Trafficking and Principles for Promoting the Health Rights of Trafficked Women*, at **www.lshtm.ac.uk/hpu/docs/trafficking final.PDF**

Women who are victims of trafficking suffer social alienation in the host and home countries. The absence of emotional and social support has an enormous effect on the women's ability to withstand and cope with the stress of their situation. They can easily develop a feeling of worthlessness in their society. For many victims, the lack of meaningful interpersonal contact leaves them feeling alone, and serves to reinforce their belief that relief or escape is ineffective.

The traffickers' modus operandi

The traffickers use different techniques. The recruiters promise the young women good jobs with high salaries in other provinces and countries. Subsequently, trapped by the recruiters' or agents' false promises, they are usually drawn into prostitution.[15] In terms of terminology, women who are deceived and coerced into bonded labor are referred to as "trafficked" while those who migrate willingly with an agent to work in exploitative conditions are usually considered "smuggled."[16] Smuggled women illegally enter the country of destination. The "smuggling of migrants is a crime involving the procurement for financial or other material benefit of illegal entry of a person into a State of which that person is not a national or resident."[17] Such women do not have protection. If they are caught by the police they will be beaten, fined and/or jailed. There are many such cases of Ethiopian domestic workers in Lebanon for instance. Deceit is one of the methods used by traffickers to deliver many women into the hands of the hunters.

The causes of human trafficking

The root cause of the trafficking of humans can be socioeconomic realities, gender inequality and instability. The women often see the offer made by the recruiters as an opportunity to be financially independent from their parents and male partners, and/or to be able to help their families financially. Most of the young girls vulnerable to trafficking are orphans and those who have to take care of their younger siblings. Others have sick parents who are unable to feed their families or single headed households and, in

[15] Cf. **www.oit.org/wcmsp5/groups/public/---ed_emp/documents/publication/wcms_117931.pdf**
[16] At **https://www.unodc.org/unodc/en/human-trafficking/smuggling-of-migrants.html**
[17] Ibid.

most cases, there is a severe shortage of resources. Frequently the families themselves force their young girls to work as domestic workers in order to improve the family's living conditions. The openness of some families to the trafficking of their female members is symptomatic of the fear they experience in light of the difficulties they have to survive. Furthermore, it also plays a role if the family has a "normalized" view of slavery, which in some countries remains deep rooted.

At the ecclesial and spiritual levels, the classical moral teachings of Christian theology have a profound effect on people, especially in the global South. Selflessness is an ideal and the "theology of suffering" plays an important role in the religious conviction of many Christians who fall into the hands of traffickers.

The "theology of suffering" is related to the suffering of Jesus. Jesus' sacrificial death redeemed people from the bondage of sin, death and Satan. This theology is the foundation of the church. Jesus suffered for the sake of the people. His suffering became a model for the suffering of people.

In many contexts of the world, it can be observed that women from a Christian background submit to the experience of suffering because they believe suffering to be related to redemption. In this case, they accept suffering as a good thing in order to redeem someone[18] and live according to the concept of "living for another." This concept makes women feel responsible for others, especially parents and families, and even their community. Although many family members share this feeling of responsibility, it has a particularly profound effect on women. It implies submerging one's own self to the other's identity, needs and interest and results in the women losing their identity. As a result, "a woman's self-actualizing potential is often anesthetized. She is taught to wait for someone to find her [...]."[19]

Among the moral virtues traditionally articulated by the Christian tradition, tolerance and obedience for instance can be interpreted in a way that helps to oppress women and lead them to subordinate to human trafficking. Tolerance is defined as the willingness to accept torture.[20] In the end, it leads the women to tolerate their problems and to lose self-esteem. They submit to trafficking as domestic workers although they know that they will experience oppression. The word obedience, meaning willingness to do what one is told to do, implies submission which can also easily

---

[18] Gemma T. Cruz, *Into the Deep, A Theological Exploration of the Struggle of the Filipina Domestic Workers in Hong Kong* (Manila: UST Publishing House, 2006), 70.

[19] Joanne Wolski Conn (ed.), *Women's Spirituality. Resources for Christian Development* (Mahawi: Paulist, 1986, 1992), 11.

[20] Haddis Tiruneh, *The Works of St. Yarde In the Light of the Holy Bible* (Ethiopia: Addis Ababa, 1999), 8.

be misused. If one is obedient to someone this means that one is submissive to that person. The patriarchal dominance in the church implies that women are subject to the authority of men in all aspects. If the church's moral teachings are unbalanced, then it is easier for men to dominate women. Their identity becomes invisible and they lack self-direction, self-affirmation and self-reliance.

In many regions of the world, the church's misuse of moral teachings contributes to the discrimination against women, social segregation, racial and ethnic discrimination, cultural and religious differences, work exploitation and economic violence, sexual exploitation and abuses.

Many women believe that God is with them and gives them strength and patience in their suffering. In actual fact, this strength and patience would be necessary to resist oppression rather than submitting to exploitation. The Christian God is a liberating God.

Theology of resistance as a way out

> Enlarge the site of your tent, and let the curtains of your habitations be stretched out; do not hold back; lengthen your cords and strengthen your stakes (Isa 54:2).

The theology of resistance is the theology that helps human beings to be conscious of themselves and to fight against trafficking: the selling and buying of humans as objects for the benefit of the traffickers and the employers. Human beings need to become more self-confident–no more holding back and waiting for other persons to speak up for them. It is time to "strengthen their stakes" to resist trafficking. They need to be fully aware of their human dignity and what they are subjected to–both in the positive and the negative sense–and to deal with it rather than simply submitting to it. The theology of resistance enables them to seek their full humanity and liberation instead of limiting their scope to a particular reality which they are tied to.

The journey of resistance is a journey from:

- Lack of self-esteem to self-definition: being aware of one's objectification and reacting against it by developing self-worthiness.

- Submission to anger: anger is better understood as a feeling signalling that all is not well in our relation to ourselves or groups or to the world around us. Anger needs to be understood as recognizing that our self needs love and compassion in spite of difficulties. In this context, it is to be understood as the will to change the oppressive circumstances under which one is forced to live.

- Shame/guilt to self-acceptance: women are created with dignity. Developing self-pride is rescuing women's self from guilt and shame feelings and resisting the damage, trauma and self-rejection that come with the experience of being mistreated as a human being.

The churches finding a new way of communicating moral teachings that leads human beings to self-awareness is a new way of resisting the submission to human trafficking. Women relate the suffering of Jesus to their experience of suffering and accept it due to the strong emphasis laid on suffering in the church's moral teachings. Therefore, suffering becomes normal and naturalized in human life. Christ's sacrificial death is interpreted as a model for sacrificing human beings, especially women. God's liberating power is not announced and suffering becomes life's final destiny. In the name of being a good Christian woman, silent and obedient, this teaching is not encouraging women openly to speak about their suffering and to denounce the violence they are victims of.

It is therefore necessary to:

- Reexamine the theology of suffering where the victorious image of the divine should be addressed in the churches' teaching and counselling. God is a liberating God. Suffering is a struggle from transformation to liberation. Suffering is not final for human beings.

- Revisit the biblical teachings of crucifixion. This will empower women to see that death is not the final answer in the gospel. An interpretation of the theology of the cross can motivate us to see Jesus as a model to overcome suffering.

- Review the moral teachings of churches that force humans to submit to trafficking.

The moral teaching of churches impact women's lives. In light of the fact that some societies are inclined to be positive toward trafficking, there is an urgent need for a change in attitude. Sociological studies on human trafficking have shown that socioeconomic factors lead some societies and the victims' families to turn a blind eye to the trafficking of their daughters, sisters, brothers and wives.

From their unequal social locations, gendered stereotypes that present men as powerful and in control, and women as passive and primarily relegated to the private sphere, feed the misconception in many societies that women are socialized to do housework. Such stereotypes contribute to the trafficking of women as they are socialized to be obedient and quietly to obey their husbands/men.

It is the church's responsibility to ensure that our young girls and boys, men and women, are educated; education can be a powerful tool to overcome the gender stereotypes that are keeping women in a subordinate position. Awareness building in the congregation includes identifying available resources, support services and organizations that can provide support for the victims, both with regard to their physical safety (shelter, food, medication and hygiene) and psychological well-being; to advocate for the equitable treatment of men and women. This will contribute to understanding the dignity of every human being and that God did not create human beings for sale.

Conclusion

It should be self-evident that the church as a community of believers should be disturbed by human trafficking and the appalling ways in which this affects the rights of individuals. The violation of a human being constitutes a violation of God's temple. When a person is oppressed, the human family is diminished. When contemplating human trafficking and its effects, we quickly realize that change is crucial. This includes changing certain attitudes, still prevalent in many societies and churches, such as associating men with human characteristics defined as superior and dominant, and women with those defined as inferior and passive. Patriarchal domination contradicts the liberating message of God's grace that has come to us in Jesus Christ.

Over the centuries, the churches have occasionally adopted moral teachings of non-Christian origin (like the teaching of Aristotle about the role of women). The churches' teachings that enforce the suffering and oppression of women can be challenged by teaching the equality of men and women as created in the image of God and by addressing God's liberating power. Creating an environment in which people find sustainable work and live from their income is also important. By truly embracing the principle of equality and avoiding misconceptions, a glimpse of light can be seen at the end of the tunnel.

Questions

What do you know about "human trafficking" today in your own context?

How might our understanding of "being created in the image of God" impact the way in which we live today?

What are the challenges that the church faces in putting this understanding of being created in the image of God into action and how do we interpret this in the light of human trafficking?

Church, Politics and the Use of Power: Some Examples from Hungary

Tamás Fabiny

Historical background

After 1945 Hungary became part of the Soviet sphere of interest. Over the next couple of years, people enjoyed relative freedom under Hungary's coalition government. The Communists seized power by widespread electoral fraud in 1947. Using so-called salami tactics, also known as salami-slice strategy, they divided and destroyed the other political parties and, in some cases, absorbed the left wing of these. With the substantial help of the Soviets, they nationalized the factories and forced the agricultural workers into kolkhozy, collective farms. During the same period, church schools were secularized. Historically, the churches had been responsible for managing many public schools in Hungary. Bar a few exceptions, church schools were closed and the Evangelical-Lutheran Church could retain none of its schools. With some delay, the world-famous Lutheran school of Fasor was also taken away. Religious orders and deaconess associations were dissolved and many church people were imprisoned. During the one-party system, the media were censored and thus paralyzed. The compulsory ideology of so-called real socialism impacted the arts and Soviet atheistic propaganda infiltrated the intellectual circles of the time. A specific term was coined during this era, namely the so-called "bell-freak": innocent people were paralyzed by fear when the doorbell rang late in the evening, because it might be the police coming to take people away, without giving any reason. At that time, being a pastor also meant taking a risk. The best known bishop of my church, Lajos Ordass, was imprisoned and many of his colleagues were relocated or forced to give up their ministry and to make a living as blue-collar workers. At the time, there seemed to be no prospects for pastors. But vocation conquered circumstance. Let me give you an example from my own family. My father had a very strong calling from God, and although he had an excellent position as a lawyer, he wanted to be a pastor because the Holy Spirit had touched him. He did not care that if he was lucky he would be called to serve as a pastor somewhere in a godforsaken village. He was ready to face suffering. As a theological student he and some other students had participated in an evangelization campaign and had distributed small booklets containing John's Gospel in the street. On the booklets it said "printed in the USA." Because of this, they were arrested by the police. He told us that they spent the night praying to the Lord just as Paul and Silas had done. In the morning they were rebuked and could go home. The interrogating officer said to them, "Give me a piece of that booklet, my wife likes to read these kinds of writings."

The 1956 revolution or uprising was an attempt to put an end to this totalitarian situation. Freedom ruled only for a few days until the Soviets occupied the country and quashed the revolution. A period of so-called "soft dictatorship" followed. People often referred to this as "goulash Communism" or "the happiest barrack in the Socialist camp" because, compared to the other Socialist countries, the standard of living in Hungary was relatively high. Today we realize that in fact these decades led to a greater deterioration in the life of the churches than an open dictatorship might have done. In an open dictatorship, the difference between good and bad is clearly defined and therefore Christian believers are ready to suffer. In a soft dictatorship, the boundaries are not so clear and many people, including church leaders, made unprincipled compromises in order to survive.

This situation impacted people serving in the church: no one had to risk their life anymore. While there were boundaries it was possible, and perhaps sometimes too easy, to find a *modus vivendi*. The relationship between church and state was like that of a patron and a client: one would receive smaller or bigger favors thanks to the cooperation between a loyal church leadership and the State Office for Church Matters (originally created for the persecution of the church): one could get a better job; one was granted a possibility to travel abroad; and pastors' children were admitted to university provided everybody agreed to the rules of the so-called real socialism. One can imagine what a distorting influence this had on some pastors' personalities. For many being a pastor meant adapting to the external framework, often having to make decisions against one's conscience and not to touch on certain taboos (1956, the Soviet presence, one-party system) in exchange for practicing one's vocation as an outcast in society, but within the confines of the church in the form of a "vestry-Christianity."

It is therefore hardly surprising that at the time of the regime change in 1989 the churches were unprepared. During those months, we often used the term "the last forty years." This metaphor, which drew a parallel between the era of oppression and being squeezed into boundaries and the forty years' wandering of the Jewish people in the desert, seemed particularly appropriate at the time. It was an alluring image for us because we could talk about slavery and plagues and about the fact that God's people had to cross the Red Sea. It was possible to mention the different kinds of idolatry and infidelity and finally we could point to a new generation. However, we could not see either a Moses or an Aaron ahead of us, or a Joshua belonging to the new generation–not to talk about Canaan.

If we want to find a biblical metaphor, then a series of events that occurred a couple of centuries later seem to be much more appropriate in order to depict the situation of the churches at the time: the end of the Babylonian captivity of the Jewish people. In the sixth century BC the political and social situation, believed by the superpowers to be extremely stable and unshakeable, changed so radically that the Jewish population, which had been taken to captivity some decades earlier at the time of Nebuchadnezzar, could return home. There is a visible parallel at least at two points. First, it was not the chosen people who fought heroically and thus gained their freedom back with their desperate prophets and members of the nation faithful until the end, but simply that the "constellation of world politics," "the structure of great powers," "the historical reality" had changed. Of course we cannot deny that the Lord of history is hidden; God can steer God's people's lives in very secular ways as well. With some confidence we can also suppose that the witness of some to a certain extent contributed to the fall of a great power at the time of the Babylonian captivity and to the system change that took place in the satellite nations after the Soviet occupation.

The other parallel we can draw between this historical situation and the Hungarian regime change is that the returning Jews did not find their country in an orderly state: it was not a situation conducive to peaceful work. Rather, they found ruins–ruins everywhere. Ezra and Nehemiah began to tackle the situation by removing the debris and rebuilding the Temple. The political changes in 1989–1990 found the churches in Hungary in the same situation: they were in ruins and a long and tiring process of reconstruction had to begin. It was impossible to continue from the point at which God's people had been before being taken into captivity or before the cessation of religious freedom. In the words of a Hungarian writer, one more biblical metaphor became part of every-day language, "there is a big crowd on the way to Damascus." This was a rather sardonic expression related to political conformity and not an indication of people joining the church in huge numbers. The difficulties of having to start afresh are well described in the four-line poem by the Hungarian poetess Ágnes Nemes

Nagy, which she wrote when, after a period of forced silence, her poems could once again be published.

> In his left shoulder, as he rose again,
> each muscle felt a lifetime's every pain.
> His death was torn from him, as was his dressing,
> For resurrection is just as distressing.[1]

Present situation

Twenty-five years have passed since then. The relationship between the elected governments and the churches has undergone a series of changes. There were and still are political parties that regard the role of the churches as being a merely spiritual one rather than one of participating in public life. This is what I call "vestry-Christianity": that is, when religious communities are pushed to remain within the confines of the church. Conservative church circles do not object to this interpretation since they feel that the churches should only deal with spiritual questions in this "sinful world."

There are, on the other hand, some political parties that regard the churches (or to be more exact, their preferred churches) as "natural partners." It seems as if they want to compensate the churches for the loss of church property, prestige and intellectual influence.

I find both attitudes rather dangerous. In a radio interview during the time of the Socialist (practically post-Communist) government in Hungary I described my position as follows: "I can hardly wait to critique a Conservative government." This was a twofold idea: on the one hand, I was dissatisfied with the Socialist government and wished for a change; on the other, the presence of the church in society must be characterized by a critical relation to political power. The church has to fulfill a prophetic role as we can see from Isaiah, Jeremiah or Jesus. The church should not follow the current political power without critique. Since the regime change and even more so since the period between1990–1994 there is the suspicion that politics tries to influence the churches: they want to tell us how to practice our faith.

In 1997, in order to deal with earlier conflicts, the Hungarian government brokered an agreement first with the Roman Catholic Church, and afterwards also with other churches. The so-called normative support system, which later caused much tension, was actually aimed at domesticating the churches. Later governments made similar attempts. Relations

[1] Translation into English by Peter Zollmann.

were sometimes friendly, sometimes less so. Over the last years there have been many issues, such as the new church law and the criminalization of the homeless, on which the church had to take a critical stance. I could not remain silent when the name of God was being inserted into the constitution and had to speak out against the increasing popularity of the extreme right. I have direct experience as a bishop in a district the majority of which lies in North-Eastern Hungary where a radical right-wing party has been especially strong in the last four years.

Nowadays we often talk about the risks of political Christianity, which refers to a situation in which those in power try to exploit the churches in a paternalistic way when they want to use the churches as a tool for reaching their own goals. This cannot be expected from any party—not even from the mayor who wants to treat the churches as his natural partner and demands political support from us. We can cooperate with several partners to create a common set of values but we are not anyone's "natural partner." The churches have suffered enough during the dictatorship when they were expected to support the state without exercising any form of critique. Luckily, even at that time, there were some people who resisted. We must not forget that the churches also experienced serious humiliation and unjust exclusion while the present opposition parties were in office.

Nevertheless, we cannot deny that the churches themselves have from time to time flirted with power. If the financial system in Hungary were healthy—which is not the case now—the churches would not be forced to lead constant financial negotiations with the government. I am here thinking of a transparent and reliable system of financing the churches that would remain untouched by changes in government, based on an understanding that churches are not only carrying out tasks in education and the social sphere but also that their spiritual work potentially has a healing effect on society.

In the Evangelical Lutheran Church in Hungary, we try to promote social sensitivity in many ways. In our educational journal, we strongly underline the topic of teaching tolerance and accepting each other in our schools, so that we are not only tolerant in our words but also our actions (i.e., the inclusion of Roma people, Jews, homosexuals, the disabled). We need to affirm that the church has zero tolerance of intolerance: the directors of our church schools have been asked to react immediately when they hear any anti-Semitic, anti-Roma or homophobic comments.

Today, intolerance not only characterizes party politics but there is also a tendency in Hungarian society not to be able to deal with those who are "different" from us, be that a blind person with a white stick or someone in a wheelchair. Perhaps the renewal of society could start with minor things such as noticing the other in need and not being ashamed to help; organizing many small communities and providing meaningful programs; giving something altruistically, without compensation, etc. Or by discovering that real love does not seek value but creates it. I would like people to find such a community in our churches.

Conclusion

The human being is not for sale

The LWF has chosen "Human Beings—Not for Sale" as one of the subthemes of the 500th Anniversary of the Reformation. I have included some examples from my personal life in this essay and have referred to historical eras in which people were deprived of freedom, both individually and collectively. The dignity of individuals or certain groups of society was violated; respectability was for sale and could be bought. In some cases the secret police, with the collaboration of ordinary people or those working at some level in the one-party system leadership, blackmailed or directly harmed both the young and the elderly. Nonetheless there were also good examples of how some retained their inner freedom, despite being constricted externally. They can be understood as having been guided by the Apostle Paul's words: "For you did not receive a spirit of slavery to fall back into fear, but you have received a spirit of adoption. We can cry, 'Abba! Father!'" (Rom 8:15). We know a form of slavery that is actually freedom. Just as the Apostle Paul remained free in prison and proudly declared himself to be "the prisoner of Christ Jesus," many confessors resisted putting their independence on sale. Luther, who was ready to question any authority of state or church, happily confessed that his conscience is "captive to the Word of God." That's why he could be really free!

Practical application of the teaching of the two realms

Besides the teaching on freedom, Luther's understanding of the two kingdoms can also be applied to our situation. Under the totalitarian system, one had to be on guard and notice when the oppressing power put demands on people and when God's governing intention was at play. For the church leadership (and in a way for each Christian), it was a temptation to merge the two. In the life of the Protestant churches in Hungary during the so-called real socialism it was widely accepted that God punishes the churches for sins committed under Nazism and for collaborating with the political power of the time. According to this understanding, churches must accept God's anger, even in the most anti-godly decisions of the Communist state.

Consequently, the so-called “diaconical theology” of the time refrained from criticizing the political power of the time or even suggesting the slightest correction to them.

After the regime change, the churches suddenly found themselves on the beneficiary side, which now and then astonished even themselves. A number of pastors felt the urge to praise the current system from the pulpit and saw God’s direct will in the regained political freedom. ”God is the Lord of history” became the justification for the political (sometimes even party-specific) presence of the church. The situation in which the churches managed to share in positions of power was not always consistent with the concept of the two realms. There were signs of mixing the kingdom of God with the actual world. The prayer “your kingdom come” was put on a par with the realization of a worldly state providing freedom. Going astray theologically was combined with the blasphemous effort of the political power to legitimize itself by using biblical metaphors. Politicians ending their speeches with *soli Deo gloria,* or others claiming that we, the Hungarians, are the chosen people, are simply misplaced in the public space.

The theology of the cross

As the third pillar of Luther’s theology, the theology of the cross can orient us. It is an interesting paradox that while the church was suffering under real oppression, it was not possible (or at least not in public) to speak about the importance of a “cruciform church.” Rather than talking about this topic many lived it out. When the time of freedom came, the church fell into the temptation of getting on the bright side, the side of glory and power, leaving a Christ-like and cruciform way of life. A well-fed, comforted church adapting to a consumer society falls short of the theology of the cross. In a world where “all-is-for-sale,” churches easily become part of consumer mentality. Therefore, in our times the church has to be alert not to give up shouldering the cross and not to make dangerous compromises.

I am convinced that the theme of 2017 Assembly—a genuinely biblical and reformatory theme—will help us to find our way back to the cross. What happened in the crucifixion of Jesus Christ is not comparable to any human deed or business enterprise. It is the acting God who is present there. Therefore we confess to be “Liberated by God’s Grace.”

Questions

Do you know similar examples of ways from political oppression to freedom?

How relevant is Luther's teaching of the two realms in different political contexts?

How can the emphasis between the two elements of "critical solidarity" change?

Life with the Other: Migration, Displacement and Gender Justice

Munib A. Younan

As we move toward 2017 and our commemoration of 500 years of the Lutheran Reformation, I am grateful for the theme we are following: Not for Sale! The message of hope and love, proclaimed from the beginning of our evangelical tradition to the present, is truly Good News. As the Apostle Paul wrote in his letter to the Romans, "if while we were enemies, we were reconciled to God through the death of his Son, much more surely, having been reconciled, will we be saved by his life" (Rom 5:10). As Paul assures us, this salvation is a free gift. It is not for sale!

The three "Not for Sale" themes—salvation, human beings and creation—are all related to one another. Because God created the heavens and the earth and was "in Christ [...] reconciling the world to himself" (2 Cor 5:19), all of creation has been sanctified with God's redeeming love. Because "by grace you have been saved through faith, and this is not your own doing; it is the gift of God" (Eph 2:8), the inherent value and dignity of every human being have been confirmed. The prophet Isaiah proclaimed God's invitation for "everyone who thirsts, [to] come to the waters" for all who "have no money, [to] come, buy and eat! Come, buy wine and milk without money and without price" (Isa 55:1). The message of God's salvation in Christ Jesus is a message of profound equality before God, where everything is given freely, where nothing is for sale. Creation is free. Redemption is freely given through the cross.

This message confronts a world where everything—from human beings to the gifts of the earth and even to the promise of salvation itself—is constantly offered in exchange for money and goods. From the exploitation of natural resources and official efforts to prevent further climate change to human trafficking, the earth and all that is in it are offered up for sale. While these things are now happening on a larger scale, the same dynamics were present in the eras inhabited by Jesus and Martin Luther. In their historical periods, both the earth and human beings were degraded. Both confronted systems of false religious belief that claimed God demanded certain sacrifices in order to smooth the passage to salvation. Each of us is free because of Christ's sacrificial blood on the cross, which continues to set us free to this day. The message of the gospel was as clear then as it is now: neither salvation, nor human beings, nor creation itself can be purchased. All are expressions of God's good and gracious gift.

The refugee crisis

In our world today, human competition over resources is driving ever greater conflict. As a result of these conflicts, human beings are displaced and driven to desperation. At the end of 2013, the United Nations High Commissioner for Refugees (UNHCR) estimated that over 51.2 million persons worldwide had been forcibly displaced. Of these, 11.7 million were refugees living under the mandate of UNHCR, while another 5 million Palestinian refugees are registered with the United Nations Relief and Works Agency (UNRWA).

The Lutheran World Federation (LWF) has a strong heritage of outreach to refugees. Our global communion was founded with the purpose of providing aid and relief to people in Europe suffering displacement and poverty after World War II. After that conflict, one out of every six Lutherans in the world was either a refugee or internally displaced person. Since then, we have built on that heritage and expanded our witness of serving the needy and vulnerable. We provide our services and resources for all who are in need, regardless of their religion, creed, or their national and tribal identity.

I am a Palestinian and a Christian. My home is in Jerusalem. My mother tongue is Arabic. We Palestinian Christians have lived in the Holy Land since Pentecost, the very beginning of Christianity. Today, we are not as many as we used to be, but we are nevertheless an integral part of Palestinian culture. My family belongs to the 1948 refugees. I still carry an UNWRA refugee card. My home is in Beit Safafa, near the Gilo settlement built on confiscated Palestinian land. With other Palestinians, I seek the just establishment of a Palestinian state within the 1967 borders, living alongside Israel in peace, justice and reconciliation. This goal includes the clarification of internationally recognized borders, a just resolution to the status of Israeli settlements and a just resolution to the chronic crisis of

Palestinian refugees. I seek these things not as part of a political program, but because I seek dignity for my people and for my neighbors.

I first learned about the LWF through a cup of hot chocolate given to us at the Martin Luther School in the Old City of Jerusalem. I remember wondering, "Why do these Lutherans love us and sustain us with food and drinks?" Today, I know that the global Lutheran church was embracing me as a Palestinian refugee. This love touched my heart; I felt challenged to pay back to the Lutherans all the good they had done for me, my family and other Palestinians. Later, I understood that the Lutheran theology of justification by faith alone drives us as Christians to serve freely even as we receive gratefully. We have received everything through God's gracious love. It is a free gift that can never be repaid.

The LWF, which since 1948 has been active in Palestine, eventually empowered our church to emerge from a German mission heritage. I admire how the LWF empowered us but did not create ways to control us. It empowered the Evangelical Lutheran Church so that we could find our path to being an independent, sustainable church. We are indebted to the global Lutheran communion for its participation in the mission of God throughout the Middle East.

As a refugee myself from the 1948 war between the newly formed State of Israel and its neighbors, I know what it is like to live with profound uncertainty and fear. I know the reality of poverty. Most of all, I know what it means to live in a situation where circumstances and, sometimes, other people, are seeking to steal from a person their very dignity.

We do not honor this dignity when we see the refugee as anything but a charity case. Refugees do not exist so that we can help them and feel better about ourselves. Instead, the Christian disciple is invited to experience the face of God in the refugee, just as we see the face of God in other people who belong to our families and our congregations. I can attest to the fact that it is when we are at our most destitute, our most hopeless, that we are most conscious of our standing before God. With and through the refugee, we are invited into God's presence. Through that presence, we are renewed and empowered in our motivation not only to give food, clothing and other resources, but to address the inequalities and structural injustices that force so many people into lives of vulnerability and fear.

Our Lutheran communion's commitment not only to diakonia informs our commitment to alleviating suffering and addressing the root causes of oppression. Beyond this commitment to service, we also practice prophetic diakonia. The prophetic nature of our approach is found in our commitment to empower refugees, migrants, and all who struggle for justice, strengthening and amplifying their voices as they seek to change their own conditions and contexts. This is the prophetic diakonia our global communion is so well-suited to provide.

The LWF has a strong presence in the Middle East. Our communion's legacy of service in East Jerusalem is grounded in the witness of the Evangelical Lutheran Church in Jordan and the Holy Land (ELCJHL) and in the diakonia of Augusta Victoria Hospital, led for several years now by a Palestinian Christian CEO. This legacy has been extended into Jordan, where the LWF is helping establish and manage the Za'atari Refugee Camp for Syrians fleeing the civil war in their country. The continuing conflict has forced us to expand our reach even further, into Iraq.

In this global Lutheran communion, I have always found sisters and brothers in Christ working to help refugees and other persons in need keep their dignity as human beings and as children of God. Our human dignity is given by God alone. Each individual human being is blessed with the image of God in which all humanity was created. We are each of priceless worth in the eyes of God. No human being can ever be for sale!

Christ's disciples, welcoming the other

The LWF is at present serving about 2 million refugees in the world. That means that every group of seventy Lutherans is tending to the needs of one refugee. We are serving in Dadab, Syria, Iraq, Jordan, Sudan, Peru, Nepal, Mauritania and many other places. Wherever we are present, we are focused on the practical needs of development and the prophetic call of empowerment.

Refugee empowerment goes far beyond providing the necessities of life. Supporting children's and adult education, providing meaningful activities and strengthening refugee capacity for protecting their rights all move us toward the goal of empowerment rather than providing charity alone.

In 2012, the UN High Commissioner for Refugees, António Guterres, invited religious leaders to discuss the religious foundations for receiving refugees. How, he asked, can we best care for others who need our assistance? It was my idea that we could develop a code of conduct based on our many different scriptures and traditions. Guterres took the idea very seriously and, as a result, we developed a document entitled "Welcoming the Stranger: Affirmations for Faith Leaders"[1] which offers the religious foundations for caring for refugees. For me, Christians are called for two specific reasons: (1) because Christ himself, with the Holy Family, was a refugee in Egypt; and (2) Jesus' call in Nazareth, that "The Spirit of the Lord is upon me, because he has anointed me to bring good news to the poor. He has sent me to

[1] At **www.lutheranworld.org/content/resource-welcoming-stranger** and **www.unhcr.org/51b6de419.html**

proclaim release to the captives and recovery of sight to the blind, to let the oppressed go free" (Lk 4:18). This was Jesus' understanding of his own call.

"Welcoming the Stranger" begins and ends with the simple affirmation, "I will welcome the stranger." The document acknowledges that this commitment sometimes takes courage. But every faith tradition has the core action at the center of its commitments. "My faith teaches that compassion, mercy, love and hospitality are for everyone: the native born and the foreign born, the member of my community and the newcomer."[2]

Our shared dignity and equality with people who are refugees and other people experiencing great need are shared also within our global communion. Together, we model what it means to live as equals before God, accepting one another with our strengths and our weaknesses intact. There is no doubt that there are many forms of inequality within our global communion. Some of our churches come from very rich countries while others, like my own ELCJHL, come from places others will not allow to be called a country!

These material inequalities do not change our relationship as equal members of the global communion any more than an individual's poverty or wealth affect their status as a child of God. As the late bishop Josiah Kibira, one of my predecessors as president of the Lutheran World Federation, was fond of saying, there is no church so small, so poor, so young in age that it would not have something to give to other churches; and there is no church so old, so rich, and so old in tradition and history that it would not depend on these gifts from others.

It makes no sense from a Lutheran perspective to claim that one person is a stronger or better believer than any other. Each one of us is *simul iustus et peccator,* no more and no less, each in equal measure before God, through Christ Jesus. The danger in both of these forms of inequality is that our communion could become divided. One constructive response to these divisive challenges is to emphasize a discipleship of equals.

In the Christian tradition, the great signs of our profound equality before God can be found in our holy sacraments. Holy Baptism is the foundation of our shared witness. Our human tendency–in the church as well as in political relations–is to emphasize what divides us rather than what brings us together. Through water and the Word, we are engrafted into the church, the body of Christ. In Baptism, we are sent out into the world together for the sake of God's holistic mission, in diaconal purpose. In 1984, our global communion agreed to the principle of pulpit and altar fellowship. The sacrament of the altar sends us out into the world as baptized members engrafted into the body of Christ to proclaim the Good

[2] Ibid.

News of God's freely given love through word and deed. Our sacramental hope sends us out into the world as Christ's disciples engaged in prophetic diakonia for the sake of our neighbors.

We must all remember that our neighbors experiencing vulnerability and need are not always in far-away places. Refugees and impoverished migrants can be in our communities as well. In broad strokes, the problems of migration today are twofold. First, migrants are escaping political problems, often caused by the postcolonial experiences of their home countries; the problems they face have been caused by the legacy of Western colonization. The situations being fled by many migrants—including extremism, occupation, threats to life and dignity, and the lack of any economic optimism—often drive them toward the very countries that helped create their misery.

While they can often stay in those countries, they are faced with a second problem: the lack of any possibility of normal integration into the cultures of the host countries. In Europe especially, we see difficulties in fully accepting and receiving migrant populations. Many factors contribute to these difficulties. It is a challenge for our global communion not only to address the root causes of economic migration, but to assist those migrants and refugees struggling to live in the host countries. One real issue related to the lack of legal, economic and cultural integration is that migrants are moving all over the world, serving the wealthy. This leads to the exploitation of unprotected laborers. If human beings are not for sale, they must be respected in every context. The exploitation of labor is unacceptable in the eyes of our Lord.

Grounded in Baptism and strengthened through the Eucharist, we are sent out into diaconal service. For centuries, Christians of all confessions have engaged in vital, holistic ministry throughout the world. It is time for us to consider practical ways this work can be done together. The call to service and the call to mission cannot be separated. If we are doing one together, we are no doubt engaging in both together. Ephesians calls us to bear "with one another in love, making every effort to maintain the unity of the Spirit in the bond of peace. There is one body and one Spirit, just as you were called to the one hope of your calling, one Lord, one faith, one baptism, one God and Father of all, who is above all and through all and in all" (Eph 4:2–6).

The Lutheran emphasis—one we share with many other churches and communions—is that the grace we receive in our sacraments is a free gift given to us by a gracious and loving God. As another theme of our Reformation commemorations highlights, salvation is not for sale. The free offer of God's grace in the sacraments confirms our fundamental equality before God. None of us is of greater worth than any other. We are all priceless. No human being can ever be thought of as being for sale.

Working toward gender justice

I am very proud that the 2013 meeting of the LWF Council unanimously accepted the LWF Gender Justice Policy.[3] This is an important step forward for our global communion. The policy emphasizes the Lutheran theological foundation that each of us is equal in creation and in redemption. Everyone has the right to experience equality and justice, regardless of gender.

While this is an important document, we must still ask what this step means in practical terms. The question is how we can introduce and implement the Gender Justice Policy in all member churches. As it stands the policy provides an excellent foundation. It can be an example for many other churches and global communions. But it must not remain a general statement without contextualizing its commitments. In order to achieve this contextualization, it must be studied in every context.

In order to achieve the vision of gender justice in every context, we must commit to one another that we cannot hide behind culture, tradition or certain interpretations of the Bible in order to justify continued gender-based inequality. Those who use such arguments in order to continue discrimination are diminishing or even misrepresenting the biblical tradition and God's policy of equality. All culture is made by human beings; it was never made by men alone. Those who hide behind culture in conversations about gender justice and the ordination of women only make their chauvinism more apparent. In order to challenge those perspectives, it is my hope that every church within our global communion will study the Gender Justice Policy and take steps to tailor it to their contexts.

Our concern for the dignity and equal value of every human being finds positive expression in our communion's work to support gender justice. We do not only give good speeches; we are to practice these commitments in our governance and executive bodies. We hope that each one of our member churches will do this for the sake of the humanity we share. This work is important in the Middle East, where gender justice will be an important step toward healing the overall conditions of our societies. In the Middle East, the growth of extremism has had immediately negative effects on women throughout the Middle East.

The ELCJHL is committed to promoting the role of women in church and society. The Women's Desk—run by a women and directed by a committee of women leaders—has accomplished many things. First, in both Palestine and Jordan, the committee has run many workshops and gatherings on the topic of domestic violence. There has been a noticeable increase in domestic violence in our society, but the issue is not often openly discussed. The group

[3] At **www.lutheranworld.org/content/resource-lwf-gender-justice-policy** .

has asked how they can help empower women to address the issue, even if they face domestic violence themselves. Their goal is to build a community of empowered women who will not keep quiet so they can live their lives without fear. But they also know that addressing women's empowerment is not a matter for individuals alone. For this reason, the Women's Desk is coordinating efforts to include gender justice policies in the constitutions in both Jordan and Palestine. They have organized several workshops with civil society leaders and are leading the efforts in both countries.

Building on these successes, the Women's Desk is now moving toward a third goal. In cooperation with the Secretary for Women in Church and Society at the LWF, they are now working on contextualizing the LWF Gender Justice Policy in the Palestinian and Jordanian contexts. The first step is to translate it into Arabic. This contextualizing strategy will allow us effectively to put the policy to work in our context. I endorse this process for all member churches of the LWF. Without being contextualized in Palestine, Brazil, Indonesia and other regions of the LWF, the Gender Justice Policy would simply be a document on a shelf. But gender justice is too important for us to let that happen.

In many cultures a broad acceptance of the LWF principles for gender justice will take a long time. This is also true for my own context, Palestine. Nevertheless, that does not stop the ELCJHL and its related ministries and programs from building the structures now. We are taking important strides toward realizing gender justice. In our context, it is difficult not to recognize that the strongest voices for achieving a just and enduring solution come from politicians who are women.

The issue of gender justice is a vital challenge for the churches today. All persons—men and women, boys and girls, regardless of gender identity—are equal before God. They are of equal worth. Human beings are not for sale. I hope that as we commemorate the Reformation in 2017, we will come to the table with all of our member churches having contextualized the Gender Justice Policy so that we shout together in the face of the world, "Human beings are not for sale!"

Conclusion

Today, our world is struggling to honor the equality of each human being before God. Our God-given equality and dignity mean that no human being can ever be accepted as being for sale. No human trafficking scheme, no sexual exploitation, no unjust system of labor can ever escape God's judgment through the critical engagement of God's church. Neither refugee crises nor the wars that give rise to such emergencies are ever acceptable in God's eyes.

We live in a fallen and broken world where human beings and the conditions in which humans live are bought and sold on a daily basis. Our shared future is being sold to benefit corporations that pollute our atmosphere and accelerate the change of our shared climate. The church must stand strong, rejecting the callous calculations of profit alone.

Our dignity—and indeed the dignity of creation itself—is found in the image of God. Because the Son of God, Jesus Christ, became incarnate of the Virgin Mary, we know that the image of God is not found in strength alone, but also in weakness and vulnerability. Because Jesus dies on the cross, shedding his blood, we know that he made all of us—regardless of gender, ethnicity, race, religion, ability or any human characteristic—free and equal. We thus strive to preserve the dignity of each and every human being we encounter. The Reformation is not yet finished. The church still needs to be purified and brought into greater alignment with the gift of God in Christ Jesus.

Questions

Are there refugees present in your community? In what ways do government or church agencies respond to their needs?

In what ways is it meaningful to you that the president of our global Lutheran communion is a refugee?

The first mission of the Lutheran World Federation was to care for refugees affected by wars in Europe. What implications does this have for your understanding of our mission together for the sake of the world?

Leaderships Capable of Responding to God's Call

Gustavo Driau

Between 2010 and 2013 the Latin American and Caribbean Sustainability Program of the Lutheran World Federation accompanied various Lutheran churches in Latin America and the Caribbean that requested support for their own work on organizational sustainability. During that period, some forty accompaniment events took place, including workshops, encounters, group meetings, one-to-one meetings, the production of reports and materials, recording experiences, etc.[1]

This paper is to a large extent based on the presentation made at the Informants' Encounter/Seminar on Management and Leadership in Sustainable Churches, which took place in August 2014, at São Leopoldo, and was jointly organized by the LWF's Latin American and Caribbean Sustainability Program and the Sustainability Institute of Latin America and the Caribbean.

Models and changes

Let me start with the question, Why are some organizations, churches and faith communities capable of surmounting the challenges of their context and succeed in going forward with their mission, while others fail to respond to changes and put their viability at risk?

Churches and their organizations rely on experienced leadership, have companions on the journey who advise them, and are also accompanied

[1] At **http://issuu.com/programasustentabilidad/stacks.**

by partner organizations and churches. Even so, many go into periods of decline and crisis. We see how some are capable of turning around, while others find it difficult to recover.

One of the crucial elements in being able to respond to the contextual is the ability to perceive the problems. Contexts change, are uncertain, complex, interrelated and varied. This requires the ability to discern the local context, as was expressed in the 2004 LWF document *Mission in Context*:

> For an effective contextual and holistic mission, the church is challenged to engage in context discernment and analysis at local and national levels, keeping in mind the impact of global and regional factors on local contexts.[2]

It is thus necessary to understand, take note of and interpret changes in the context, with the aim of producing responses that are focused on contextual mission.

In light of the sustainability processes within the churches, we need to assess whether our leadership is capable of perceiving the challenges of contexts or, on the contrary, whether our paradigms, mental models and previous judgments hamper or slow down our perception and the actions that we need to take.

The vastness of what surrounds us is immeasurable, as can be seen in the Psalms (i.e., Ps 8, 96, 144), and human beings have a limited capacity to process the facts arising from their contexts. We cannot know everything, we cannot perceive everything and, in order to make sense of our world, we need simpler images of our situation. These simplified images—what some call "mental models"—are deeply rooted suppositions and representations, influencing our way of understanding the world and of making decisions.

This representation of reality functions like a retina, which, while helping us to see certain facts about our situation, holds us back from perceiving others.

In light of our limitations in perceiving and processing everything that is happening around us, these representations enable individuals and organizations to give meaning to their contexts (understanding them), which then allows one to decide how to act in that particular setting. Thus, some of these "retinas" or mental models help us to discern, to have a panoramic view of and to understand our context, while others stand in our way of it.

When we are thinking about leadership in sustainable churches, we need initially to become critically aware of these retinas through which we read reality, and to note that we carry with us certain particular mental models.

---

[2] *Mission in Context*, at **www.lutheranworld.org/sites/default/files/DMD-Mission-in-Context-EN-low.pdf**, 10.

Obviously, if we were to recognize that we are carrying with us a particular retina through which to read reality, then we could choose to change it.

In the biblical experience of the People of God, changes are initiated by a vision inspired by God. Moses, on his journey to the Promised Land, Paul, in his missionary work, and Jesus himself are guided by visions that are not merely human but inspired by God.

As stated in 2007:

> The basic sustenance of the church is ensured by the redemptive action and the continued creative action of God in time. It is in this confidence that men and women in all ages have dared to take on their own role and responsibility in the different aspects of the life of the church, in that way responding to God's call to become a new community (baptism), to build it and as such to share in God's mission, offering their own gifts for the work.[3]

As human beings we are confronted with the paradox of being at the same time both dependent and responsible. Sometimes, we tend simply to abdicate our responsibility, leaving it to God to do it all for us, and thus not to take any action. At others, we tend to forget our dependence and take on responsibility without God.

The church's activity is paradoxical in so far that, as it carries out its contribution to God's mission, it is called to stress both our human dependence on God and our human responsibility of being those who carry out the task.

Processes of change, empowerment and reconciliation are essential experiences in the lives of individuals, society and the church. It is God who imparts the vision for change and guides and empowers the process of transformation.

The grace of God that stimulates processes of change, empowerment and reconciliation is not limited to the church alone but available to all. At the same time, as baptized persons, we have been given the responsibility to be stewards and to implement these changes. Throughout the Bible, God frequently entrusts individuals with the task of achieving change, a task which is sometimes lifelong or requires one or more generations. Change, empowerment and reconciliation do not happen in an instant but are long-term and costly processes.

---

[3] *Con Confianza en el Porvenir* [With confidence in the future], Sustainability Program document, COL, 2007. See **www.est.edu.br/sustentabilidad/pdfs/Con-confianza-en-el-porvenir-extenso.pdf https://sustentabilidad.files.wordpress.com/2010/08/trusting-in-the-future-eng.doc**

Contexts

Churches are located in particular places, and places change, including shifts in social life, culture, the economy, science, politics and also in aspects of faith and spirituality. We live in a world community in which there is little solidarity, with the poorest members of the community, who suffer exploitation, oppression and war and, even worse, exclusion. Individuals, and whole social groups, are written off as expendable, unemployable, non-citizens.

In a world system where the extreme interests of finance and the markets predominate, human life, justice, dignity and rights do not easily find their way onto the world agenda as priorities, and questions regarding the purpose of human life have little room.

We live in the midst of a culture misused for instant gratification, entertainment and excessive leisure that attempts to fill people's entire lives. It is a culture of success, of coming out on top—even if this is achieved through corruption and crime—one which worships prestige, power and social status. The predominant individualism weakens community ties, since in urban areas many forms, values and lifestyles exist side by side and do not relate to one another. Urbanization and migration caused by poverty result in a breakdown in identity, solidarity and healthy relationships.

In face of these challenges, **God is in mission**:

> This God in mission, who creates and sustains the universe and yet becomes vulnerable in and at the hands of God's own creation, is a Triune God. Trinity describes "God in mission" as always a God for others; namely, the whole of humankind, the world, the entire creation.[4]

In face of these challenges **God is not idle**:

> The Holy Spirit transforms human words proclaiming the Good News, the water of baptism, and the bread and wine of the Eucharist into signs of Christ's presence in the church, empowering the church for God's mission. The Holy Spirit equips Christians and the whole church with a diversity of gifts (1 Corinthians 12; Romans 12; Ephesians 4). Equipped with these spiritual gifts (charismata), they are able to proclaim the gospel and share the life described by the gospel with all peoples in every place. All of the Spirit's gifts – preaching, teaching, healing, prophecy, administration, and others given to women and men – are intended to strengthen the communities of God's gathered people, congregations, for inner growth and holistic mission.[5]

---

[4] Op. cit. (note 2), 24

[5] Ibid., 27

> Through baptism, individuals are included in the new covenant of the people of God and are changed and empowered by the gifts of the Spirit (charismata), as instruments of God's loving purpose for all creation. With that, Luther forcefully links his theology of the universal priesthood of all believers with the 'missio Dei', God's mission, as it is particularly expressed in the work and merits of Christ. Through baptism and by means of the gifts of the Spirit, each individual participates in that mission, which originates in God and is incarnated in the world in Christ.[6]

One of the contributions to God's mission is working to improve the sustainability of faith communities and churches. This involves being able to count on a leadership capable of perceiving the challenges of the context, leaving aside the retinas that obstruct and restrict our vision. The call God makes to us requires a leadership capable of foreseeing future scenarios, analyzing problems and long- and medium-term possibilities, building networks, developing resources and facilitating processes and not simply dealing with day-to-day problems.

Changing contexts present communities and churches with new interrelated and complex problems. In this context, leadership cannot be developed if individuals or groups in the organization behave as if they were silos, that is, enclosed spaces, connected only among themselves. Sustainable leadership is developed by identifying, making visible and connecting the different sectors and levels of churches and their organizations. There is an obvious incompatibility between the idea of the church as the body of Christ (as described by Paul in 1 Corinthians 12) and the development of a leadership based on individuals, segments or groups as if they were such silos.

That term silo is a metaphor suggesting a similarity to the tall grain storage cylinders that keep one type of grain separate from another and from the outside world. Parts of the church do all they can to remain separate and isolate. In an organization suffering from this silo syndrome each part interacts mainly within the silo, and not with other groups in the same organization, nor with the outside world, or its context.

This silo syndrome makes it impossible for relationships between congregations, districts, synods, programs, projects and civil society, etc. to produce healthy growth in the church. It is, however, one of the mental images that we carry with us: each part is isolated and considers itself more important than the whole.

Another of the mental images that we carry with us is the one that regards leadership as being located in the individual traits of a particular

---

[6] Martin Junge, *Baptism, Universal Priesthood and Ordained Ministry, 2007*, at **http://issuu.com/programasustentabilidad/docs/baptism__universal_priesthood__and_/1**

person or the characteristics of a particular position. This is a retina that, when it thinks of leadership, thinks in terms of individual leaders. That presupposes an idea of leadership as residing in a person, who takes on the directing and coordinating of an activity or ministry in the church and who has been appointed to that role by one or a group of persons. Such a person is confident of the approval of the church, but only until problems arise and their work is criticized, and competition and power struggles arise.

Being church in the present challenging context demands joint leadership, group involvement and collaborative work with the commitment of and participation by all the groups and parts constituting the church and contributing to processes of change, in which vision, mission and values are shared.

Leadership in sustainable churches is a whole collection of processes that motivate the action of many individuals toward fulfilling the call given by God in that context. Leadership is thus a dynamic interactive process that takes place within a group or organization or a network of organizations. It is thus a leadership that is aware of the wide extent of inter-relations, perspectives, limits, encouragement, discouragement, collaboration and conflict in the midst of which the work has to be done.

Leadership in sustainable churches is a leadership that is mainly collaborative and collective, with a range of abilities to encourage, help and organize, facilitate processes, motivate baptized members and create networks within and outside the church.

Thus, with regard to sustainability in the church, when we think of leadership, we are not thinking exclusively of individuals, but in terms of the effectiveness of the leaders as a whole, i.e., paying attention to developing groups, teams, bodies and meetings, bearing in mind all the baptized who are part of the community (whether it be a congregation, parish, church or world communion).

There is, without doubt, a need to help leaders, or potential leaders, to develop their own abilities, but there is a real danger of defining leadership training exclusively, or mainly, in terms of the aptitude of individuals. In the area of organizational sustainability we have to think of developing leadership abilities in working groups, governing boards, committees, councils, pastoral and ministerial groups, etc.

Jesus and leadership

Thinking in terms of leadership development for a sustainable church is a much wider issue than thinking merely of leadership training or ministerial training. Leadership as a process in the life of a community involves sharing responsibilities and decision making and encouraging commitment between baptized members.

The hierarchical concept of leadership results in a structure of positions. Thus elder, prophet, bishop, pastor are all titles designating positions in the church. However, the vision that emerges from the New Testament is focused on functions. Authority comes from the Holy Spirit and from gifts, spiritual maturity and the service given by each member. Leadership as service focuses on functions instead of on positions, is task-oriented and not based on titles or responsibilities. The stress is on what is done—catechizing, pastoring, preaching—and not on the person responsible, such as the catechist, pastor, preacher. The hierarchical concept of leadership uses nouns, whereas the model of leadership as a function uses verbs.

After the disciples James and John had asked Jesus to allocate to them the most important seats beside his throne, he answered, "It will not be so among you."

> But Jesus called them to him and said, "You know that the rulers of the Gentiles lord it over them, and their great ones are tyrants over them. It will not be so among you; but whoever wishes to be great among you must be your servant, and whoever wishes to be first among you must be your slave; just as the Son of Man came not to be served but to serve, and to give his life a ransom for many (Mt 20:25–28).

> But he said to them, "The kings of the Gentiles lord it over them; and those in authority over them are called benefactors. But not so with you; rather the greatest among you must become like the youngest, and the leader like one who serves. For who is greater, the one who is at the table or the one who serves? Is it not the one at the table? But I am among you as one who serves (Lk 22:25–27).

Jesus' words call into question not only the leaders of the nations as such, but also the hierarchical form of leadership in that context. Jesus rejected leadership on the basis of power and the exercise of authority from above.

"It will not be so among you," emphasizes that it is the community that is responsible.

The community of the faithful, the church, is called to organize itself. There is a phrase that often appears in the New Testament: one another. "Love one another"; "support one another"; "pray for one another"; "forgive one another"; "bear one another's burdens." That phrase, one another, is an image of the Triune God, and it is the image that Jesus used for the constitution of the church. This image, left to us by Jesus, shows us that exercising leadership is a mutual, reciprocal and interdependent relationship of one to another.

Leadership in the sustainable churches lies in each baptized member of the church and not in a distinct person or group. Leadership in sustainable churches is based on a relationship of mutuality, companionship, participation, belonging, fulfilling obligations, authority, celebration and the mutuality of giving and receiving.

Leadership in sustainable churches implies lay persons, ministers, women, youth, elderly, people with only one talent and people with many talents relating to one another and mutually sharing tasks—tasks that will never be perfect. They will reach agreements, plan, carry out joint activities, be mutually accountable and together celebrate, one with another.

Leadership within the framework of the Latin American and Caribbean Sustainability Program

Leadership is a dimension of the development and sustainability of churches that would deserve much more reflection and biblical, theological and organizational study. Meanwhile, within the framework of the Latin American and Caribbean Sustainability Program, we have identified, albeit in a practical way, some of the marks and features of leadership that make a powerful contribution to the sustainability of churches. At present what we are in a position to communicate is mainly empirical knowledge, based on our experience during the years 2010–2013, together with those Lutheran churches of Latin America and the Caribbean that requested some sort of accompaniment under the Latin American and Caribbean Sustainability program.

Aptitudes and abilities

Within the framework of the Sustainability Program we have been able to identify some features of the ways in which leadership contributes to sustainability processes in the churches. We have put them into two groups:

- Aptitudes: an inclination, tendency or spiritual aptitude and (mental) understanding for seeing, perceiving, distinguishing and relating to the various aspects that make for the organizational sustainability of one's church.

- Abilities: the resources of individuals and the church to carry out a task and to perform certain activities.

Aptitudes

The church leadership that has gone through processes of change and development in its organizational sustainability has a certain aptitude, predisposition, inclination and pro-active quality in some aspects. It

- **Reads its context (both immediate and more distant) and reflects on it.** This form of leadership is not afraid to reflect on and recognize the changing context in which there is increasing complexity and interdependence between actors and issues; reflects on these challenges together with others, and not only on broader contexts (at a distance), but also on immediate contexts–its own neighborhood and community of faith, i.e., parish life. The opposite of this aptitude to read the context is to look down, remain inward looking, enclosed as in a silo. The aptitude to read the context contributes to understanding the call which God sends us here and now, and visualizes and analyzes the situation of the community vis-à-vis the challenges of the situation.

- **Discerns out of awareness of its identity.** This form of leadership seeks to discern its context out of its confessional, ecumenical and cultural identity and thus contributes to a shared vision and values that keep organizations cohesive and provides a sense of direction and discernment. It will place its identity in context, with moral integrity and inspire solid trustworthy models in the organization. It thinks critically in order to reflect out of its identity with an awareness of its role and the present moment and seeks clearly to understand the contribution that the church can make to God's mission.

- **Has a sense of continuity in the long term, and a sense of the church body as a whole.** This form of leadership has a long-term vision and a sense of continuity. It examines the history of its faith community, the church, and communion (the past) and at the same thinks long term (the future). It does do not remain trapped in the day-to-day. It can be characterized as having a long-term horizon, common purpose, decentralization processes, and passing on responsibilities to successors.

  It does not only think of individuals or groups (my congregation, my pastoral work, ministries), but cherishes the hope of having an impact on the body of the church. It does not only keep in mind the constituent parts of the church but also of the church as a whole. It enables individuals to work together, exchange information, combine knowledge and skills and take decisions as a team in order to confront strategic working challenges to build up organizational resilience and improve sustainability. It focuses on developing leadership across the whole church (not only ordained leaders or only paid workers), seeking to develop mutual, reciprocal (one to another) abilities (coaching and teaching). It is aware that focusing on change, based on the whole body (according to 1 Corinthians 12), results in efforts and changes that will endure.

These capabilities function as a propensity, a collection of ideas and attitudes, generally based on previous experiences, which individuals bring to a situation in order to interpret it. They are the retinas used by the leaderships to give meaning to its situation.

Abilities

Three significant abilities that have been identified stand out because of their implications in the field of contextual mission, which, when they are present in the leadership of churches and act in synergy, produce a clear breakthrough and a qualitative leap forward. These are the ability to

- **Develop connectivity, manage networks and facilitate processes**: This implies identifying other players with similar purposes, dialogue and effective collaboration to bring people together, mostly on a temporary basis, to achieve common objectives; working in relationship with networks and systems in the Lutheran communion, ecumenism and local and global civil society.

  The leadership that is able to connect with others is aware that sustainable organizations are built on collaboration in alliances and networks, and require a vision formed and shaped by many players, parties and stakeholders. It is capable of seeing relatedness between parts of systems and sub-systems, and how they combine to create an emerging ownership of the whole. It facilitates participative processes that are instructive, increase understanding and stimulate empowerment. Developing the ability to work with others implies becoming aware of the concept of God's mission and putting it into practice.

- **Work in creative and innovative ways**: Creativity and innovation are understood as the ability to find innovative and original ways to solve problems, using the gifts and talents, wisdom, courage and prudence that God gives us to find solutions in a different way. A creative and innovative leadership reshapes sustainably the services that the church is mandated to provide: *diakonia, liturgia, kerygma.*

  This kind of leadership stimulates the development of abilities and fresh thinking, not only in groups of traditional, ordained leaders, but also in leadership teams and among staff members. It takes local management initiatives and, at the same time, initiatives to develop systems that strengthen organizational sustainability. It is capable of keeping change in mind, willing to risk taking initiatives and of using the resources available to the full. This kind of leadership is able to adapt and be resilient.

- **Plan, carry out plans and be accountable**: It is important to anticipate what needs to be done and how it will be carried out in order to achieve the goals that have been set. Strategic, participative planning, producing an annual work plan, monitoring, follow-up and evaluation give direction and multiply gifts, abilities and capacities in faith communities, create higher levels of participation, use scarce resources in a better way and make room for follow-up so that plans succeed. Both internal and external factors that might impact the achievement of desired aims are kept in mind by planning. The plans are implemented realistically, setting successive short-term milestones.

  This leadership is aware that giving account means the obligation to inform, justify and accept responsibility for the use of the resources put at one's disposal and for those decisions and actions that have had positive or negative impacts.

  Producing accounts implies the ideas of responsibility, transparency, legality and budget control and auditing.

Summary

Within the framework of the Latin American and Caribbean Sustainability Program we were able to identify, albeit in a practical way, some of the marks and features of leadership that make a powerful contribution to the sustainability of the churches. As an outcome of this process, we have classified them (a) as aptitudes, i.e., a certain retina that enables people to distinguish; and (b) as abilities or skills. Although based on the Latin American and Caribbean experience, we are confident that the same abilities and skills play a crucial role also in other contexts.

The leadership abilities that contribute to the churches' sustainability include resources and attitudes to carry out the necessary tasks for managing the organization of church communities and organizations. The abilities needed are many and varied, yet three of them play a crucial role: the ability to develop connectivity, manage networks and facilitate processes; to work in creative and innovative ways; to plan, carry out plans and give account of one's actions. These three pinpointed in this analysis are the ones which, when combined, produce a significant, qualitative breakthrough or leap forward.

They presume certain aptitudes; we have pointed out three: the ability to read one's context (both immediate and more distant) and reflect on it; to discern out of an awareness of one's identity; to have a sense of continuity in the long term, and a sense of church body as a whole.

As mentioned above, the experiences we analyzed enabled us to compile only a list of practical learnings, i.e., knowledge based on experience and practice, and thus on what we have observed. It is not based on academic research and further research is needed to analyze the leadership characteristics in the churches involved in sustainability processes in Latin America and the Caribbean.

The next, medium-term, objective would be for the churches themselves to be able to regard those characteristics as necessary to develop leadership in their organizations and contribute to their sustainability. This means that faculties, study centers and seminaries that train church leaders should include courses on these aspects of leadership and management in their curricula and programs.

Questions

How would you describe the role of the church leadership in your context?

How could laity support participatory leadership in the church? What kind of abilities and aptitudes should it have for this?

According to Lutheran understanding, why is it important to have a governing structure in the church that is synodical and includes laity?

Conviviality: A Core Value of Diakonia

Ulla Siirto

Introduction

Globalization and the principle of the maximization of profit constitute a global challenge to which the worldwide Lutheran church is trying to respond. At the experiential level, everything—including the human being—appears to be for sale. What can people do to protest against this harsh reality?

From its very beginning, the Lutheran church has been a protestant church. In other words, the Lutheran church is one that does not content itself with the experienced "order" of the world that is defended by the agents of the respective order either verbally or, if this does not suffice, by use of force.

"Protestant" does not only imply opposition. It derives from the Latin "protestare," meaning "to testify in favor of something or somebody." The New Testament is the testimony of God's love for people that manifests itself in Jesus Christ's words and deeds. To a great extent, Christ's deeds are deeds of compassion. His whole being can be understood in terms of *kenosis*—Christ leaves heaven in order, out of mercy, to share people's earthly existence. He becomes a human being with all that this implies (Phil 2). In his resurrection he empowers people for a new existence and renewed relationships with their neighbors.

"Conviviality" is a diaconal concept that expresses this renewed Christian and evangelical way of life. In the following, I shall outline some aspects of conviviality, as they are understood by modern diaconal and social science research.

Processing diakonia from different realities

Diaconal actors from all over Europe are taking part in preparations for the 500th Anniversary of the Reformation. In a participatory process, facilitated by the Lutheran World Federation, a group of diaconal workers, the solidarity group, reflected on diaconal work in the context of a changing Europe under the motto, "Seeking Conviviality–Re-forming Community Diakonia in Europe."[1]

Mapping the changing European context, the solidarity group recognized that various social, economic and political changes have become increasingly globalized and therefore, in one way or another, affect all European countries. Some of these changes have, for example, driven entire nations to the brink of bankruptcy, created new flows of migration and have led to rising income inequality. At the same time, local communities and many neighborhoods have become home to people from very different cultural backgrounds.

Stories from different working contexts, background reading and research enabled the solidarity group to look at the changing realities in Europe and challenged the group to look at its task from different perspectives. First, the group named economic, social and political changes, even crises, as contextual challenges which affect people's daily lives. Second, the group noted that the young and the elderly have to pay the highest price for these changes. Third, the group acknowledged the impact of worldwide migration and the fact that some people are forced to endure extreme conditions. Last, but not least, a growing number of people are being excluded and thus remain "hidden" from mainstream society and the organizations that offer social support.

After looking more deeply and analytically at different contexts, the solidarity group identified some common themes that were visible in different realities and from which they selected four core themes: vocation, justice, dignity and conviviality in light of which the group started to study diakonia in a changing society and in different communities. The first three themes are very often connected to diakonia, but the latter provides a new perspective for looking at the core of diakonia. Its meaning is close to the Spanish word, *convivencia* and the German word, *Konvivenz.*

Conviviality was first mentioned by Ivan Illich in his book *Tools for Conviviality.*[2] Illich underlines that the concept describes the autonomous and creative communication both between people and between people and their environment. The solidarity group further developed the concept of conviviality, defining it as the art and practice of living together in solidarity. The art and practice of living together has given rise to a new challenge, especially in light of increasingly diverse communities.

---

[1] Tony Addy (ed.) *Seeking Conviviality–Reforming Community Diakonia in Europe* (Geneva: The Lutheran World Federation, 2013), at **www.lutheranworld.org/sites/default/files/DMD-Seeking_Conviviality_Diakonia_Europe.pdf**

[2] Ivan Illich, *Tools for Conviviality* (New York: Harper & Row, 1973).

From hospitality to conviviality

While the concept of hospitality has repeatedly been featured in the discussion on strangers and immigration, we can also understand it in relationship to all relations with the "other"—with people who are "strange" or "different." For instance, an example would be the way in which the understanding of conviviality challenges the use of the concept of hospitality in the context of migration. Hospitality plays a prominent role in the biblical tradition and according to it guests or strangers should be treated better than one's own people or family representatives (i.e., Gen 18–19; Heb 13:2). The concept also provides a basis for understanding the way in which we treat other people.

In 1997, the philosopher Jacques Derrida, himself also an immigrant, wrote about hospitality in *De l'Hospitalité* (published in English in 2000 under the title *Of Hospitality*).[3] For Derrida the concept of hospitality is a problematic one. He points out that, on the one hand, once guests have been integrated to the extent that they become similar to the population they cease to be guests and hospitality disappears. On the other, hospitality also disappears there where the "native" population does not set any conditions for the newcomers and lets them live their lives however they want.

The concept of hospitality has a further problematic connotation. It involves the assumption that the guest is merely visiting and will be leaving some day for another place. But, what about the situation when the guest has come to stay? Would they not become co-residents? In this event, is hospitality still a valid concept?

Instead of hospitality, the concept of conviviality implies that in one way or another all communities are diverse and residents must learn the art and practice of living together and respecting each other's differences. In a convivial society people not only tolerate but accept differences, and have mutual respect for one another. Day-to-day sharing enables us to learn from one another and by exposing our identity to other identities we can build mutual relationships with those who are different from us.[4]

A number of studies have shown that people like to be with those who are similar. This is visible in the segregation of neighborhoods, the forming of friendships and the way in which people spend their free time. Yet, the art of living together involves a conscious learning process. Members

[3] Jacques Derrida, Anne Dufourmantelle, *Of Hospitality*, transl. Rachel Bowlby (Stanford: Standford University Press, 2000), at **www.clas.ufl.edu/users/burt/shipwreck/derridahospitality.pdf**

[4] Cf. Theo Sundermeier,"Konvivenz als Grundstruktur ökumenischer Existenz heute," in *Missionswissenschaftliche Forschungen*, Neue Folge 3 (1995).

of a community have to transcend the barriers that they have constructed between different people and worldviews. Very often this involves leaving one's own comfort zone.

The notion that people are too different to live together also needs to be called into question. In today's changing societies, the art and practice of living together have to be learnt. People cannot continue to erect barriers; we have seen that this is a recipe for disaster. Conviviality is part of the essence of every human being. All people are created in the full diversity of God's own image and by getting to know one another and by acting together people join in God's creative work. However, the art and practice of living together require curiosity and a willingness to learn from one another. Research has shown that communities living side by side generally are more tolerant than those communities that do not have this experience. This would suggest that conviviality is learnt over time.[5]

Conviviality: living together in solidarity

The word "solidarity" adds a further perspective to the concept of conviviality. Solidarity means sharing, and giving up one's own self-centeredness. This, however, is not charity. Charity can easily imply a control dimension. Solidarity implies a mutual effort to create a better environment for living together and, by extension, to create a better world. Solidarity implies joint activities for the common good. It assumes that everyone tries better to understand their own motives and hopes as well as those of others. Such joint learning processes can help to identify shared understandings and differences which, in turn, will help to build community and raise awareness of topical issues.

In *Why Can't we Live Together?*,[6] the award-winning professor of social psychology Miles Hewstone, who has studied conflict areas, distinguishes between the possibilities for encounters and meaningful encounters. He believes that possibilities for encounters do not constitute commonality. Rather, it is meaningful encounters that are significant since they prevent prejudice and create empathy. Already knowing one "different" person will help increase the understanding and acceptance of those who are different.

---

[5] Cf. Madeleine Bunting, "If you don't think multiculturalism is working, look at your street corner," in *The Gurdian*, 16 March 2014, at **http://timeli.info/item/1227726/The_Guardian_Comments/If_you_don_t_think_multiculturalism_is_working__look_at_your_street_corner___Madeleine_Bunting___...**

[6] **www.thersa.org/large-text/events/video/vision-videos/why-cant-we-live-together**

In turn, Paul Gilroy suggests that the concept of conviviality brings a new aspect to the discussion on diversity. According to Gilroy, conviviality is associated with living interactive processes. He claims that many problems can be solved by mutual encounters that help to create a feeling of "sameness." When people are united by a common cause they can move beyond other differences. It is possible to identify these kinds of common causes or issues within local communities such as, for instance, when people start to work and fight together in order to improve their situation.

Alongside this, it is important to note that conviviality relates to the atmosphere and feeling between people.[7] Sharing and learning together inevitably lead to joint celebrations in communities.

Convivial diakonia

As societies change, churches are challenged anew and social problems become increasingly acute. Diaconal work (and the wider work of churches) must be open to the social realities such as poverty and marginalization that affect many people and, in some instances, whole communities and regions. Members of churches should live as a church in the midst of the people and work with them toward bringing about social change.

Change can be implemented in the diaconal church that builds bridges between local communities and people from very different walks of life. A diaconal church can create space for and processes of learning. Furthermore, it can engage those who are unemployed as community builders and in voluntary community-based work. The diaconal church is rooted in motivation, attendance and participation which arise from experience, relationships and faith.

The solidarity group noted that in diakonia reflection and action are based on the four themes mentioned above: vocation, justice, dignity and conviviality. On the one hand, the call comes from God and, on the other, from those who are suffering. To recognize the other and different kinds of realities requires awareness which enables us to start working together with local people in order to bring about change. Living together in solidarity is based on respectful interaction and reciprocity.

---

[7] Amanda Wise, "Hope and Belonging in a Multicultural Suburb," in *Journal of Intercultural Studies* 26(1) (2005), 171–86. Amanda Wise & Selvaraj Velayutham, *Conviviality in everyday multiculturalism: Singapore and Sydney compared, European Journal of Cultural Studies* (2013), at **www.academia.edu/4391937/Conviviality_in_everyday_multiculturalism_Singapore_and_Sydney_compared,**

Through diaconal activities, church workers and volunteers encounter many people who pay the price of social injustice. One of the aims of diakonia is to strive for equality and justice. It also implies that diaconal workers practice non-discrimination in relating to people in need and are careful not to misuse their power either in relationships or decision making. Following diaconal values implies that the decent life means applying basic human rights in relationships and structures. Diakonia in practice stands in stark contrast to the consumer society and the market economy by expressing its values in action and promoting alternative ways of meeting needs. It always stays on the side of those who are the most vulnerable. In doing this diakonia underlines that nobody is for sale.

Towards the 500th Anniversary of the Reformation

The starting point for reshaping of community-based diakonia is the local situation. The diaconal vocation is based on the local church and community life. By working with those who are involved in identifying diaconal activities within the framework that has been developed as a result of the "Seeking conviviality" process, communities that include also those who have been excluded can be created. The art and practice of living together in solidarity is the basis for the diaconal congregation and local diaconal practice. The search for justice is based on a diaconal community where the entire community is looking for justice. Human beings in their diversity are created in the image of God and thus possess a God-given dignity. Moreover, the existence of Christ, who incarnated under the terms of *kenosis*, encourages us to become humane ourselves and to stand up against the commercialization of our fellow human beings. "For freedom Christ has set us free. Stand firm, therefore, and do not submit again to a yoke of slavery" (Gal 5:1). Therefore, all are valuable. The re-formation of diakonia also requires that local actions are supported. It is important that people receive training in order to practice in this new context and in future also advocate for themselves.

The process of re-forming diakonia continues. It fits well under the main theme of the Reformation Anniversary, "Liberated by God's Grace." Conviviality only describes one aspect of this liberation. The European solidarity group has been divided into three thematic areas that reflect its work on salvation, the human being and creation, all sub-themes of the Anniversary, underlining that none of them—neither salvation nor human beings or creation—is for sale. One of the thematic groups is considering concrete steps related to conviviality; another is exploring the understanding of what is needed for a convivial economy; the third is working on a convivial theology, carried by the *kenosis* of Christ and the liberation he brought to people. In the years leading up to the Reformation Anniversary the solidarity group will work in these three concrete areas, which will assist in the diaconal activities of the churches.

Questions

What does conviviality mean in your local context and what can you do together with other people in order to strengthen it?

What are the issues which might pose a threat to conviviality in your context?

What added value does the concept of conviviality bring to theology and spirituality?

God's Repentance—Human Beings are not Interchangeable Commodities

Douwe Visser

> The Lord said to Moses, "Go down at once! Your people, whom you brought up out of the land of Egypt, have acted perversely; they have been quick to turn aside from the way that I commanded them; they have cast for themselves an image of a calf, and have worshiped it and sacrificed to it, and said, "These are your gods, O Israel, who brought you up out of the land of Egypt!'" The Lord said to Moses, "I have seen this people, how stiff-necked they are. Now let me alone, so that my wrath may burn hot against them and I may consume them; and of you I will make a great nation." But Moses implored the Lord his God, and said, "O Lord, why does your wrath burn hot against your people, whom you brought out of the land of Egypt with great power and with a mighty hand? Why should the Egyptians say, "It was with evil intent that he brought them out to kill them in the mountains, and to consume them from the face of the earth'? Turn from your fierce wrath; change your mind and do not bring disaster on your people. Remember Abraham, Isaac, and Israel, your servants, how you swore to them by your own self, saying to them, "I will multiply your descendants like the stars of heaven, and all this land that I have promised I will give to your descendants, and they shall inherit it forever." And the Lord changed his mind about the disaster that he planned to bring on his people (Ex 32:7–14).

Moses in dialogue with God

In this passage we read about an exchange between God and Moses that is within the limits of what can be said about and to God. The translation softens it considerably but God says something that God regrets and withdraws in the same passage. The words "the Lord changed his mind" are a weak translation of the original Hebrew that clearly implies that God regretted what had been said. This is a far cry from a theological thinking about God according to which it is impossible for God to regret something because God is omnipotent and omniscient. Therefore, many claim that this passage is a rather primitive anthropomorphic way of speaking about God. It is a way of keeping theological thinking apart but, like others, I prefer to read the passage in that rough and "primitive" understanding. What we read is that God says something terrible and that Moses wants, by all means, to prevent God from being unfaithful to the promise of salvation. For God the people of Israel seem to be interchangeable. The Israelites will not only be destroyed (except for Moses) but God will create a new and even better nation. The words "for sale" are perhaps not applicable in the literal sense, but the aspect of being an interchangeable commodity certainly is. God can do without Israel.

God repents

From the perspective of the covenant, what Israel did is unacceptable. The Israelites regarded God as a commodity; for them, God is for sale. They regarded the golden calf as something better. So is God not allowed this *quid pro quo*? The answer is no, God is not. In Matthew 7:11 Jesus says about God, "If you then, who are evil, know how to give good gifts to your children, how much more will your Father in heaven give good things to those who ask him!" Is there ever a parent who would want to destroy their child? It can and does happen but is destroying one's own child not the most awful thing that can happen? Children can sometimes make their parents' lives very difficult but destroying is not part of a parent's vocabulary when talking about their children. Parents are the child's source of life. How could they ever willingly take away that life? Whatever the child does, this is not allowed. A child is not a commodity that one can simply eradicate.

God is the source of life for the people of the covenant, Israel. God is in fact the source of life for the earth and all who live on it. For God, every person is a unique being. And the words of Isaiah are fully applicable: "I have called you by your name, you are mine" (Isa 43:1). Being their source of life, God cannot do away with them. That would go completely against the essence of God's being.

Moses has to "correct" God even though it seems to be strictly off limits for human beings to correct God. In the Bible it is usually the other way around, congruent with the general understanding of the relationship between God and human beings. Nevertheless, in this passage God clearly has to be corrected, which is what Moses does. And to this plea follows the reaction described in verse 14: "And the Lord repented of the evil which he thought to do unto his people" (King James Version).

Of course the word repented, a literal translation of the Hebrew word, is stronger than the words "change of mind." But even that already goes against a concept of God as the perfect, sacrosanct being. Article 1 of the Belgic Confession, a sixteenth-century Reformed confessional document, states clearly that God is "unchangeable." God cannot have a change of mind. However, the conflict between a theological concept of God's "unchangeability" and this passage wherein God clearly has a "change of mind" is in the end of less importance than the conflict between God's promise to Israel to be their God forever and the change of mind to destroy them and to create a new people. So there is always a conflict between the changeability and unchangeability of God. About God Paul says: "[...] if we are faithless, he remains faithful—for he cannot deny himself" (2 Tim 2:13). With the destruction of the Israelites God would have become unfaithful and that cannot be.

The meaning of God's repentance

Unless this passage is put away as, in Nietzsche's words, "Menschliches, Allzumenschliches" (human, all too human), the message of God's repentance is very strong and extremely meaningful. No one can deny that while this repentance is difficult to understand, it almost brings God down and is also unique in its appearance, it means in the end that something very special is said here. The word "repentance" connected to God can only mean that something is out of the question.

Words such as "repent" of "regret" are not the most popular in a society that prefers self-confident people. Managers are not allowed to repent publicly. For instance, when the worst effects of the credit crisis came into the open one hardly heard any bankers openly repent for the evil they had caused. As the former Archbishop of Canterbury, Rowan Williams, said: "There hasn't been what I would, as a Christian, call repentance. We haven't heard people saying 'well actually, no, we got it wrong and the whole fundamental principle on which we worked was unreal, was empty'."[1]

Also, repentance in less public environments is not easy. It is even difficult to "repent" openly to one's wife, husband and, above all, one's children. But one has not failed when one repents. One fails when one does not regret one's failures. When evil is not regarded as evil and we no longer

---

[1] **www.telegraph.co.uk** .

call a sin what cannot be called otherwise. We should therefore never give up thinking about sin and its consequences. The biblical consequence is repentance but also forgiveness. And most of all: a new way forward. As there was a new way forward for God with the people of Israel and that new way forward had to come. Because, also for God, humans are not disposable. They are not for sale! They are never ripe for destruction; they are not interchangeable goods. What Moses did would in the end have been the task of every praying person: to keep God faithful to God's promise! Our prayers to God should be strong. We should come close to God. When our prayers are said out of the desire for salvation for the earth and those who live on it, then we should not be too modest. The Book of Psalms can inspire us to be radically direct in our prayers.

Based on the firm conviction that for God we are never a disposable commodity, it can also be affirmed that God, also, is not for sale. That God loves us does not mean that evil is not brought to light. God is "corrected" by Moses as a consequence of God's threat to destroy the people of Israel. God's anger itself is not corrected because the Israelites cannot be excused for what they have done.

This passage strongly asserts that God cannot be exchanged. This can be said because of God's reaction to destroy Israel, notwithstanding the fact that God is made to repent for what God has said. This shows that the Israelites have gone too far, but it also affirms that humans are not for sale, because God regrets what God threatened to do. It may indeed be an almost too anthropomorphic way of speaking about God but the message clearly is: for God, human beings are not a commodity; they are not for sale. The conflict within God results in this strong message.

Repentance and God's sovereignty

The words that God showed repentance have been part of numerous exegetical discussions. Certainly, for those who are reading the Bible in a more traditional, i.e., literal way and also from a rather dogmatic perspective when thinking about God, it is difficult to understand that God can repent. That seemed to be so much unlike God! On the other hand, in the same tradition, the fact that God had repented could not simply be brushed away. In the Reformed tradition, certainly, the traditional understanding was for a long time the standard understanding. After seriously struggling with this passage, it was, in the end, understood as a very meaningful sign of God's love for the people of God's covenant. God cannot do away with them and when it seems that God will, God can even be corrected and brought to repent for the evil God has said. But, on the other hand, is this not contradictory to what, for Reformed theology, is fundamental, namely the sovereignty of God over all life? Does it not mean that God is free to do what God wants?

In Reformed thinking the principle of God's sovereignty went together with God's election and, connected to that, the concept of irresistible grace. Without any doubt these concepts have been subject to serious misunderstanding and even misuse. It has led to a certain degree of fatalism and feeling that we humans have no role to play. God as the sovereign is far above us and does with us what God wants. But, in line with the dialogue between God and Moses, sovereignty is first of all the unchangeable faithfulness of God to keep God's promise of salvation. God will not give that up and therefore we cannot lose faith in God as the ultimate source of life for the earth and all who live on it. That is not for sale.

The earth and those who live on it belong to God. God will not, and cannot, do away with them. For Reformed Christians, it is crucial to underline this message. It is vital to do so in situations where human beings are being offered for sale. Even God cannot do that, let alone us—this is the message we have to proclaim. That is evil one cannot be silent about. It is a situation of great injustice. It denies the sovereignty of God over all of life. This is why Reformed Christians feel so strongly committed to advocating for justice to be done. The commitment to justice is in the genes of Reformed Christians, so to speak. What needs to be added though is that of course this is not unique to Reformed Christians and it is not always done best within the Reformed tradition.

God's sanctification of life

This commitment to justice has to be embedded in the awareness of God's justification, the basis of our life before God, that life is sanctified and that sanctification can only be made visible in a life of justice. Human justice—*iustitia humana*—is a holy matter. When a church, or an organization of churches, cries out for justice, that cry for justice can only be made clear with the assumption that this cry for justice is a holy matter. In a document that deals with the cry for justice one should, however, always start with the biblical and theological foundation of this cry for justice to make clear that this is part of God's work. God has sanctified us to cry out for justice. For an organization of churches, only this biblical and theological foundation can give weight to the cry for justice. It should not start with an economic or political analysis of the situation or, worse, it should not limit itself to such an analysis only. A church statement does not gain importance from a "secular" analysis but, rather, from a thorough biblical and theological foundation. If, with regard to their commitment to justice, Reformed Christians feel inspired by Calvin they can only make reference to him if they work on the basis of this broad perspective. Otherwise they have a very limited understanding of Calvin.

Not much has to be said in reference to the often critical and negative opinions about Calvin and his theology. In many aspects we cannot follow Calvin uncritically and there is certainly no need to make a saint of him. But it goes too far to see Calvin as a negative thinker. The ultimate goal of Calvin's theology is to serve the whole of life.

Committed to justice

The World Communion of Reformed Churches (WCRC) has raised its prophetic voice against situations of injustice. One can hardly question the legitimacy of this. But there is the risk that this becomes a repetitive process and we need to seek alternatives and solutions. The theme of the 2004 General Council of the WCRC's predecessor, the World Alliance of Reformed Churches, was, "That all may have life in abundance." This theme comes from John 10 where Jesus calls himself the good shepherd. It is quite clear that the abundant life the good shepherd gives to his sheep is that they will find pasture. They will not live a life without hardship. The thief, the hired hand, the wolf–they will all come. They could be seen as symbolizing injustice that has to be resisted. But the pasture symbolizes life. Following in his footsteps, Jesus' community will seek to resist injustice. But it will also try to find the pasture. Both are part of the church's live-giving ministry. Also here we have to be aware that it starts with grace. God is the giver of life. There is no need for us to be stressed life seekers. The grace of God sets us free but "the grace that frees is also a grace that forms."[2] It is important to develop practices that will be foundational for what already elsewhere has been called a life-giving ministry. Many of these practices will not be found only in the Christian community. However, within that community they cannot be developed without theological discernment: "A practice must pursue a good beyond itself, responding to and embodying the self-giving dynamics of God's own creating, redeeming, and sustaining grace."[3] On the other hand, this should not mean that Christian practices have to be set apart from other human practices or that the Christian com-

[2] See Dorothy C. Bass, "Ways of Life Abundant," in Dorothy C. Bass (ed.), *For Life Abundant: Practical Theology, Theological Education, and Christian Ministry* (Grand Rapids: Wm. B. Eerdmans Publishing Co., 2008), 28.
[3] Ibid., 30.

munity has to be set apart from non-Christian communities. God is present in the world and not only in the church. It is obvious that the Christian community can never participate in the life-giving ministry without God. The life-giving ministry of the Christian community is not just a political program but one that will have major political consequences.

It cannot be denied that putting human beings up for sale is unjust. The prophetic voice has to be raised against that. The unique conflict within God, who wanted to do away with God's people, and God's repentance, can only lead to the firm conviction that humans are never a disposable commodity. We should speak out against this evil with the same commitment as once Moses pleaded with God not to put the people of Israel for sale, because that is an evil God repented of.

Questions

Is it possible to say that "God regrets what God has threatened to do"?

Should words such as "sin, repentance and forgiveness" be used more often?

Is it first of all the task of the church to give a theological and biblical foundation of the commitment of justice?

Bible Study: Galatians 3:25–29

Susan Johnson

Opening Prayer

Begin by praying together:

> Gracious God, as we prepare to read and study your Word, open our eyes to see, our ears to hear, our minds to think and our hearts to feel. Help us to hear you speaking to us through the text and through each other. In Jesus' name we pray. Amen.

Text

Read aloud Galatians 3:25-29:

> But now that faith has come, we are no longer subject to a disciplinarian, for in Christ Jesus you are all children of God through faith. As many of you as were baptized into Christ have clothed yourselves with Christ. There is no longer Jew or Greek, there is no longer slave or free, there is no longer male and female; for all of you are one in Christ Jesus. And if you belong to Christ, then you are Abraham's offspring, heirs according to the promise.

Discuss: What are your first thoughts on reading this text? What words or ideas stick out for you?

The Lutheran World Federation and the 500th Anniversary of the Lutheran Reformation

Together, the whole Lutheran World Federation—all 72 million members and 144 member churches—are preparing to commemorate the 500th Anniversary of the Lutheran Reformation. We are doing this together and with ecumenical partners under the theme "Liberated by God's Grace." In this Bible study we are focusing on one of the sub-themes, "Human Beings—Not for Sale."

When we think about "Human Beings-Not for Sale," one of the first things that we think about is slavery. There are some that would think that slavery no longer exists in our world, but they would be wrong. Slavery still exists and it takes on different forms in different parts of the world.

According to the International Labour Organisation (ILO), 20.9 million men, women and children around the world are in slavery. Someone is in slavery if they are forced to work through mental or physical threat; owned or controlled by an "employer"; dehumanized, treated as a commodity or bought and sold as "property"; physically constrained or has restrictions placed on freedom of movement. Slavery exists today despite the fact that it is illegal in all the countries where it is practiced.[1]

Forms of slavery include bonded labor, child slavery, early and forced marriage, forced labor, descent-based slavery and human trafficking.

Discuss: Think about your context? What forms of slavery occur in your region?

Read Galatians 3:2-29 again.

> But now that faith has come, we are no longer subject to a disciplinarian, for in Christ Jesus you are all children of God through faith. As many of you as were baptized into Christ have clothed yourselves with Christ. There is no longer Jew or Greek, there is no longer slave or free, there is no longer male and female; for all of you are one in Christ Jesus. And if you belong to Christ, then you are Abraham's offspring, heirs according to the promise

Discuss: What is the text saying to you in your context given the forms of slavery that are present?

[1] www.antislavery.org/english/slavery_today/what_is_modern_slavery.aspx

Our Baptism defines us

Martin Luther lectured on the book of Galatians in both 1519 and 1535. As he discussed the verses of our text he focused on how our Baptism into Christ becomes the one thing that defines us. Our Baptisms make us equal to each other, regardless of the ways that others would try to define and demean us. Here are some of his words:

> Therefore Paul teaches the Baptism is not a sign but the garment of Christ, in fact, that Christ Himself is our garment. Hence Baptism is a very powerful and effective thing. For when we have put on Christ, the garment of our righteousness and salvation, then we also put on Christ, the garment of imitation.[2]

> It is characteristic of human and legalistic kinds of righteousness to be divided into sects, and for distinctions to be made according to works. Some profess, advocate, and pursue this; others, that. In Christ, however, all things are common to all; all things are one thing, and one thing is all things.... Therefore there is neither rich nor poor, neither handsome nor ugly, neither citizen nor farmer, neither Benedictine nor Carthusian, neither Minorite nor Augustinian.[3]

Discuss: If we are one in Christ, equal in the eyes of God because of the righteousness of Christ which we wear, what difference does that make in the way in which we view and treat each other?

Global advocacy

In his "Small Catechism (1535)," Martin Luther explains the fourth petition of the Lord's Prayer and expands on the definition of "daily bread" to include everything required for the "necessities and nourishment for our bodies."

Similarly, our understanding of "Human Beings–Not for Sale," might be expanded to include anything that detracts from the necessities and nourishment of our bodies. Depending on your context, these might include poverty, war, being a refugee or internally displaced, female genital mutilation, domestic violence, rape, honor killing, unchecked disease, as well as bonded labor, child slavery, early and forced marriage, forced labor, descent-based slavery and human trafficking.

---

[2] Martin Luther, "Lectures on Galatians, 1535," in Jaroslav Pelikan (ed.), *Luther's Works*, vol. 26 (Saint Louis: Concordia Publishing House, 1963), 353.

[3] Martin Luther, "Lectures on Galatians, 1519," in Jaroslav Pelikan (ed.), *Luther's Works*, vol. 27 (Saint Louis: Concordia Publishing House, 1964), 280–81.

Here is some of what the LWF is doing to care for the needs of people. The LWF Strategy 2012–2017 priority themes for global advocacy include: religious freedom and interfaith relations; climate change and environmental protection; gender justice; refugees, internally displaced persons and other forced migrants; oppressed minority populations and indigenous peoples; economic justice; HIV and AIDS.

Discuss: How do these priority themes relate to Galatians 3:25–29 and to "Human Beings—Not for Sale"?

Gender justice

The LWF has adopted a Gender Justice Policy and is encouraging its implementation across the communion and in all member churches. It states:

> As a community of equals, through baptism, the church is called prophetically to announce and practice inclusion. As we read in Galatians 3:27–28, As many of you as were baptized into Christ have clothed yourselves with Christ. There is no longer Jew or Greek, there is no longer slave or free, there is no longer male and female; for all of you are one in Christ Jesus.[4]

and,

> Humankind, regardless of gender, biology or other conditions, is transformed in Jesus' grace, forgiveness and new life. Differences of power based on ethnicity, class and gender are changed and transformed through baptism. All are one in Christ.[5]

In a previous LWF document, *Churches say "No" to Violence Against Women*, we were encouraged to "highlight Paul's commendation of women as co-workers and Galatians 3:28, which emphasizes the end to differences and our oneness in Christ."[6]

Read the text again. How might it be calling you to act for justice and human dignity in your context? Discuss.

---

[4] At **www.lutheranworld.org/content/resource-lwf-gender-justice-policy**, 4–5.
[5] Ibid., 26.
[6] **www.lutheranworld.org/content/resource-churches-say-no-violence-against-women-action-plan-churches**, 39.

Closing prayer

Close your Bible study with the following prayer from the USA or another prayer of your choice.

Jesus Heal Us[7]

Leader: Jesus, lover of humanity, you healed the daughter of the Syrophoenician woman, a foreigner who came to you, a Jewish teacher. By your gift of life you showed us that we are one people, all worthy to be loved. Now we come to you, as mothers in spirit, praying for the healing of the world, saying:

All: Jesus, heal us.

For this country, suffering from the self-inflicted wounds of racism, greed, the genocide of its native people, and the oppression of the poor, teach us that greatness can only be found in justice, generosity and compassion. We pray:

All: Jesus, heal us.

For peace among all nations, that the dry bones found in battlefields and the mass graves dug by tyrants rise up as a resurrected humanity, committed to peace and the well being of all on earth. We pray:

All: Jesus, heal us.

For your church divided, blundering, often intolerant, we rub our eyes, hoping to clear our vision and keep it ever on you. But we lose ourselves in the mists of delusions, fears and doubts. Send us the guiding light of your wise spirit, the healing of your love. We pray:

All: Jesus, heal us.

For all we name now in this assembly who need healing and our prayers: (*those assembled offer names*) And so today as we celebrate the feast of redemption we lift up all the living for your mercy, and thank you for the lives of all our loved ones who now celebrate your glory in heaven.

All: Amen.

---

[7] By Irene St Onge, San Francisco, California, USA, in ibid., 56–57.

List of Contributors

Ayana, Ebise, M.A., Lecturer in Theology, Mekane Yesus Seminary of the Ethiopian Evangelical Church Mekane Yesus, Ethiopia

Driau, Gustavo, Facilitator of the Sustainability Programme LAC, United Evangelical Lutheran Church (IELU), Argentina

Fabiny, Tamás, Rev. Dr, Bishop, Northern Diocese of the Evangelical Lutheran Church in Hungary, LWF Vice-President for Central Eastern Europe, Hungary

Johnson, Susan, Rev., National Bishop, Evangelical Lutheran Church in Canada, Canada

Nüssel, Friederike, Prof. Dr, Director of the Ecumenical Institute, University of Heidelberg, Germany

Siirto, Ulla, Principal Lecturer, Diaconia University of Applied Sciences, Järvenpää, Finland

Visser, Douwe, Rev. Dr, Executive Secretary for Theology and Communion, World Communion of Reformed Churches, Germany

Younan, Munib, A., Rev. Dr, Bishop, Evangelical Lutheran Church in Jordan and the Holy Land, LWF President, Jordan

Salvation—Not For Sale

Edited by
Anne Burghardt

Bibliographic information published by the German National Library

The *Deutsche Nationalbibliothek* lists this publication in the *Deutsche Nationalbibliografie;* detailed bibliographic data are available on the internet at http://dnd.dnd.de

Printed in Germany · H 7924

This book was printed on FSC-certified paper

Editorial assistance:	Department for Theology and Public Witness
Layout:	Department for Theology and Public Witness
Design:	LWF-Office for Communication Services
Printing and Binding:	Druckhaus Köthen GmbH & Co. KG

Published by Evangelische Verlangsanstalt GmbH, Leipzig, Germany, under the auspices of
The Lutheran World Federation
150, rte de Ferney, PO Box 2100
CH-1211 Geneva 2, Switzerland

Parallel editions in German and Spanish

ISBN 978-3-374-04160-2

Inhalt

Introduction

Anne Burghardt

This booklet is part of a small collection published by the Lutheran World Federation on the occasion of the 500th Anniversary of the Reformation in 2017. "Salvation—Not For Sale" is one of the three sub-themes of the Anniversary's main theme, "Liberated by God's Grace." The popular essays in this booklet were written by authors from all regions of the Lutheran World Federation; the ecumenical voice is here represented by a Roman Catholic theologian.

The essays included here question practices and theological concepts that could be described as attempts to commodify salvation. Endeavors to commodify salvation differ widely, ranging from prosperity gospel to attempts to "guarantee" salvation by following certain practices, rituals, etc. Today, one of the crucial aspects in many contexts is the intense pressure to respond to the requirements of a certain social or professional status in society. This leads to the questions from where human beings expect their salvation today and before which "institution" they feel the need to justify themselves.

The essays in this booklet address different topics, ranging from whether Luther's search for a "gracious God" is still current today, to the issues related to prosperity gospel, identifying oneself with one's work, expecting salvation from consuming etc. The list of the topics discussed in this volume is far from being exhaustive yet it hopefully offers some impulses for further discussions.

How Do I Find a Gracious God?

Bernd Oberdorfer

Paradise rediscovered: Luther's discovery of the free gift of righteousness

In 1545, the year before his death, Martin Luther returned to past events that had turned him into the Reformer that he had become. Reading his report, we can sense the strong emotions that continued to move him, even after thirty years had passed. He wrote how repeatedly he came across the term "God's righteousness," and how he "hated" it. He had thought that it meant the righteousness with which God judged and punished. Luther became a monk because he took God's commandments particularly seriously, which meant that he felt that he could never do everything right for God. Despite all his efforts, he continued to feel like a sinner and feared God's wrath. He saw Christ not as a savior but a severe judge, who convicted him for good reason. However, soon he came to understand the phrase "God's righteousness" in an entirely new way, namely, as the righteousness that God grants us, although we do not deserve it, the righteousness that God allows us to share in freely, i.e., by grace alone and without us having to do anything for it. "I had the feeling," he would write later, "that I was born again and entered into paradise through opened doors."[1] This joyous experience is the very core of Luther's theology, and would become the driving impulse for the entire Reformation. Luther's desperate question, How can I find a gracious God?–what can and must I do for my salvation?–was answered with the promise of redemption: We cannot and do not have to do anything for our salvation as God has already given us everything that we need in Christ. Christ took the deadly consequences of our sin upon himself on the cross so that we no longer need to bear it ourselves, and grants us new

[1] *WA* 54,186.

life. Luther used the image of an unequal marriage to illustrate this: A rich man marries a poor, indebted woman and does not only take on her debt but allows her to have a share in his entire wealth.

Salvation for sale? Luther's critique of the sale of indulgences

It is no wonder that Luther's conflict with the church of his time was ignited by the practice of indulgences which brought economic thinking into the realm of faith. It was of course (at least theoretically) plain to see that it was not salvation itself that was "for sale" with the indulgences. They only provided believers, whose sins had already been forgiven through their confession, with the opportunity to purchase "letters of indulgence" as a means of reducing the amount of time they would have to spend being cleansed of sin in purgatory. It was also emphasized that God would only reward this payment by grace. Nevertheless this doctrine allowed it to appear as if it were the path to salvation itself that was on sale. Moreover, it created the impression that the church could arbitrarily place the gift of salvation through Christ on the market. Luther protested against this on 31 October 1517 with his Ninety-Five Theses, in which he stated that, with his call to repentance, Christ did not mean a particular church ritual but, rather, an attitude that should permeate every Christian's life. The church, Luther added, did not have the right to intervene in how believers fared after death. It would, furthermore, contradict God's goodness, if the church were only to pass on part of God's gifts of grace to its flock if they were to pay. God grants salvation completely and unconditionally. Luther also criticized that the sale of indulgences was being used to finance St Peter's Basilica, and thought the pope should have used his own fortune instead.

The Ninety-Five Theses demonstrate how the theological understanding of freely granted righteousness became, for Luther, a standard to gauge and position church doctrine and practice. Luther further developed and defined this understanding in the course of subsequent disputes. This would lead to what is now described as the Reformation doctrine of "justification by faith alone," an outline of which will be presented in the following.

Justification by faith alone

Already medieval theology shared the conviction that we cannot actually earn our own salvation. It, too, regarded salvation as a gift of grace. The idea that God expected a least an initial step on our part was, however, popular during Luther's lifetime. If we did the little that was in our own meager power, the idea went, God, in God's pure grace, would reward us with something infinitely greater, namely eternal salvation. This may sound very good at first. The Reformers recognized, however, that we ultimately turn our gaze inward with a view to our own abilities. The question then remains, Have I done enough? Have I truly done the little that God expects of me? It then becomes unclear as to whether God will really reward us. Or it is just the other way around: We gaze inward and believe ourselves to be leading good religious and moral lives and conclude that we have done enough. Proud of ourselves, we expect that God will reward us with eternal life because we have deserved it. This inward looking can consequently lead either to desperation or to pride, desperation in the sense of not even living up to God's modest expectations, or pride in having fulfilled them. This pride, however, can give way to desperation at any time, whenever doubts arise, about whether we have actually deserved our salvation.

When people look only at themselves it results in this vacillation between pride and desperation. For Luther the way out of this hopeless situation was to turn one's gaze from oneself to look solely toward God. God is not waiting for us to approach God; God does not link our salvation to the condition that we first do something to achieve it. "Justification by faith alone" means not trusting in our own abilities but solely in God. Faith means trusting that God has already done all that is necessary for our salvation when Christ took everything upon himself that we ourselves have to answer for.

The reason why God views us as righteous does not lie within ourselves. Righteousness "before God" derives entirely "from God." The Reformers expressed this with the expression *iustitia externa*, i.e., our righteousness comes from outside of us, or *iustitia aliena*, "alien righteousness." This does not come thanks to a quality or achievement that we find within ourselves, but instead by God imputing Christ's righteousness to us. This means that God, as it were, "views" Christ "into us." When God looks at us, God sees Christ in us, or, more specifically, God sees the sinless Christ in us sinners. With his "creative" vision, God "views" the salvation into us that Christ has won for us.

Distinctions were made later between an "effective" and an "imputative" justification, and between "making" people righteous and "speaking" them righteous. It was often claimed that only "speaking" people righteous was appropriate for the Lutheran understanding of justification. This could be meant either positively or critically. On the positive side, one could say that "alien righteousness," according to Lutheran doctrine, could never truly become a quality of one's own, never a property of people themselves. We "are" righteous only in the eyes of God, and we "experience" ourselves to be righteous only by allowing ourselves to be spoken so by God's Word and by trusting in this Word. The criticism was lodged, however, that nothing in fact happened when people are spoken righteous, as they are not changed in the process. Is being spoken righteous not then in fact ineffective?

The Reformers would have thought this distinction to be artificial and inappropriate. They were indeed convinced that God's Word was always creative. When God "speaks" someone righteous, God also "makes" them righteous. If we trust and believe in God's Word, we can be assured that we are also judged to be righteous by God. This assurance that God's judgment is valid and true without any limitations is, at its core, what the Reformers ultimately understood as "faith." It was not mere chance that Luther, in his Small Catechism, translated the word "amen" as: "This is most certainly true."

The Reformers, however, also maintained that the gift of righteousness can never be established objectively. We cannot "prove" that we are righteous. That is and remains an act of faith that cannot simply be translated into demonstrable knowledge. This applies even more with regard to others: There are no empirical traits that allow us to know, without a doubt, whether someone is in a state of grace—or not.

This is indeed the meaning of the famous Lutheran phrase *simul iustus et peccator*, "simultaneously just and sinner." While this is often understood as if justification does not change anything in our status as sinners, it is not meant that way. It is in fact meant to express that we are only righteous when we look at ourselves, as it were, through God's eyes. We are truly and fully righteous in God's eyes. If we look directly at ourselves, however, we will recognize that we are sinners and that we do not live our lives in accordance with our Creator's will. The phrase makes it again clear that our salvation comes entirely thanks to God; justification does not give us possession of anything either that we could bring before God, if need be. Salvation is and remains unearned.

JUSTIFICATION AND ETHICS

Luther's doctrine of justification by faith alone was, from the very beginning, vulnerable to the critique that it meant that human action does not matter. If God grants us salvation "for free," if we cannot and need not do anything for it, do we not lose an important reason to do good and avoid evil? Why should we help our neighbor if we no longer need to fear God's wrath? From the early days of the Reformation, Luther grappled with this objection and explained the significance of "good works." He maintained without reservation, however, that we cannot earn salvation through our actions. This does not make "good works" unnecessary or unimportant, though. On the contrary, they are important, but they are not a precondition but a consequence of salvation.

Luther expanded on this particularly eloquently in his writing "On the Freedom of a Christian." Because God has already given us everything we need for our eternal salvation through Christ and in Christ, we are freed from worrying about ourselves. We no longer need to work hard to secure our own lives and to grab ahold of what we think we need to this end. Fear is the strongest reason for the greed in which the Apostle Paul already recognized the nature of sin (cf. Rom 7). Relieved of this fear for our own well-being, we can be there selflessly for others and look out for their well-being instead. Luther explained that it was precisely because we were free in Christ that we could act in service to others. And because we do this now freely, we no longer understand the commandments as being an external compulsion; we do them gladly and of our own accord. Justification is therefore the source of our love for our neighbors. We essentially pass on the joy to our neighbors that we receive by being accepted by God in Christ. Luther was thus able to say that we ourselves become "Christ" to our neighbors.[2]

Luther was enough of a realist to see that this does not always work out. He often spoke of our earthly lives being a series of new beginnings. We are often our own worst enemies and need to come to terms with a still incomplete world. Selflessness must therefore be relearned time and again. Luther was even able to derive a good reason for asceticism from this. He no longer, however, meant the particular self-denial of monks, but also and especially the "every-day service," i.e., the dutiful fulfillment of tasks in our social lives, as when parents bring up their children, farmers till their fields, or public servants carry out their various duties. In doing so, they do not focus on their own interests but use their energies for others. The Lutheran work ethic is thus an expression of fulfilled selflessness and love for one's neighbor put into practice.

This does, however, involve one particular danger: If the "freedom of a Christian" is translated into the selfless fulfillment of duties, it can also get lost in that context. The "freedom from ..." threatens to be suffocated by the "freedom to ..." Justification must not be reduced to a mere initial step toward action (freed only to serve) as the liberating gospel could then again become a restrictive law.

[2] *WA* 7,35.

Church dividing no more? The Joint Declaration on the Doctrine of Justification

In the sixteenth century, justification by faith alone marked a distinction between the Reformation doctrine and that of the Roman Catholic Church. While religious dialogue did lead to some degree of rapprochement (e.g., Regensburg in 1541), Lutherans would continue to perceive Catholics as seeking justification through works. At the Council of Trent, the Roman Catholic Church, for its part, expressly rejected the doctrine of justification by faith alone. This appeared to them to deny human responsibility. The two positions thus distinguished themselves from one another. The twentieth century would, however, see a great variety of new experiences of ecumenical community. This has cast doubt on the continuation of the old state of mutual rejection and led to new dialogues. One question that arose in the process was whether the mutual doctrinal condemnations of the Reformation era were really based on a proper understanding of the other side, or whether positions were in fact being rejected that they did not even hold. Another question was whether essentially the same objectives were perhaps being pursued, but using different manners of thinking, speaking and nuance. Following several decades of intensive research and dialogue, the Lutheran World Federation and the Pontifical Council for Promoting Christian Unity signed the Joint Declaration on the Doctrine of Justification in Augsburg in 1999. While the declaration does not pretend that there do not continue to be serious differences between the confessions in their understanding of justification, it attests to a consensus in basic truths on the doctrine of justification, which, in turn, permits us to view any differences as no longer posing a strict division between the churches. Even the Roman Catholic Church now emphasizes that nobody can "earn" salvation, while Lutherans are clear about faith becoming palpable and manifesting itself through how we live our lives. This allows for a common description of the basic fundaments of the process of justification.

Justification today

It has been asked, time and again, whether the Lutheran doctrine of justification can still have meaning for us today. Unlike the sixteenth century, not many people today live their lives in fear of God's severe and final judgment. The question of God's grace, which Luther grappled with so extensively, has often lost its ability to torment us, or does not even come up in the first place. The idea that we are held accountable by God and therefore need to confess our failure, and that we can only place our hopes in God's unfounded forgiveness, now appears to many to be a dark shadow that darkens our lives and prevents us from having a basic positive attitude. Viewed from this perspective, it is that type of pessimism that itself leads to the dire situation and the need for Christ as a redeemer in the first place, while what humanity actually needs is to be saved from the oppressive idea that it requires salvation. Many Christians even question whether God's creation is actually given enough appreciation when human sinfulness is emphasized so strongly. Others ask critically whether Luther's rejection of active human participation in their salvation does not in fact disregard human freedom, the very freedom, however, in which human dignity is itself rooted. Neither Luther's questions nor his answers would thus appear to remain applicable to us today.

But people of course still live in fear for themselves, even today. They yearn to be accepted unconditionally just as they are confronted by demands and fear not being able to meet them. They experience pressure, both in their work and in their domestic and family lives, and although they try hard and do everything they can, they are still often left with the feeling of not having met expectations. Other people sense that their gifts and abilities are not recognized or put to proper use when they cannot find work or are seen by society as "unproductive" due to their age, illness, or weakness. Still others suffer as poverty robs them of the opportunity to participate actively in society or to train their skills to put to use there. And there are those who feel marginalized due to their ethnic background, their gender, or their lifestyle. The yearning to be accepted and dignified as a person is in no way less strong than it was in Luther's times. This applies to guilt as well. People today also live with a sense of guilt, are ashamed of their behavior and are plagued by self-chastisement. They know that they cannot undo what is done or make it better, and yearn for forgiveness and a new beginning, even as they know that they have not deserved it.

One often hears that "justification by faith alone" focuses too strongly on the negative experience of failure and guilt, is too one-sided, and no longer meshes with the way modern people feel about life. Even Christians today can feel more open than in earlier times to a yearning for earthly happiness, and recognize in it a reflection of eternal salvation. This needs not, however, contradict justification by faith alone. The experience of happiness also includes the understanding that success and fulfillment remain beyond our control, despite all of our efforts, and thus remain an unearned gift, giving us reason for joyous thanks.

The doctrine of justification by faith alone can thus continue to have a meaning for us today that liberates us, provides us relief and gives us courage. The doctrine can raise our awareness for how God affirms us unconditionally. God has already accepted us before we can do anything for it. God respects us even when we are not able to find any respect for ourselves. God offers dignity even when people degrade and despise others. God opens up new horizons when situations seem hopeless. God frees us to take new action when we are otherwise paralyzed. "By faith alone" can mean that this affirmation, this acceptance, this dignity, this encouragement, this new hope–all of this is a gift. And like every true gift, it is voluntary, beyond our control, and cannot be coerced or sold. "By faith alone" is a message that remains important today: Salvation, a new and authentic life in faith is "not for sale," we do not need continually to recalculate whether we have enough of our own "capital" to purchase it.

Filled with fear, Luther asked, How can I find a gracious God? And he wrestled long and hard with the question. The answer that ultimately emerged is simple and continues to hold great significance today: We do not need to find this God–we already have this God.

Questions

What does it mean to you, to be "justified by faith alone"? How does this impact your understanding of life?

Where do you experience "gifts of grace" in your life?

How do you see the role of "good works"?

What would you describe as your "everyday worship"?

Human Will—Free or Enslaved?

Jaan Lahe

> For I know that nothing good dwells within me, that is, in my flesh. I can will what is right, but I cannot do it. For I do not do the good I want, but the evil I do not want is what I do (Rom 7: 18–19).

Discussions on free will, on the freedom of a human being to choose and to decide, and on the question to what extent human beings are able, of their own volition, to shape their own lives have lasted for as long as the human being has reflected on the meaning and purpose of life and its possibilities. The freedom of the will has been a subject of debate in the history of philosophy as well as of theology and, to an even greater extent, in the history of religion.

The bondage of destiny

Already the Greeks believed that there is a force that even the immortal gods had to obey, namely destiny. Faith in the power of destiny deepened during the Hellenistic period (4–1 BC). During the period of the Roman Empire (1–5 AD) destiny or inevitability (Greek: *ananke, heimarmene*) became a "cosmic power" governing the entire universe. It was commonly held that every person's life was predetermined from birth until death by destiny and governed by seven planets or seven "governors," whose government or disposition was called Fate or Destiny. According to Origen (ca. 185–253/254) and Augustine (354–430) these planets were feared by both Christians and heathens. Astrology, which according to various sociological studies remains very popular among many people, is also based on the belief that we are governed by celestial objects. It has become detached from its original attachment to religion (planets were considered to be divine or demonic beings) or, at least, modern mass culture has forgotten the religious roots of astrology.

In philosophical terms, the faith in destiny was founded by the Stoics, according to whom destiny or fate represents a general law determining the world, a fact which a wise person would not ignore. The perception of a human being as a puppet in the hands of almighty destiny is widespread, even beyond Antiquity. The Persian mathematician, astronomer, philosopher and poet Omar Khayyám (1048–1131) got to the heart of the matter by equating fate with infinite time:

> We men are puppets, whose steps God ordains;
> The time is short in which we dally there,
> Then in death's casket one by one we fall,
> The game is played and earth must cover all.[1]

The poet suggests that the rotating firmament which is governed by the planets is a visible manifestation of destiny or infinite time. Time creates beings, including human beings, gives them the opportunity for a brief moment to appear as marionettes on the stage of the "great world theatre," and brings them back to the dust they were made of. Thereafter time would use the very same matter to create new beings and it would repeat itself time and again, forever.

It is not easy to live with the knowledge that one cannot change anything. Khayyám's reaction to the realization that everything is predestined is a hedonistic one: drink wine and enjoy the company of your beloved one. The Epic of Gilgamesh, an epic poem from ancient Mesopotamia, "Harper's Song" (or Song of the Harper) from Ancient Egypt, several Greek and Roman poets and the unknown author of the Book of Ecclesiastes in the Old Testament from the Hellenistic era–they all express a similar reaction. However, this has never been a satisfactory solution for profound thinkers. Ever since Antiquity there have been attempts to refute the belief in predestination by using rational arguments. Carneades (214/3–129/8 BC), an Academic skeptic (so called because this was the type of skepticism taught in Plato's Academy in Athens), proved astrology's arguments to be wrong by stating that the fate of twins born under the same constellation of planets can be different, whereas two people having at their birth a different constellation of planets may share the same fate (e.g., in the case of

[1] *The Ruba'yat of Omar Khayam*, trans. H.M. Cadell (London, New York: John Lane The Bodley Head, 1899), at **www.omarkhayyamnederland.com/vertalingen/engels/cadell/index.html**

a shipwreck). The ancient Greek philosopher Epicurus (ca. 342-270 BC) argued that the basis of free will lies in the freedom of atoms falling into an empty space—they do not fall in a straight course as previously believed, but deviate from it. According to Epicurus, the bearer of the human will, the soul, consists of atoms too. This means that human beings are free to make their own decisions.

Not everyone can be convinced by rational arguments; hence their eyes will be turned to supernatural forces in the quest to find a remedy against fate. Papyrus manuscripts dating back to the Roman Empire contain magic spells to break the power of the fate. Some gods were also believed to be able to save from the chains of fate. One of these gods was the Egyptian goddess Isis, who was popular in the Greco-Roman world, and who promised her devotees liberation from the power of fate and a prosperous afterlife. Many Christian teachers of the first centuries believed that Baptism can set a person free from the power of fate—that anyone who is baptized belongs to Christ (Christ owns them) and not to fate (fate no longer owns them), and the planets do not have any impact on them. However, this faith has not proved to be a satisfactory solution to many Christian thinkers who have tried to find an answer to the question about freedom of the will.

Free will?

Paul confesses that "I do not do the good I want, but the evil I do not want is what I do" (Rom 7:19) (the "I" here does not mean specifically Paul, but may refer to the humankind in general) and explains it by the fact that sin rules over human beings. The "sin" Paul talks about has many similarities with the "fate" of the Greeks and Romans. He describes it as a "cosmic force" that has ruled humankind since Adam (e.g., Rom 5:12ff.). A few centuries later, it was adopted in a similar way by the church father Augustine, who shared Paul's conviction that only God's grace can save us from sin. Almost 1000 years later, the Reformer Martin Luther (1483-1546) drew the same conclusion as Augustine. His discussions with the humanist Erasmus of Rotterdam, (1466 or 1469-1536) like Augustine's with the British-born ascetic moralist Pelagius (ca. 390-418), focused on the role that human beings will play in the process of salvation. Augustine's and Luther's views largely coincide in this matter; human will cannot save a human being and even the human ability to believe, considered to be the only way to salvation, is a gift of God and therefore, out of the reach of human will. According to Luther, human will is enslaved by sin, and when the Augsburg Confession of 1530 touches upon the issue of free will, it says that human will "has some freedom for producing civil righteousness and for choosing things subject to reason."[2] As a witness to this teaching, Book III of Augustine's *Hypognosticon* is quoted here.

> We confess that all human beings have a free will that possesses the judgment of reason. It does not enable them, without God, to being —much less complete—anything that pertains to God, but only to perform the good or evil deeds of this life. By "good deeds" I mean those that arise from the good in nature, that is, the will to labor in the field, to eat and drink, to have a friend, to wear clothes, to build a house, to marry, to raise cattle, to learn various useful skills, or to do whatever good pertains to this life.[3]

Whereas the Reformers were more occupied with thinking about freedom of the will and predestination regarding the relations between God and human beings, the question about free will in relation to the way in which human beings act and decide in their everyday life has been extensively discussed by psychologists and neurologists. For example, Sigmund Freud (1856–1939), the father of psychoanalysis, claimed that the behavior of human beings and their decisions are not free and thus free will exists in the imagination only. In reality, a human being's behavior and decisions are controlled by the part of the human psyche that Freud describes as "the unconscious" (German: das Unbewusste). In this layer of the human mind, according to Freud, lie sexual desires and traumatic childhood experiences, repressed by our consciousness, that affect day to day human behavior. In behaviorist psychology there is little scope for free will as it states that human behavior can be analyzed only on the basis of objectively measurable mental processes, which, according to behaviorists, do not include free will. However, some psychologists are convinced that the will as many other mental functions can be developed. They argue that this is why a human being is never determined always to behave in the same situation in one and the same way—they have the freedom of choice. No matter how the freedom of will is conceptualized, from the perspective of psychology the will is not something supernatural ("divine origin in the human being"), but a mental function psychophysically based on the activity of the frontal lobe and on the functional connections between the speech centers and the frontal lobe of the brain. As such the will is subject to experimental research that has led to remarkable results. The pioneering American scientist Benjamin Libet (1916—2007) has researched the activity of the

---

[2] "The Augsburg Confession—Latin Text—Article XVIII: Free Will," in Robert Kolb and Timothy J. Wengert (eds), *The Book of Concord. The Confessions of the Evangelical Lutheran Church* (Fortress Press, Minneapolis, 2000), 51.
[3] Ibid., 51.

brain cortex during volitional acts and concluded that the changes in the cortex that indicate the start of a volitional act occur an instant before the human being acknowledges their volitional act. Hence, the will precedes consciousness (being conscious) of the volitional act, meaning that the brain determines volitional acts and only a little later it becomes conscious of the volitional decision. The results of Libet's research seem to provide evidence against freedom of the will, but one should not forget that the experiments concentrated only on the most basic volitional decisions (i.e., to move the hand or leg). Are these results transferable to more complex decisions that influence our whole existence such as the choice of profession or life partner?

We see today an ever increasing demand for and popularity of so-called self-help books that emphasize the boundlessness of human will—if you truly want something and convince yourself of it, you can achieve wealth and fame; find an ideal life partner, your dream job etc. These books attribute to human will almost supernatural powers that can bring about the fulfillment of every human desire (provided that the person concerned is committed to influence their own will)—a concept where one can almost recognize the pattern of magical thinking.

Between freedom and predestination

Nonetheless, there are a great number of things in this world that do not depend on us nor on our will, and we have to accept them as a given. We do not choose the moment we are born and even the healthiest lifestyle and greatest cautiousness does not allow us to choose the moment and the way of dying. In his book, *Immortality. The Quest to Live Forever and How it Drives Civilization,*[4] Stephen Cave demonstrates that throughout history, humankind has constantly been devising strategies to remove death from the picture, but none of these strategies seem to have fulfilled this dream. Similarly, we are not able to choose our parents, our place of birth, nor the environment that we are born into. At the same time, these factors have the strongest impact on the shaping of our personalities and our volitional decisions.

Today we know that the factors impacting the shaping of our individual personalities do not start with the home and environment, but are already present at the moment of conception. We inherit from our biological ancestors the genes that influence our mental, psychological and physical health

[4] Stephen Cave, *Immortality. The The Quest to Live Forever and How it Drives Civilization* (New York: Crown Publishers, 2012).

as well as the development of our characters. It is probably impossible to define the exact proportion of the role that our genetic constitution plays vis à vis the environment and education. Depending on the prevailing ideological mindset, attitudes and values in society the one or other may be more strongly emphasized. This then actually leads to the greater impact of either genetic constitution or environment and education on the human being in the particular context as it influences the concepts of anthropology, education, training, etc. Thus the role of the prevailing ideas in a particular society may never be underestimated in the discussion about free will and predestination. This is true even there where the ideas and values do not reflect the mainstream of society but a subculture. A person can be considered as a human being only in relationship to fellow human beings. Whether willing or not, being in an "I and Thou" relationship (Martin Buber, 1878–1965) obliges us to take into consideration the other "I-s" and "Thou-s" since otherwise there could not be any coexistence. Even choosing the life of a hermit and severing all ties with other people would not set us free of our personality that is shaped by earlier relationships with other people. The hermit would take along memories from the life before and ideas acquired in a previous environment. Even in a state of mind achieved through certain mental techniques (i.e., meditation, fasting, prayer) where a person experiences complete liberation, these ideas may reemerge at a certain point. Might these be the demons that according to early Christian tradition attacked the ascetics in the desert?

In today's globalized and commercialized world, we are coactors in larger economic schemes that we are often not even aware of. The notion of collective sin pertinently describes the way in which we are caught into the global network of unjust structures without often actually realizing it. We ourselves consider our decisions to buy, sell and consume to be made freely whereas they are actually frequently shaped by clever commercial manipulations and standards set by companies who try to sell their products and by groups who set the standards for living.

Unfreedom which is not perceived as such is most dangerous, and therefore critical thinking is crucial in order to increase our actual freedom of choice there where it is possible, for instance in regard to our consumer habits, the environment, etc. And, indeed, almost all of us, even if to different degrees, do have the possibility to choose between different options in our everyday lives. And these decisions can change the world we live in. Without this option to choose it would also be rather cynical to make human beings morally and legally responsible for the consequences of their volitional decisions, i.e., their actions.

We can therefore conclude that while human beings have free will with regard to their everyday decisions the scope seems to be rather more limited than was previously assumed. In view of our relationship to God, Luther's conviction that it is not our conduct or performance, but God's grace that moves God to save us, is still valid. We are not saved by God's grace plus our good works or anything we do. We cannot so to speak "buy our way to heaven."[5] We are saved by God's grace alone.

Questions

Why is the question about the existence of the freedom of the will important for us? What depends on the answer to this question? Which impact does it have on our lives?

Why is the question about the freedom of the will so complicated that until now different thinkers have not been able to agree on this? Is there a chance that this might change one day?

Does the existence or non-existence of the freedom of the will have an impact on the relationship between human beings and God and if yes, then how?

[5] See also Luther's argumentation in his famous Ninety-Five Theses, e. g., thesis 27 in regard to buying the indulgences: "They preach only human doctrines who say that as soon as the money clinks into the money chest, the soul flies out of purgatory": Martin Luther, "Ninety-Five Theses," in Helmut T. Lehmann (ed.), *Luther's Works*, vol. 31 (Philadelphia: Muhlenberg Press, 1957), 27–28.

God's Promises and Human Prosperity

Sarah Hinlicky Wilson

America has made quite a number of significant contributions to world culture, for good and for ill, from cornflakes to modern democracy to the nuclear bomb. Fitting right into this legacy of ambiguously important contributions is the prosperity gospel. Though it has since gone viral around the planet, its origins are in America. Some historical background will make its theological claims a little easier to grasp—and to reject.

The American background

Nineteenth-century America started out optimistic. It saw a chance to create a new Christian civilization in a continent considered to be "empty" without all the baggage of the bloody European past. No longer saddled with state churches, the "revival" became the new locus of Christian life: large public meetings dominated by powerful preaching and equally powerful emotions. At the same time, newly developing industry and the colonization of the West gave American Christians the sense of being a new Israel, establishing a righteous society, one that was getting bigger and better all the time. Success and victory were signs of God's favor.

But it was not enough to conquer the earth and the passions of the body. There was a longing to conquer the realm of the spirit, indeed to say that spirit alone was real while the body and the earth were mere illusions. In this environment, marginally Christian movements emerged, such as Christian Science (a sect that denied the reality of the body and believed that all illness could be cured by pure mental effort), Transcendentalism (a Unitarian philosophy that believed in the inherent goodness of human beings as opposed to corrupt society), and New Thought (a form of pantheism that claimed people were divine and could overcome all difficulties by right thinking). All of these believed in mind over matter. But by their account, mind and spirit were as mechanistic as body and machine: they operated according to immutable laws. Crack the code behind the spiritual laws, and you could tame everything else according to your desires.

The American Civil War (1861–1865), and subsequent military conflicts at home and abroad, put a dent in American optimism but did not squash it completely. As long as the economic system rewarded those who worked hard, optimism kept a firm hold on American culture. Those who failed to thrive did not disprove the promise of success: they only proved that they had failed to live by its laws. And that is where Essek William Kenyon came in.

E. W. KENYON AND THE "WORD OF FAITH"

Kenyon was well acquainted with New Thought and other forms of metaphysical mastery popular in the nineteenth century. His only objection to them was that they were not tied closely enough to the Christian faith. So he simply borrowed their reasoning and added some extra Jesus. For example, Kenyon argued that Jesus' death overcame all negative things in this life, including poverty and sickness. Thus, "faith" means taking advantage of the new spiritual law of victory in Christ. You could not just hope for something from God; you could not just **ask** for something from God; no, you had to name it and then you had to claim it–and, as a result, it would be so. God was guaranteed to give it to you. That was real faith.

A corollary of Kenyon's teaching was that physical signs are deceitful, distractions from Satan to lead you astray. Thus, true believers suffering from illness simply assert their victory over illness, and from then on disregard the symptoms, which are temptations, not truth. True believers confess that they will be rich, and in due course they will indeed be rich. In fact, according to Kenyon, true believers avoid even mentioning negative things, because talking about bad things might make them come true. Done right, though, "the word of faith" always gives you what you want–and what you want is, of course, good. Obviously, God does not want anybody to be sick or poor. So name your health, claim your wealth, and God will automatically grant it to you. If you do not get what you want, the problem is on your end, not God's. You probably did not believe hard enough.

Kenyon did not become a widespread influence in his own time. He operated at the margins of church life; many people have mistakenly thought him to be a Pentecostal, though he was not. It was not until the second half of the twentieth century that Kenyon was rediscovered by another American evangelist, Kenneth Hagin, who started popularizing Kenyon's thought through preaching tours and TV programs. Matching a new burst of postwar optimism, other evangelists picked up on his message and started preaching their own variations on the theme of prosperity.

Variations on the prosperity theme

By and large, non-denominational preachers have promoted the "word of faith" movement, with some Evangelical and Pentecostal participants. But because prosperity has always worked through networks of influence rather than formally structured denominations, it has reached every corner of the church and every nation of the world. Members of churches that formally renounce prosperity will read books or listen to radio programs by prosperity preachers without recognizing the conflict in the teaching. There are even Roman Catholic variations on the theme, as in the El Shaddai movement in the Philippines. Prosperity earns the unfortunate honor of being the most widespread and successful heresy of the twenty-first century.

There is much to criticize about the prosperity gospel, but one word of caution must be spoken. Prosperity has a very different impact depending on where it is preached. It is obviously repulsive when uttered by rich American preachers who extract life savings from naïve believers and then use the proceeds to buy a $23000 toilet seat (as evangelist Joyce Meyer did). It is positively criminal when such preachers dissuade parents from giving their sick children the medicine necessary for survival, leading to an early and completely preventable death—as has happened far too often.

But prosperity is a popular message also in places that are not at all prosperous. It has a different texture when it is preached by and to people who are destitute, starving and denied access to any medical care at all. In such situations, there is often a fine line between legitimate divine healing and illegitimate promises of believer-induced healing. Likewise, the message of prosperity can have the effect of pulling a marginalized community together to support each other in creating the stable economic and social relationships that allow the entire group to rise out of its poverty. Finally, most people who preach and practice the prosperity gospel are not even aware of it as a distinct Christian movement with serious problems: it is simply the Christian faith as they have heard it and continue to proclaim it. Discerning critics need to separate out the real flaws from the real benefits that have come to people through such preaching.

A Trinitarian critique of prosperity

Here we will begin with a Trinitarian approach to countering the claims of the prosperity gospel. As you can see at the origins of Kenyon's teaching, there is a very faulty understanding of "spirit" at work. "Spirit" is made to be the enemy and the opposite of "matter," which is low, misleading and unimportant. Such attitudes are very ancient; Christians have been fighting them in various forms since the earliest days of the church, whether in the form of Neo-Platonism or Gnosticism or Manichaeism. By contrast, in the Nicene Creed we profess our faith in "the Holy Spirit, the Lord, the giver of life." This same Spirit hovered over the waters at creation and called matter, earth, and living creatures into being (Gen1:2). This same Spirit raised up the crucified body of Jesus to new life (Rom 8:11): risen, transformed, but still a body, still matter, still something that could eat and drink and speak and even bear wounds. To be spiritual is not to be an enemy of the material.

And that therefore also means that we who live by the Spirit are called to be stewards of the material, not exploiters of it. The prosperity gospel proclaims infinite greed to be rewarded with infinite accumulation, for the material world is purely an object to be used. But the Holy Spirit created and sustained the world for the glory of God and for the flourishing of all, not for humans at the expense of the earth or for some people at the expense of others.

The mention of our crucified and risen Savior leads us to another aspect of prosperity's false message. Prosperity preachers often assert that Christ already did all the suffering for us, thus believers should expect nothing but success and wholeness. This is an extreme misreading of the whole testimony of Scripture, both of whose Testaments witness to the reality of suffering in the lives of the faithful. The Book of Job is the most sustained biblical protest against the idea that those who suffer must be unrighteous—and equally against the idea that righteousness is a guarantee of happiness. Jesus was a shocking savior precisely because of his suffering on the cross, and his earliest disciples and apostles shared the good news about this savior at great personal cost, even death. Martyrdoms have followed the faithful in all ages—and the last century has seen more Christian martyrdoms than any other period—but we understand them as testimonies to the faithfulness, not the failure, of God. The Epistles also commend churches to be strong amidst persecution and trials, poverty and illness.

The most destructive thing the prosperity message does is convince people that, if they have not received the healing or wealth they have claimed, it is their fault. In such cases, there is no comfort for the bereaved: they can only assume that their loved ones failed and that is why the illness won. Prosperity preaching destroys the community: the wealthy are assumed to be the true believers while the poor must be doubters, so the strong are encouraged to cast off the weak in the name of holiness. Prosperity cannot endure the scandal of the cross. It cannot abide Jesus, the crucified savior of the world.

To reject the crucified Son is also to reject the Father who sent him. Wrong as it is, it is perfectly understandable: human beings have always raged against their weakness and dependence, their vulnerability to suffering and death. Much religion now and throughout history is simply magic, an attempt to figure out the secret laws of the universe and exploit them for our own gain. Prosperity is twenty-first-century Christian magic. It wants control. It does not want a God who is Lord over all, who may call us to suffering for the sake of the gospel, who cannot be explained or predicted or bribed. Prosperity wants a God who can be bought off with "faith" or with generous giving in hope of an even bigger return. But God is not for sale any more than salvation!

The Christian message does not take away the agony, frustration, or unanswered questions of human life. It does not promise victory or success now. Instead, it declares that "the sufferings of this present time are not worth comparing with the glory that is to be revealed to us" (Rom 8:18). Jesus' vindication came after his death on the cross, when he was raised from the dead by the Father: so shall it be for us. To be a Christian is to share in the death and resurrection of Christ, not to avoid death or to disdain the flesh that will be raised. In life and death and new life, the Father can be trusted to bring all things right.

A law-and-gospel critique of prosperity

What does the gospel promise? Not health, not wealth, not a successful career or a solid marriage or a just government or happiness. All of these things are good, and they have their place—but in the law. The holy law of God is what governs our this-worldly life, directs us toward justice, curbs our sin and reminds us of our constant need for God's mercy and forgiveness to get us back on track. The law teaches us to make good use of the gifts of creation and community.

Here in the realm of the law, prosperity misleads by being a half-truth. It is true that sin can lead to suffering. But God hardly needs to punish sins directly in this life: they tend to be their own punishment. To be an idolater is to be enslaved to a mute, dead, unresponsive thing, instead of being in a life-giving relationship with the life-giving God. Likewise, as Jesus said on the night of his arrest, "all who take the sword will perish by the sword" (Mt 26:52): violence begets more violence. The Proverbs in particular warn that greed, abuse of the poor, laziness and general unrighteousness will have severe consequences. God's law is against sin not least of all because it is destructive of people and the whole creation.

However, we are not allowed to reverse this logic. Bad things, suffering and disasters are not therefore always caused by sin. People tend to assume that suffering is always a result of evildoing, as a punishment, but Jesus forbids us to make that leap. He clearly stated that those who died in the collapse of the tower of Siloam were no worse than anyone else, thus their death was not caused by their particular sins (Lk 13:4). Likewise, the man was born blind not because he sinned or because his parents sinned; Jesus cut off that interpretation entirely (Jn 9:3). Nor is abuse at the hands of other human beings due payment for sin: for Jesus the sinless one was handed over to death on the cross. Quite often it is righteousness, not unrighteousness, that leads to suffering. Thus the prosperity interpretation of suffering blasphemously distorts the law's good purpose of warning against evil deeds, and its interpretation of success ignores the wrongdoing that often leads to wealth.

But we still need to go one step further in our critique of the prosperity gospel. The gospel is neither the created gifts of God nor the law that protects them. And the gospel is not conditioned on our doing anything right, whether in obedience to God's law or mastery of supposed spiritual laws. The gospel is nothing other than God's self-giving for us and for our salvation, purely gracious, purely entirely on account of who God is—a friend of sinners and lover of enemies. As Martin Luther put it in his summary of the Creed in the Large Catechism:

> in all three articles God himself has revealed and opened to us the most profound depths of his fatherly heart and his pure, unutterable love. For this very purpose he created us, so that he might redeem us and make us holy, and, moreover, having granted and bestowed upon us everything in heaven and on earth, he has also given us his Son and his Holy Spirit, through whom he brings us to himself.[6]

The gospel is God for us, with us and in us: Father, Son, and Holy Spirit.

This is a gospel by which we can live in strength and die in hope. It sustains us through doubt, persecution, failure and suffering. It is a promise that does not mislead but fortifies and enlivens. Such is the testimony of Tsehay Tolessa, an Ethiopian Lutheran woman tortured and imprisoned for ten years under a violent regime on account of her faith:

> God's hand is great; it reaches so far. It is there even where no friends can reach, no neighbors, no family. But He still comes in. In the midst of filth, He is there, in humiliation, in blood, in stench. Through everything He went along with me, so close by me. I felt His nearness the whole way.

[6] Martin Luther, "The Large Catechism," in Robert Kolb and Timothy J. Wengert (eds), *The Book of Concord: The Confessions of the Evangelical Lutheran Church* (Minneapolis: Fortress, 2000), 439.

With such a God, we are so rich that there is no need to chase after the false promises of prosperity!

Questions

All Christian believers ask God for blessings of all kinds, both physical and spiritual. What is the right way to ask? What is the right way to receive? What is the right way to respond when we do not receive what we ask for?

Think about how you and the people in your society and church respond to the rich and successful, and to the poor and struggling. Do these attitudes reflect Jesus' teaching and example?

Imagine how you might respond to another Christian who perceives God as a means to this-worldly success. How might you articulate the truth that the gospel is enough, that God is enough, even in the midst of struggle and suffering?

Your Will Be Done

Chiropafadzo Moyo

Prayer is not only a phenomenon of Christianity; it is also practiced in most other religions such as Islam, Judaism, African Traditional Religions and many more. The term generally refers to addressing a divinity for different purposes. Christians also use prayer as a means to communicate with God. According to the Christian faith, it is also one of the ways in which God communicates with human beings. For the purpose of this paper I shall confine my discussion to Christian prayer.

Prayer is meant to be intimate and to establish a reciprocal relationship between God and humankind, for we are commanded to love God with all our hearts. This means that prayer should come from the heart as we read in Deuteronomy 6:5, "You shall love the Lord your God with all your heart, and with all your soul, and with all your might." God commands us to pray. Prayer can be performed either verbally or non-verbally—for example through sacrifice[1] or dance. In Genesis 3, we read that God came down to walk on earth and command God's creation. After they had sinned, Adam and Eve hid from God; they did not want to see or communicate with God. God took the initiative to continue to communicate with God's creation as God wants to be and stay in communication with us.

An example of God's direct communication with human beings is Abraham's call (Gen 12). That encounter demonstrates a two-way communication. God called and Abraham answered the call. God made a promise to Abraham and this promise was an incentive to continue the dialogue.

[1] Watson E. Mills (ed.), *Mercer Dictionary of the Bible* (Georgia: Mercer University Press, 1990), 706. Sacrifice in Christianity is only understandable as a means of thanksgiving. It is never performed by sacrificing living beings in order to achieve God's benevolence. It is the answer to the granted benevolence of God.

God initiated the dialogue but, increasingly, it became reciprocal and was sustained by God's promise. God promises humankind God's ear and response. According to the Christian faith, God's ear and response have become a human being–Jesus Christ.

There are three reasons why we should pray:

- Already in the Old Testament we are instructed to pray as we are by Jesus who tells us to "Be alert at all times, praying"(Lk 21:36). Christians pray for God's sake. We pray because God promises to hear us (Ps 50:15) and seeks to communicate with us. Christians pray for their own sake.

- We pray for God to grant us power over evil and to heal the world. Christians pray for the sake of the world.

All this is not undertaken from a deep human resource of spirituality, from a mere human desire to achieve some things and avoid others. The author and sustainer of Christian prayer is not the Christian him or herself, but according to the Christian understanding, it is the Holy Spirit who drives us and helps us to pray.[2]

Since there are different reasons for Christian prayer, there is also a formal freedom in how to pray. However, prayer is to be undertaken with humility and a repentant heart. Prayer must be constant. How can this be achieved? It is achieved through a lifestyle,a constant communication with God that often expresses itself nonverbally. It could be described as living in the conscious knowledge of God's presence. This would be a prayerful life. Such a prayer carries its "reward" in itself: it is the faithfulness in God's certain presence that strengthens us and helps us to overcome evil within and around ourselves.

The New Testament tells us that we can pray everywhere (Mt 6:6; 1 Cor 1:2); the temple is one possible place of prayer (Lk 24:53; Acts 3:1; 22:17). The character of prayer can be personal or communal; prayers can be offered in private or in the community of faith. There is need for fellowship in prayer since praying with others enriches spiritually and praying together as the church unites all Christians in their individual search for God's presence. It is important to notice that the New Testament clearly invites everybody to pray, regardless of social status and gender (cf. 1 Sam 1:10) and that there is no need for an external mediator between God and

---

[2] Cf. "The Large Catechism," Third Part: The Lord's Prayer, in Robert Kolb and Timothy Wengert (eds), *The Book of Concord. Confessions of the Evangelical Lutheran Church* (Minneapolis: Fortress, 2000), 440ff.

human beings, be it a priest or a person with special charisma. Both in a Jewish and a Christian prayer the barriers caused by gender and hierarchy are rendered invalid (cf. Lk 2:37f; 18:13; 1: 46–55).

In Philippians 4:6 we learn that we may pray for everything that concerns us on earth and in heaven. There are different ways to perform a prayer and different kinds of prayers. God wishes us to express our needs and to lament, if we are in trouble. God wishes us to carry our needs and sorrows before God. But God also wishes us to express our gratitude and praise for the liberation from death and for giving us a sense and purpose in our lives.

The Old Testament Psalms, which were also the prayers of Jesus, offer wonderful examples of both praise and of lament. And those Psalms still talk to people; Christians lament and praise God also today, creating new hymns and new "psalms" that can be spoken or sung. Some Christians praise God with a very poetic language. God needs to be praised for what God has done for God's people. Some people prefer to praise God before they put forward their petitions. Prayers of praise also follow a general pattern in which the heart of the prayer gives reasons for the praise. Good examples for this kind of praise from the classical Psalms can be found in Psalms 8 and 33.

Learning how to pray—the Lord's Prayer

Jesus Christ commands us to pray in his name. For a Christian it is not possible to pray in any way other than in Jesus' name, because Jesus taught us to call God "Our Father in heaven" and it is his spirit that makes us pray. So, whether or not we mention his name, any honest Christian prayer will always be in the name of Jesus.

The third article of Martin Luther's "Large Catechism" explains the meaning of the Lord's Prayer, the prayer Jesus taught his disciples who had asked him to teach them how to pray (Lk 11:1). This is the most central of all Christian prayers; it is the very essence of Christian prayer. We can observe in it the reciprocity, the will of God, our needs and the deliverance from evil: The Lord's Prayer takes our hearts to God, praising God for God's holiness, God's realm that is among us and the fulfillment of God's will both on earth and in heaven. Then the prayer takes God to us, lets God meet our needs—both the physical and the spiritual ones. Forgiveness and salvation are asked for the whole of humankind.

The way God is addressed in the Lord's Prayer: "Our Father who art in heaven," is significant. Jesus teaches us that we are invited to relate to God in the closest possible form of human address. The "Large Catechism" identifies seven petitions in the Lord's Prayer that help to identify the core characters of Christian prayer.[3] The first petition, "May your name be hallowed," relates to what God demands in the Second Commandment: God's name should not be taken in vain by swearing, cursing, deceiving, etc., but used to the praise and glory of God. God's name must thus not be misused for purposes that are actually driven by ideological, political, economic and private interests, which are falsely legitimized by using God's name. The second petition, "May your kingdom come," calls us to accept God's grace given in Jesus Christ, and asks for the realization of God's Word within us and our fellow human beings. Explaining the second petition, Luther writes,

> [W]e must [...] let the kingdom of God be the first thing for which we pray. Then, surely, we shall have all the other things in abundance, as Christ teaches, "Strive first for the kingdom of God and his righteousness, and all these things will be given to you as well."[4]

The third petition, "May your will come about on earth as in heaven" continues to ask for the realization and actualization of God's will within us. Luther adds the following prayer into his explanation of the third petition in Lord's Prayer:

> Dear Father, your will be done and not the will of the devil or of our enemies, nor of those who would persecute and suppress your holy Word or prevent your kingdom from coming; and grant that we may bear patiently and overcome whatever we must suffer on its account, so that our poor flesh may not yield or fall away through weakness or sloth.[5]

The following petitions: "Give us our daily bread," "And remit our debt, as we remit what our debtors owe," "And lead us not into temptation," are requests that relate to human needs. "Daily bread" refers to human needs in the broadest sense, including life on earth. "Remit our debt" refers to the importance of the central Christian message, of forgiveness, in our daily lives. "As we forgive our debtors" expresses the need to be gracious and merciful to our neighbors just as God has been to us. The petition not to lead us into temptation calls us to think about the various forms of temptations that we experience in our daily lives, from "fondness for

[3] Ibid., 445ff.
[4] Ibid., 448.
[5] Ibid., 449.

luxury, honor, fame, and power" to "unbelief, false security, stubbornness,"[6] etc. The "Large Catechism" explains: "This, then, is what 'leading us not into temptation' means: when God gives us power and strength to resist, even though the attack is not removed or ended".[7] The last, the seventh petition, is a petition for deliverance from all the evil, ending with Amen: "But deliver us from the evil. Amen." "Amen" is the affirmation of faith, meaning that we have no doubt that our prayers are heard. It is a sign of the personal affirmation of our trust in God.

With the Lord's Prayer, Jesus asks us not to fall into the misunderstanding of prayer: there are the prose prayers which are made up of petitions. Most people are caught up in these kinds of prayers as they think that to pray means constantly to request something. Some petitions are presented with lengthy elaborations and in colorful language, which is meant to persuade God. The elaboration is meant to provide an incentive to God. Yet Jesus teaches us that long prayers may suggest hypocrisy. These long prayers are usually meant for blessing, healing or remembrance. When people want something from God they use long prayers that plead with God. However, we must bear in mind that God is aware of what we want, even before we say it and that our prayer could be quite selfish if it restricts itself to the mentioned topics. It may turn God into being a servant to our needs.

ANSWERED PRAYERS—MAGIC AND PRAYER

Christians believe that God hears and answers all their prayers. Jesus promises that also pleading prayers will be heard by God, like by a loving father. God gives us what is good for us. Petitions are sometimes fulfilled differently than the praying person thought. How God hears our prayers and how God fulfills them remains a miracle. Jesus' saying, "Ask, and it will be given you" (Mt 7:7) is frequently heard in a very simplified way, creating an expectation for immediate answers to our prayers. Some try to make God hear their prayers by forcefully exerting lots of energy. Others make commands that can provoke admonishment, when they "speak" as if they were God. In such cases, we can often see that they forgot to call upon the name of Jesus while praying. It is not a prayer that Jesus would pray.

In the Lord's Prayer we are taught to ask for the will of God. It is God's will that should be done on earth as it is in heaven. Christians may wish for things to happen in a certain way, but the will of God might be different. We may ask for healing, but God may have a different answer altogether. If

[6] Ibid., 454.
[7] Ibid.

death results after praying for healing, has God not answered our prayer? The Bible instructs us to pray and ask with faith and trust and wait for God to answer in the best possible way. The prayer is not about dictating to God what to do. Often the answers to our prayers are very different from what we actually asked for. And it may be extremely difficult to believe in an answered prayer when one is faced with strong expressions of evil.

Those who practice magic make things happen immediately, and because we live in a world full of magic and magical answers to life, people expect also religion to respond magically. People experience many pressures in their lives and, as a result, they want immediate answers to everything. As a consequence, some Christians, in Africa for instance, use elements such as water and stones to "hold" their prayers. In some cases, a true "prayer business" has started, where holy oil, water, etc. are being sold with the promise that by using these material means prayer will become more effective and more or less "guarantee" being heard. External signs or material elements that accompany prayer may sometimes be useful yet one must be extremely careful not to cross the line to idolatry. Salvation as well as prayers cannot be for sale because what is essential to Christian prayer are not the magic elements but faith and the readiness to entrust your life into God's hands. Christians are advised to seek the Lord with all their heart and to do everything in faith: "Then when you call upon me and come and pray to me, I will hear you. When you search for me, you will find me; if you seek me with all your heart" (Jer 29:12–13). God knows what is good for each one of us at a given point in time "For my thoughts are not your thoughts, nor are your ways my ways, says the Lord" (Isa 55:8).

Jesus says that everything that you will ask the Father in my name will be granted to you (Jn 15:7, 16:13). At the same time, the reference to the name of Jesus is a critical remark on what we pray: is it really something Jesus would pray for as well? Christians should not only pray in Jesus' name but also trust in him. One needs to have faith in Jesus when praying so that one's prayers might be answered.

CONCLUDING REMARKS

Christian prayer cultivates the relationship between God and the Christian. Hence, Christians cannot experience spiritual growth without prayer. Also nonverbal forms of prayer such as silence, music and dance help us to explore and express our emotional and physical dimensions as people before God. God wants to be loved and adored for God's sake and for our sake and for the sake of the world. God leads us in prayer to Godself and comes to us, accompanies us in our needs and troubles, but also in our joys. God has called us to pray always, as a lifestyle of faith in God. We pray to God and God answers; we do not pray to ourselves, thus we should not prescribe answers to our prayers, but await everything from God, who is present in Jesus Christ and is praying in us through God's Holy Spirit. We have learnt from Jesus to address God as "Father." That means we are invited to relate to God in the closest possible form of human address. This address is a sign of intimacy of the relationship to which we are called.[8] If we take this intimacy seriously, we will not dictate to God in prayer and will not try to "buy" the responses to our prayers, but we will trust God, just as Jesus did.

Questions

In which ways have you experienced prayer as empowering and transformative?

What would you think of as being the most frequent misuses of prayer?

Why should Christians pray and why is communal prayer important?

[8] Werner G. Jeanrond, *Call and Response: The Challenge of Christian Life* (Dublin: Gill and Macmillan, New York: Continuum, 1995), 120.

“I am because I work”—Identifying Oneself through Work

Busi Suneel Bhanu

Introduction

The popular Sanskrit saying *Udyōgampurushalakshanam* [work is the identity/characteristic of human beings] is a popular, reflective statement on the Indian perspective on work, irrespective of caste, creed and gender. According to the Indian understanding, work is a human necessity, a religious expression, a reflection of human existence and integral to one’s identity. For the average person, work, within the Indian religio-cultural framework, also denotes human relations based on power and authority as well as submissiveness and subjugation. One may understand work as a positive and progressive channel that offers glimpses into the purpose and meaning of life, thereby becoming an enriching experience. Or, one may come to the negative conclusion that work is a dehumanizing and life-negating instrument that shatters the hope and aspirations of life itself. As such, this reflection tries to understand the dignity, identity and ability of a human being through work from an Indian socio-religious perspective, namely the perspective and way of life of those who are popularly known as untouchables/*harijans*/Dalits. In the search for identity through work, the following experience of a Dalit highlights the struggle.

Selfie 1. A monochrome view: “work as dharma”

Since I became a Christian I have been reflecting on the meaning and purpose of human life in general and my life in particular. In fact, I am the first person in my family to receive and accept the gospel of Jesus Christ and begin to experience God's faithfulness in Jesus. My parents gave me the name Raja (king). Their wish and desire, I learnt later, was that I should lead the dignified and comfortable life of a king. However, in terms of my work, I realized that I am nothing but a physical and psychological wreck. In our national language, Hindi, the designation for my work is *safaikarmachari*, manual scavenger or sanitary worker. The term and title look so grand as if it were an ennobling work without any dehumanizing connotations.

As a child, I was sent to the mission (Christian) primary school, situated where we lived along with the rest of the *safaikarmachari* community. After completing my primary education, on the insistence of some of my teachers, my parents reluctantly enrolled me in the secondary school, run by the same Christian organization and located in the center of the town where we had lived for generations.

When it was time to go to college, I vividly remember that in spite of my varied tactics of protest, my parents emphasized the need and *dharma* (duty) to follow the family occupation. They invoked two compelling reasons. First, even if I were to graduate from the university with distinction, it would not be easy for me with my family background to secure employment in the highly competitive Indian society. Therefore, in order to avoid the unnecessary frustration of being unemployed, it would be wise to follow and continue the family occupation (something like a bird in the hand is worth two in the bush). Second, and most important, in order to attain *mukti* (salvation/liberation])from *karma-samsara* (the cycle of births and deaths based on the fruit of one's actions in life) one needs to perform the work assigned to one. Further, we are born as "untouchables" in the present birth and the only way to be born as upper caste in the next birth is to perform our assigned duty as *safaikarmachari* without complaint or protest and complete submissiveness. To dispel my frustration and displeasure at this turn of events and to shatter my ignorance of the social structures, sustained by religious philosophies, they patiently explained the Vedic creation narrative that justifies our plight as "ritually impure" people and hence as "untouchables." For my parents, who remain Hindus, the possibility of climbing the hierarchical social ladder, achieving an honorable identity and ultimately securing release from the bondage of *karma* and *samsara* is attainable only through following the assigned work (*dharma*).

While the saying, *udyogampurushalakshanam* has become a reality in my life, the despicable scavenger shattered my dreams of life. The work I am assigned to is obnoxious. We have a twofold responsibility: we are the guardians and protectors of environmental cleanliness within our own villages and towns. Our communities are responsible for cleaning the dry lavatories of hundreds and thousands of households and toil day and night to keep the crisscrossing sewage lines of the villages, towns and cities of our country clean. In my traditional caste assigned work, I have to collect in a bamboo-basket the night-soil (human excreta/feces). I carry it on my head, deposit it in the bullock cart waiting at the roadside and empty it away from the village or town. Moreover, I have to climb into the manholes and with my naked hands clear away the filthy obstacles in order to allow the sewage to flow freely so that it will not dirty the surroundings and thereby cause and spread disease (vector control). But in the process, the sewage water drenches my whole body and, as a consequence, stench emanates from me, driving onlookers and passersby away from me with their scornful looks. Moreover, I often fall prey to illness. I am indeed, an untouchable with work as my *dharma*.

Manual scavengers are one of the living symbols of the dehumanizing reality of caste and untouchability. Because of the obnoxious work they are forced to perform they are the most exploited, rejected and marginalized community in Indian society. In spite of provisions under article 17 of the constitution (abolition of the practice of untouchability), and several acts of legislation such as the Protection of Civil Rights Act 1955, Prevention of Atrocities Act 1989 and the Employment of Manual Scavengers and Construction of Dry Latrines (Prohibition) Act 1993, the practice of manual scavenging continues unabated. It is an undeniable fact that "I am because I work." *Udyoga* in its popular understanding means work and something worth doing. However, according to the Hindu religious philosophical understanding, it also means *ud* (higher) and *yoga* (spiritual discipline) oriented towards the realization of the goal of life, namely liberation. For my illiterate and gullible parents, entrenched in such a religious view and conviction, if not today, then one day, maybe one birth later or after several births, one will achieve that unique identity as the "perfect human being." In the words of our very own Nobel Laureate Rabindranath Tagore, "What harm is there if thy clothes become tattered and stained? Meet him and stand by him in toil and in sweat of thy brow."[1] This untouchable scavenger identity is only temporary and not permanent. For them, work is not simply for the sake of work, but something unique that brings out passion and offers meaning to life. I, on the other hand, have found a new tomorrow here and now in Jesus, and wish not to let this life pass by without this new understanding of work that has become worship and offered me an authentic and liberative human identity. Today, I am slowly and steadily coming out of my stigmatized "untouchable" identity and the appended "work ethic" and have begun to feel proud of my Dalitness and cherish my Dalit Christian identity.

[1] S. K. Paul, *The Complete Poems of Rabindranath Tagore's Gitanjali. Text and Critical Evaluation* (New Dehli: Sarup & Sons, 2006), 58.

SELFIE 2. A SEPIA VIEW: "I AM A DALIT"

In Indian society, certain categories of people who were not included in the *catur-varna,* the four-fold caste system, are historically known as the *asprisya* (untouchables). There are different theories and views about the origin of the caste system in India, the most popular being the arrival of the fair complexioned āryans on the Indo-Gangetic plains, which marked the beginning of the practice of *varnā* or caste. The āryan settlers not only devised and implemented the four main divisions of people–*brāhmin* (priest), *kshatriya/rājanya* (king/ruler/warrior), *vaisya* (trader) and sūdra (artisan/servant)–but also gave the system strong religious moorings with the introduction of a creation story in the *rigveda,* which today is one of the revealed scriptures of Hinduism. According to this narrative, when divine beings sacrificed the *purusa* (the primal being) diverse categories of people emerged from different parts of this divine being: from his mouth the *brāhmin*; his two arms the *rājanya*; his two thighs the *vaisya* (trader and agriculturist); and from his feet the *sūdra* (servile category). Further, the three upper castes'–the *brāhmins, kshatryias* and *vaisyas,* known as *dvija* (the twice-born)–physical as well as spiritual birth enjoyed the privilege of being adorned with the sacred thread, a religious sign of superior birth and a qualification to learn the sacred *vedas.* The last in the caste hierarchy was the *sūdra,* the servile caste, whose only duty is to serve the above mentioned three upper castes.

While all these four categories fall within the framework of caste in the majority of Hindu religious traditions, there is a large percentage of people who are not only differentiated from the other four castes but whose social status as the lowest of all is underlined. Their segregation and their ritual pollution gradually resulted in their untouchability. Further, Manu, the *brāhmin* law-giver, through the strict imposition of certain rules and regulations, dehumanized the people known as *candālās.* Accordingly, their dwellings were to be located only outside the village proper, they must be made *apapātrās* (ineligible) in every respect, and entitled to own only dogs and donkeys. Their dress should be the garments of the dead and they should only use broken vessels to eat their food. Only ornaments made from black iron are for them and they must continuously wander from place to place. Moreover, they are expected to entertain relationships and transactions only among themselves and marry their equals. If a member of one of the casts wishes to offer them food, then it should be in a broken dish; at night they are prohibited from walking around the villages and towns. However, during the day they may enter the village/town for the purpose of their work. In an attempt to commit psychological genocide, the religiously and numerically dominant upper castes continue to use several derogatory and degrading terms to describe them including: *amānusya* (no-people/non-human); *antyaja* (last caste/exterior castes); *as-prisya/achūta* ((untouchable); *asura/rākshasa* (demon); *avarna* (casteless); *chandāla* (uncivilized); *dāsa/dāsyu* (servant); *mleccha* (locals/natives); *nisāda* (primitive hunting/food-gathering people); *panchama* (fifth caste); *svapāka* (one who cooks the meat of dead animals); etc., and some other modern terms such as scheduled castes (de-notified groups–British Colonial Government); depressed classes (*babasahebambedkar*); *harijan* (children of God–Mahatma Gandhi); and Dalit (the untouchable masses).

In this context the untouchables have chosen an identity for themselves by consciously choosing the term Dalit. Etymologically, the root of Dalit, *dal*, means things or persons that are cut, split, broken or torn asunder, scattered or crushed and destroyed. The term, Dalit reflects the existential reality and never-ending plight of those communities who suffer from caste (social and religious) oppression and the resulting (economic and political) poverty while also signifying the need to revolt against the double oppression of ritual degradation and socioeconomic and political deprivation. For the Dalit Panthers, who popularized the concept of Dalitness, the term Dalit has become symbol of assertive pride and resistance to, as well as the rejection of, the unending oppression perpetrated by caste. Furthermore, it implies change and revolution, rather than remaining perpetually subjugated to caste and its bondage. The term chosen by the Dalits themselves has become a reality reflective identity and, as such, the hallmark of self-respect, self-identity and self-assertion of the untouchable communities and their fighting slogan against the dehumanizing caste oppression. In other words, the term Dalit, identifies upper caste oppressors, who are the cause of dehumanization, and reflects the consciousness of the Dalits' own unfree existence and outcaste experience, which form the basis for a new cultural unity and Dalit ideology as well as a certain militancy. The name Dalit is a symbol of change, confrontation and revolution. However, in spite of this self-respecting chosen identity, they are to a large extent forced to follow and accept the work assigned by the evil caste system.

Three millennia of submissiveness and acceptance of discrimination and dehumanization without raising their voices in protest are the hallmark of Dalits' characteristic behavior. This silent surrender of selfhood resulted in Dalits voluntarily sacrificing their very lives on the altar of their self-respect, self-dignity and self-identity for the benefit of the upper castes, thereby becoming a "non-people." In other words, one can observe the internalization of low self-esteem, confusion of self-identity, self-hate in the very psyche of Dalits that can be summed up in the phrase "wounded psyche." Therefore, the Dalits strongly felt the need to regain their genuine identity that they are robbed and deprived of by the so-called upper castes under the complex and sacrosanct garb of religious teachings, dogmas and doctrines of ritual purity vis-á-vis ritual impurity and the avoidance of ritually impure people to maintain the moral cosmic order.

Selfie 3. A panoramic view: "I am a Christian and a Lutheran"

For a majority of Dalits, Hinduism through its multifaceted shades and dimensions—its philosophical nuances, mythical mysteries, reflections of art and architecture and culture conundrums—conveys an irrevocable message of "accept caste or perish." Thus, the imposed perennial identity of the very existential reality of Dalits as a ritually impure people, the forced acceptance of victimization through unrelenting religious discourse and the determination to seek a spirituality to wriggle out of such hopeless life situations marked the beginning of the Dalits' search for an alternate religion that offers a liberative transformation and a self-emancipating identity that spells out humanization. A majority of Dalits found liberating streams in other religious traditions such as Buddhism, Christianity, Islam and Sikhism. Unlike Hinduism, these religious traditions, with an egalitarian vision reflected in their religious teachings and practices, offered the potential to break down the oppressive structures in society and root out caste distinctions and inequalities.

Today those untouchables, who take pride in calling themselves Dalits and follow religious traditions other than Hinduism, constitute about 16.6 percent of the total Indian population of 1.22 billion. There is no agreement with regard to the actual total population of untouchables as public and private estimates vary between 225 and 250 million. For the present purpose, it might be useful to consider a conservative estimate of 225 million. The figures would be substantially higher if Dalits who embraced non-Hindu religions such as Buddhism, Sikhism, Islam and Christianity were taken into account. The Indian government however considers only those Dalits within the Hindu fold in the population census and ignores all those who embrace other religious traditions. Although estimates vary, of the 2.34 percent of the total Indian population who are Christian, between fifty to eighty percent are of Dalit background.

The gospel of Jesus Christ when planted in the crucible of Indian socio-cultural soil has taken strong roots and blossomed to offer an identity *par excellence* to Dalits. The gospel offered two powerful liberating messages. First, human beings are created in the image of God and hence divine nature is an integral part of their very being; no human being can be declared and treated as ritually impure and thereby untouchable and outcaste. Second, being created in the image of God, all human beings are equal without any hierarchical or horizontal differences. This powerful and double-edged message of the gospel penetrated deeply into the wounded psyche of some of the Dalits who have been looking for a religion that would help and support them in their quest and effort to regain their robbed identity, deprived of self-respect and spiritual enlightenment. As a result, India witnessed mass conversions to Christianity of some groups of the untouchables in search of a new identity and liberation from the oppressive structures of caste. In fact, as it is often said, the history of the Dalit liberation movement is interwoven with the history of the church in India. While Christianity in general offered people the enviable status as the children of God, created in the image of God, Lutheran teachings and doctrines opened up a new understanding of life, through work, witness and worship.

The first Lutheran missionaries to India, whether they were from Halle in Germany or Pennsylvania in the United States, brought with them the life transforming message of the gospel, replete with pietistic undercurrents. Pietism was a reform movement within the Lutheran confessional heritage that engulfed the Lutheran church in Germany and emphasized the need for a practical Christian view and way of life reflecting faith in Jesus Christ. These Lutheran missionaries with a pietistic background gradually led Indian Lutherans not only to strive for spiritual enrichment and religious renewal but also to endeavor becoming aware of social and educational issues. This kind of socioeconomic and religio-spiritual renewal was introduced through the Lutheran teachings of *sola gratia, sola fide, sola scriptura, solus Christus, soli deo gloria, theologia crucis, deus absconditus, coram deo* and the priesthood of all believers, bondage of the will, two kingdoms, etc. This unique, down-to-earth preaching of the gospel offered a transforming identity not only to those who embraced Christianity spread by the Lutheran missionaries and, later, gospel workers. Even today the same transforming identity is reflected in the work and witness of the members of the Lutheran communion in India. This continuously reformative transforming identity is evident and being experienced in the teachings of the Lutheran church in India.

God's work: "Not my merit, but by God's grace"

The church in India exists amidst the plurality of religious philosophies and ideologies and social, cultural, economic and political complexities. As a result of the teachings and doctrines of the majority religion, Hinduism, with its claim of *caturvedas* as *apauruseyas* (not authored by human beings but were of divine creation and revelation) the masses believe the evil practice of caste to be divinely ordained. Thus, the only way of attaining *moksa* (liberation from the unending cycle of births and deaths) from this ritually impure status is in the next birth either through *jnānamārga* (path of knowledge/wisdom) or *bhaktimārga* (path of devotion) or *karmamārga* (path of duty). Following one of these *mārgas* for liberation depends on the religio-spiritual temperament and capability of a person. Since Dalits are ritually impure by birth and not competent enough to choose either the *jnānamārga* or the *bhaktimārga*, the only *mārga* available to them is *karmamārga*, that is performing one's assigned *dharma* in utter obedience and without questioning or complaining. In other words, liberation is only possible through the human effort of performing one's assigned work.

In this context of descent based discrimination, Christianity in general and Lutheranism in particular offered the *triratnās*, the three jewels, *sola gratia, sola scriptura,* and *sola fide*. That is, liberation from every life threatening force is possible through the life sustaining grace of the Creator God alone, through the life giving eternal Word of God alone and through life enriching faith in Jesus Christ rather than through one's own merit and actions. This radically vibrant and dynamic reforming identity of seeking God's friendship and fellowship through work and witness as a practicing Christian rather than depending on one's own assigned work is further infused with a priestly identity to Dalit Christians which hitherto had been considered the sole privilege and prerogative of the *brāhmin*. Dalits seeking that status was anathema to the caste people and a pie in the sky to Dalits themselves.

Priesthood of all believers: "I am privileged to work as a pujāri"

In the caste hierarchy and on its scale of purity/pollution of the four castes, the *brāhmins* not only declared themselves as *bhūdevās* (gods on earth) but also placed themselves at the helm of both the temporal and religious affairs of society, with access to learning and disposition of knowledge as their birth right. Further, to impart the acquired knowledge to deserving pupils from the three upper castes was their privilege. They monopolized the right to command and demand respect, as well as to enjoy unquestioning loyalty, support and service from anyone and everyone. Even the kings were to rule and could only rule by obeying and accepting the guidance of the *brāhmin* priests. Thus the *brāhmins* elevated themselves to the top status in the social and religious hierarchy, both as temporal and spiritual leaders. The ritually impure and polluting people, the Dalits, were denied learning and realizing their religious aspirations by being forbidden to enter temples and holy places as well as the curtailment of seeking religious services from the priests.

Into such a life-context of Dalits, Lutheranism offered a radically new doctrine of the priesthood of all believers, hitherto an unthinkable and unimaginable teaching and concept for Indians in general and Dalits in particular. In "On the Freedom of a Christian," Martin Luther expressed the hope that the term priest would become popular because he believed justified by the grace of God through faith to mean that every Christian believer is a priest. For Luther, God called every human being, irrespective of profession or vocation, according to their gifts to minister unto others–whether one is an untouchable cobbler who works with the skin of dead animals or a woman who periodically becomes polluted with her menstruation or an upper caste intellectual who boast of dispelling the darkness of ignorance of others through their gift of knowledge and wisdom. Every person's vocation is nothing but a call to priesthood, ministering unto others. In this radically new *pujāri* (priestly) work identity, identity, the differences between man and woman, sacred and secular, ritually pure and ritually polluting, caste people and outcaste masses–all these are nailed to the cross of Jesus. As God's child the humun being's *pujāri* status and every individual's human dignity are restored. For Christian Dalits this major step has become an anchor in their moving away from the institutionalized caste suffering. Dignity of labor rather than division of laborers has indeed become a gift for the Dalits.

The Dalit context and the hope and aspirations of the community are reflected in Dalit theology. Martin Luther's theology of the cross offers a powerful vision of God identifying with the cry of the suffering masses and thus Lutheranism stands in solidarity with the Dalits in their quest for humanhood in the midst of their suffering.

The theology of the cross

Dalit theology is a counter theology that challenges the classical Indian Christian theology that employed the philosophical categories of Hinduism. The metaphysical articulations that are rampant in classical Indian Christian theology failed to offer any relief to Dalits. For Dalits, the gospel message of Jesus Christ, with its dynamic and ever flowing liberative streams has become an authentic channel to quench their spiritual thirst. God in Jesus Christ is ever present in the pathos and pain of Dalits, offering them liberation from caste bondage and the accompanied dehumanization. Thus, Dalit theology, a contextual theology from below, is a theology of the Dalits, by the Dalits and for the Dalits. It seeks to be relevant to Dalits based on their existential reality of dalitness, and strives to empower them in their struggle for the restoration of their human dignity, self-respect, equality and liberation, all of which have been denied and robbed by the religiously sanctioned caste discrimination.

Before the emergence of Indian contextual Dalit theology, the Lutheran congregations were exposed to Martin Luther's theology of the cross. Whether acknowledged or not, Luther's theology of the cross provided the much needed impetus to the Dalits' view and way of understanding their new found faith in God and their hope and aspiration of a new tomorrow—not an eschatological idea but a here and now reality and that God is a suffering and liberating God. God in his lowliness, through Jesus Christ on the cross, hears the cries of the suffering and identifies with them. In the theology of cross, the believer understands the church as the people of God, nurturing themselves on the faithfulness of God and sharing their gifts with their neighbor thereby moving into a wider, ecumenical community.

Conclusion: Salvation Not for Sale

For Indians in general and Dalits in particular religion is a vibrant force and for an average religiously oriented Indian, *dharma* is everything—the very basis of social and cultural traditions; the life-regulating spring of ethical values and the provider and sustainer of life-enriching spirituality. With such an understanding, Dalits in India, who have been denied a life-fulfilling religion, have been actively searching for a metaphysical force that can provide authentic human dignity, spiritual potential and moral strength, a force that could empower them effectively to fight caste-infused oppression and the resultant discrimination as well as achieving a holistic liberation and a new and enriching human identity.

The preamble to the Indian constitution declares,

> We, the people of India, having solemnly resolved to constitute India into a Sovereign, Socialist, Secular, Democratic Republic and to secure to all its citizens Justice—social, economic and political; liberty of thought, expression, belief, faith and worship; equality of status and of opportunity; and to promote among them all fraternity assuring the dignity of the individual and the unity and integrity of the Nation.[2]

But the secular credentials of this ancient civilization seem to be a fragile myth. In a culturally and religiously plural country laying firm secular foundations does not happen overnight. It is in the process of development, however, often in faltering steps, during which compromises are being made with religious institutions or beliefs. As a consequence, the practice of caste remains popular and appears to be a never ending story.

Christianity came to India with its gospel of universal love and egalitarian message. Dalits who have embraced Christianity never find a reason to

---

[2] M. V. Pylee, *India's Constitution* (Bombay: Asia Publishing House Ltd., rev. ed., 1967), 51.

renounce this life offering faith, because it firmly remains as a liberating channel to achieve self-dignity and self-esteem by offering various avenues to fight against cast invoked humiliation. Conversion to Christianity has indeed become a boon for Dalits to fulfill their long neglected and deliberately denied human rights, hope and aspirations. Christianity is helping them in their struggle to liberate themselves from the inherited disadvantages of a psychologically ingrained inferiority complex, forcefully imposed economic backwardness, political powerlessness and life-negating religious stigma of ritual pollution.

The gospel message overwhelmingly reflects Jesus' love, healing and compassionate ministries, and his care and concern for the poor, oppressed and outcastes of society, as well as his sacrificial death for the people on the margins. Some groups of Dalits readily identified themselves as subjects and objects of this liberating, life renewing and identity offering message. Along with opening avenues to learn religious truths and to nurture their faith, through the opening and establishing of educational and other allied institutions, technical training schools as well as health care centers and social projects in and around Dalit localities, Christianity has become a force to reckon with. It offers a holistic liberation to the untouchables and a channel to infuse new courage and confidence to challenge and to fight against the caste oriented assigning of dehumanizing and polluting work thereby creating new opportunities to work a giving new meaning of dignity of labor. In other words, the gospel message helps and encourages Dalits to raise their voices in protest and fight against the injustice being perpetrated by the caste system.

In addition, the teachings of the Lutheran church enrich and enhance the identity as well as the work and witness of Dalit Christians. For Dalit Christians Lutheranism has without a doubt offered a new and solid hope of the possibility of change for a new way of life endowed with freedom, self-respect, human dignity and a life renewing and transforming identity. The Lutheran teaching of the three *solas*, especially salvation/liberation through the grace of God, revealed in the Scriptures and offered through faith in Christ Jesus, has also been reflected in a new identity. The priesthood of all believers helps Christianized Dalits to overcome their wounded psyche, ritually-polluted personality and the humiliating experience of being the lowest of the low as untouchables in the socio-religious hierarchy and thus to reach new heights of a healed psyche of their work and witness as priests of God. The ascriptions and appellations of the ritually polluted and untouchables that have been forcefully handed down for over three millennia are now being eroded with the powerful gospel message and the Lutheran teachings of salvation/liberation through the grace of God. Egalitarianism that advocates and emphasizes that every person is created in the image of God is equal and thereby endowed with divine nature and precious in the sight of God. Further, in the theology of the cross Dalits experience a new *ekklesia* and with their interiorization of *koinonia*, new relations of friendship and fellowship are emerging in a visible ecumenism. This new and transformed view and way of life is a result of their understanding of the existential reality of their lives. As a a consequence of their recognition of the liberating presence of God in Jesus Christ in their very lives, they are no more "no-people" but God's people.

With Jesus Christ as their anchor, the gospel message as their firm foundation and the teachings of the Lutheran church as channels refining and continuously redefining and reforming their self-understanding of work and witness, Dalit Lutherans have begun to rewrite their own history and to enjoy and take pride in a transformed and transforming identity as children of God. Christianity and the Lutheran perspective offer this new and unique identity. Thus Dalit Christians in general and Dalit Lutherans in particular are no longer ritually polluted untouchables whose touch and even shadow would pollute others. Rather, they are human beings created in the image of God and hence, ritually pure. Like any other human being Dalits are liberated through the grace of God and called to minister unto others as priests and to initiate a new ecclesia, *koinonia* and a wider ecumenism. Salvation/liberation does not need to be earned through identity tarnishing pre-assigned work. It is God's gift. In other words, salvation/liberation is "not for sale" but offered by God who identifies with the Dalits, suffers with them and nails their suffering to the cross, thus offering a spirituality of humanhood through God's resurrection.

Questions

For an average person, "work" denotes human relations based on power and authority as well as submissiveness and subjugation. Is it true in your local context?

Do you believe that "religion" offers liberative transformation and a self-emancipating identity to those who, because of their traditional occupations, are denied of their self-respect and human dignity?

Do you agree that Luther's Theology of the Cross offers not only an eschatological hope, but also the here and now reality that God hears the cries of the suffering, identifies with the discriminated against and offers a holistic liberation to them?

Freedom of Movement and the Reality of Migrants, Displaced Persons and Refugees—A Theological Dialogue based on Acts 27

Elaine Neuenfeldt

Article 13 of the Universal Declaration of Human Rights reads:

> (1) Everyone has the right to freedom of movement and residence within the borders of each state.
> (2) Everyone has the right to leave any country, including his own, and to return to his country.[1]

In many parts of the world, migration and the forced displacement of people and refugees are components of everyday reality. While these are not new phenomena, people involved in these movements are facing increased vulnerability. The lives of migrants who are seeking a better place to live and of refugees or displaced people fleeing their own countries due to war, conflicts and environmental degradation among other causes are increasingly at risk. The world is shocked by daily news about the tragedies to which these people fall victim:

> In the space of a week, at least 750 migrants are feared to have died crossing the Mediterranean Sea. Many thousands of others have risked their lives this year, fleeing conflict and instability in Africa and the Middle East, in small, often decrepit vessels in an attempt to reach European territories. But the number of

[1] **www.un.org/en/documents/udhr/**

> fatalities has risen dramatically in a matter of months. More than 2,200 lives have been lost since June, the UN refugee agency UNHCR believes. That is because of the big increase in numbers crossing the Mediterranean. While some 60,000 reached European shores in 2013, so far more than 130,000 have arrived in 2014.[2]

> In April 2015, at least five boats carrying almost two thousand migrants to Europe sank in the Mediterranean Sea, with a combined death toll estimated at more than 1,200 people.[3]

In general, poverty, armed conflicts, social and political turmoil and situations related to climate change and/or natural disasters are among the root causes of migration and the forced displacement of people.[4] Nevertheless, it is crucial that we differentiate forced displacement and migration from other international waves of migration that originate "in the social, economic, and political transformation that accompany the expansion of capitalist markets into non-market or pre-market societies."[5] In a global economy,

> [...] international migrants do not come from poor, isolated places that are disconnected from world markets, but from regions and nations that are undergoing rapid changes as a result of their incorporation into global trade, information and production networks.[6]

The reality of the mass movement of people, either forced or freely seeking other places to live, is highly complex. It cannot be analyzed simplistically or by looking at the phenomenon as if it were only a matter of people from poor and so-called less developed countries seeking better life conditions in the so-called more highly developed countries. A critical approach to migration must question the model of society and economic development that produces vulnerability for those who are in movement. What are the dynamics in a society that exposes migrants and people on the move, especially those in forced displacement, to danger?

It is not only leaving home that makes migrants and refugees vulnerable. Arriving at another place also presents a huge challenge. Being a migrant is synonymous with being a stranger.

---

[2] *Mapping Mediterranean Migration*, 15/09/2014, at **www.bbc.com/news/world-europe-24521614**

[3] *Mediterranean Sea Migrant Shipwrecks*, April 2015, at **http://en.wikipedia.org/wiki/April_2015_Mediterranean_Sea_migrant_shipwrecs**

[4] *Root Causes of Migration–Fact Sheet–An Age of Migration: Globalization and the Root Causes of Migration*, at **https://www.weareoneamerica.org/root-causes-migration-fact-sheet**

[5] Douglas Massey, *The Political Economy of Migration in an Era of Globalization*, at **www.ucpress.edu/content/chapters/11307.ch01.pdf**, 26.

[6] Ibid., 27.

> The presence of strangers interferes with the dichotomy between inside and outside; friends and enemies. Enemies stay on the other side of the battle line, but strangers do not maintain the distance. No one knows if they are friends or foes.[7]

Women, gender and migration

When using a gender justice perspective to address the reality of migration and forced displacement, the question of how being on the move affects women and men according to gender roles and cultural expectations must be unfolded.

> According to United Nations data, in 2009 there were 213 million international migrants worldwide, corresponding to 3.1 per cent of the global population. Half of the international stock of migrants is women. The migration of women is gradually shifting from a family reunification trend to a more economically motivated strategy, in which more and more women migrate autonomously to work abroad.[8]

The reality of migration affects women according to the gender roles attributed to them—in the country of origin as well as in the receiving country. On the whole and globally, women are less educated than men, have less access to skills training and, therefore, obtain work that is less qualified and lower salaried. As a result, women are more exposed to vulnerable situations when migrating, which increases the possibility that they may suffer violence and fall prey to human trafficking.

> People's experiences of gender are central to the patterns, causes and impacts of migration. Gender roles, relations and inequalities affect who migrates, how, why, and where they end up. Migration can lead to a greater degree of economic and/or social autonomy for women, and the opportunity to challenge traditional or restrictive gender roles.[9]

Women are normally the caretakers in their families; they assume responsibility for the elderly, children and the sick, which increases their burden in refugee camps and puts them at a disadvantage in relation to men migrants.

---

[7] Alessia Passareli, "Reflecting on Migration in Europe," in *Migration–Migration–Migración*, Student World 07, WSCF (2008), 98.

[8] **www.un.org/womenwatch/feature/trade/Labour-Mobility-and-Gender-Equality-Migration-and-Trade-in-Services.html**

[9] **www.bridge.ids.ac.uk/bridge-publications/cutting-edge-packs/gender-and-migration**

About hopes and boats: Act 27, a Bible text in dialogue with the reality of migrants seeking asylum/refuge in Europe

A boat: This is the place where our dialogue between Bible text and migrants seeking refuge in Europe takes place. The boat is an image that symbolizes migration, especially the current flow of migration to Europe. In every boat, there are dreams, there is hope. Boats full of migrants attempt to cross the Mediterranean Sea, carrying people who are seeking a better life, fleeing from conflict, pursuing that tiny glimmer of hope on the horizon.

The biblical narrative of Paul sailing to Rome as a prisoner and the many events in his voyage, described in Act 27–28 will be our text in dialogue with the experiences of migration today.

Routes and geographies

As we "sail" through the biblical text, we can easily identify elements that connect with the realities of migrants and refugees, especially those who even now are attempting to cross the Mediterranean. An itinerary of fear and danger in troubled waters is described in the story. When you are trapped in a boat in the middle of a vast ocean, facing storms and harsh winds, risk and vulnerability are the only reality.

The text describes how Paul and the other persons in his boat reacted to these moments. There are conflictual situations that need to be addressed; each of the characters in the story reacts in a different way according to their own understanding and context. The narrative uses geographically detailed information to describe the journey. Yet places and cities seem to be not only physical spaces where the boat is anchoring, but also geopolitical places with a crucial role in the story.

The conflict–in the middle of the storm (Acts 27:13-26)

> As day was about to dawn, Paul urged them all to take some food, saying, "Today is the fourteenth day that you have continued in suspense and without food, having taken nothing. Therefore I urge you to take some food; it will give you strength, since not a hair is to perish from the head of any of you."

Being a refugee or a migrant normally implies a condition of vulnerability and instability due to the rootlessness of the person in that situation. Today, the normative framework of moral obligations is still based on a fixed and limited notion of territory and borders. It is governed by an institutional and exclusionary notion of sovereignty constructed and at the same time shaping a political discourse of "insiders" and "outsiders." Solidarity and hospitality are hardly part of this political vocabulary.[10]

Theology as well as churches' and Faith-based Organizations' practices and discourse can therefore play a key role in changing this concept of sovereignty. The churches' diaconal work is based on the notion of hospitality and solidarity.[11]

Engaging in a journey where one is liberated by God's grace, and affirming that salvation, human beings or creation are not for sale, the narrative of Acts 27 gives us a scenario in a boat that reproduces the larger context of the Roman Empire.

The empire's whole reality is reproduced in this boat: there are soldiers and the centurion, prisoners, sailors, workers and wheat.

What is the wheat doing in this boat? Where is it coming from? The text does not tell us, but as the boat is carrying prisoners and heading to Rome, the wheat supplying the city, was probably collected as tax in kind from the provinces and is the product of an oppressive system of taxation.

I would like to propose that in the context of a journey where life is not for sale, we learn from the biblical narrative how conflicts can provoke different reactions. It is possible to deal with conflictual moments in different ways; the approach will depend a lot on where you stand. Where your feet are will provide the direction for dealing with such situations.

What are the alternatives? What are the possible actions? (Acts 27: 21–22)

> As they had been long without food, Paul then came forward among them and said, "Men, you should have listened to me, and should not have set sail from Crete and incurred this injury and loss. I now bid you take heart; for there will be no loss of life among you, but only of the ship.

[10] Edward Newman, "Refugees, International Security and Human Vulnerability: Introduction and survey," in Edward Newman and Joanne van Selm (eds.), *Refugees and Forced Displacement. International Security, Human Vulnerability, and the State* (Tokyo/New York/Paris, United Nations University Press, 2003), 9 (sample chapter at **http://unu.edu/publications/books/refugees-and-forced-displacement-international-security-human-vulnerability-and-the-state.html#overview**).

[11] Cf. *Welcoming the Stranger: Affirmations for Faith Leaders* (Geneva: The Lutheran World Federation, 2013), at **https://www.lutheranworld.org/content/resource-welcoming-stranger**; Kjell Nordstokke (ed.), *Diakonia in Context | Transformation, Reconciliation, Empowerment* (Geneva: The Lutheran World Federation, 2009), at **https://www.lutheranworld.org/content/resource-diakonia-context-transformation-reconciliation-empowerment**

It seems that the boat is pursuing its journey in a particular but normal life situation until the storm breaks down this normality. The storm is like a button that switches on the conflict. The storm is not the conflict in itself, but a crisis that opens up the problem and requires that all in the boat take some action.

A closer look at the action taken by each person or group in this moment of crisis gives us some elements with which to analyze their different conflict resolution approaches.

The very fearful moment of the shipwreck provokes some—expected or unexpected—actions by the boat's passengers. Let us analyze these:

Paul implored them all to take food (Acts 27: 33-34)

> As day was about to dawn, Paul urged them all to take some food, saying, "Today is the fourteenth day that you have continued in suspense and without food, having taken nothing. Therefore I urge you to take some food; it will give you strength, since not a hair is to perish from the head of any of you." And when he had said this, he took bread, and giving thanks to God in the presence of all he broke it and began to eat

What does an invitation to eat together at this very inopportune moment mean? Who would want to eat when their boat is struggling to stay afloat, battered by powerful waves? What kind of proposal is this? "I urge you to take some food; it will give you strength, since not a hair is to perish from the head of any of you"—as if he were foreseeing more trouble.

Then, they were all encouraged (Acts 27: 36)

> Then they all were encouraged and ate some food themselves

The text develops similarities with the gospel narrative of feeding the multitude (Mt 14.13-21; 15.32-39); the ritual of breaking the bread, giving thanks and eating it is very similar to what happens at the institution of the Lord's Supper (1 Co 11.23).

But still, why eat in such a situation? The storm was still a danger and the boat was still being tossed about. Eating could make the passengers sick. Why the insistence on eating together?

Looking at the social relations between those who share bread, who eat together, might help to provide an answer to this question. The ritual created around food creates community, communion. The word "companion" carries in its Latin root the notion of "eating bread with"—con-pan. In other words, those who eat bread together become partners. Bread creates connectivity, relations, commitment. Sitting together, sharing bread or food creates alliances, connections. Would it be this connectivity that produces the solidarity that Paul is trying to provoke?

Can we not see the action of eating food together as giving the boat passengers the strength to decide on the next step? Indeed it was a dangerous action: they took a decision on what needs to be saved. Their action represents in practice what we affirm today: that human beings, human lives, are more important than material goods or wealth. Human beings are not for sale.

This biblical narrative provides the foundation on which to build what from a Latin American theological perspective is described as the collective memory of the passion and resurrection—the memory of God's solidarity with humankind. It is sharing bread and wine in friendship.

> Only the celebration of life and justice as a gift for all can bring one into a communion of equals. At the communion table, there is no place for the logic of exclusion. [...]. It is possible to celebrate the festival of Communion even if one's life is in danger, because in justification, the place of sorrow and lament gives way to confidence in God as a friend with whom one lives in solidarity.[12]

Eating bread in the midst of sorrow and fear has the symbolic power to bind those sharing the circle of bread and solidarity together. They are in the same boat. They need to seek solutions for their problems together. The solution will come as a collective act of survival. But not all bring the same experience to the situation. Their reactions to fear and their survival needs are connected to their own life experiences. Their decisions on what to value and what to preserve are very much associated with the context from which they come and are related.

What to carry? What to throw away? Not for sale (Acts 27:38)

> And when they had eaten enough, they lightened the ship, throwing out the wheat into the sea

Throwing food away? Why? What was the economic, social, symbolic value of this wheat? Considering that the boat was carrying prisoners and products to Rome, the wheat was probably a feature of the Roman tax collection system. It was food, but not for people's consumption. It was not intended to ensure food sovereignty; it was not an autonomous and collective system of food for all with justice. Rather, it served to guarantee the food security system of the Empire. The food that satisfied hunger was already shared.

[12] Elsa Tamez, *The Amnesty of Grace. Justification by Faith from a Latin American Perspective* (Nashville: Abingdon Press, 1993), 139.

This wheat was not meant to satisfy the people's hunger but the greed of the Empire. Therefore, in evaluating what was to be saved in the midst of the storm after having shared bread together, they could throw away the wheat.

Acts 27: 42

> The soldiers' plan was to kill the prisoners, lest any should swim away and escape.

It is difficult to overthrow a system that creates privileges and instills in some groups the belief that they must uphold the system by keeping order. The soldiers' solution for saving the boat comes from their world vision in which the lives of prisoners do not count, have no value, can be thrown away.

Acts 27:43

> [...] but the centurion, wishing to save Paul, kept them from carrying out their purpose. He ordered those who could swim to throw themselves overboard first and make for the land.

At the beginning of the story, we learned that the centurion was kind to Paul. Some kind of solidarity was already established. For the centurion, the solution was that each passenger would take responsibility for themselves, because everyone is capable of ensuring their own survival.

Acts 28:1

> After we had escaped, we then learned that the island was called Malta.

It could also have been Lampedusa, and so many other islands in the Mediterranean where migrants seek refuge today.

Acts 28:2

> And the natives showed us unusual kindness, for they kindled a fire and welcomed us all, because it had begun to rain and was cold.

Movements in the globalized market economy—sharing as counteracting a "for sale" culture

A society that is based on a capitalist market economy produces a radical rupture between humanity and nature. This has tremendous consequences for human relations, that are fragmented and transformed into commodities. People are not important because they are human beings with dignity, but because they are consumers; they have value due to their power to buy and possess. The most sacred principle of the market is that the biggest buyers are the winners.[13]

According to the perceptions that this system creates, the ones who buy and possess more are "worth" more. An economic system that is regulated by a capitalist and globalized market thus has an impact on people's values. Material status symbols have special importance not only in wealthy countries, but also in countries with little economic power.

This market economy model is oriented and moved by and through the desire—this is the "spirit" of capitalism—to consume and, especially, to ostentatiously show what is consumed; the power to consume is often equated with divine blessing; prosperity is understood as a sign of "salvation." To understand and critique this idolatrous construct[14]—the neoliberal market-oriented economic system—we need to bring in religious grammar. In a setting where buying and consumerism are highly valued, it is difficult to agree to live with less. Yet, as long as there is no readiness among the wealthy[15]at an individual as well as a collective level[16]to live with less, it will be hard to bring about a peaceful and more just coexistence in today's world.

Faith, religion and spiritual practices are fundamental territories to be taken into account in a critique of an economic system built on exclusion and oppression. In a system characterized by displacement or mobility and individualism, a faith that provides a feeling of belonging, recognition and participation is highly relevant.[17]

> Another important point that theology can and must contribute to the discussion of economic injustice is to show and strengthen the spiritual dimension of ethical indignation. Christian theology should be a critical reflection of the spiritual experience of finding and following the crucified and risen Jesus in the world

[13] B. Herry-Priyono, "Re-emebedding the Economy for the Common Good," in Martin L. Sinaga (ed.), *A Common Word. Buddhists and Christians Engage Structural Greed* (Geneva/Minneapolis: The Lutheran World Federation (Lutheran University Press, 2012), 53, and available at **www.lutheranworld.org/sites/default/files/DTS-Studies-201201-A_Common_Word_sm.pdf**.

[14] Jung Mo Sung, "Ethical Indignation and Economic Injustice," text presented at the seminar "Redeeming the Market: Theological Contributions to an Alternative Economics," John Knox Centre, Geneva, 31 May–1 June 2013.

[15] Ibid.

[16] Ibid.

[17] Harvey Cox, *The Market as God*, at **www.theatlantic.com/magazine/archive/1999/03/the-market-as-god/306397/**

> today. The spirituality that the world needs today is a spirituality that is born of and lived in conjunction with ethical indignation against injustice. Therefore, it is a spirituality that leads people to be concerned with economic and social issues and to fight within their means for a fairer society.[18]

Justification, justice and human dignity

As a communion on the move, on a pilgrimage, we journey together toward life in all its fullness. We pray for God's guidance and inspiration so that our pilgrimage will open us to one another through dynamic and creative interaction for justice.

Justification by faith alone radicalizes respect for human dignity by attributing it to God's free will and not to a market of meritocracy that all too frequently drives society. Justification, in that sense, means liberation from anxieties and self-condemnation.

> The revelation of the justice of God and its realization in justification proclaim and bring about the good news of the right to life for all people. The life granted in justification is recognized as an inalienable gift, because it proceeds from the solidarity of God, in Jesus Christ, with those who are excluded. Such a life of dignity makes human beings subjects of their own history. God "justifies" (make and declares just) the human being in order to transform the unjust world that excludes, kills, and dehumanizes that same human being.[19]

Questions

How can the biblical narratives be a light in our journey that affirms that salvation is not for sale?

What do we learn from the biblical story?

What do we learn about solidarity and welcoming migrants and refugees?

---

[18] Sung, op. cit. (note 14).

[19] Tamez, op. cit. (note 12), 14.

The Catholic Doctrine of Justification in the Ecumenical Context

Wolfgang Thönissen

After centuries of theological disputes, the middle of the twentieth century was marked by the beginning of a search for an ecumenical understanding in disputes dating back to the Reformation. At the center of these common efforts lay the core concern of the Reformation itself: the doctrine of justification. With his book on Karl Barth, published in the early 1950s, the Swiss Catholic theologian, Hans Urs von Balthasar, already made a contribution to a common understanding of the doctrine of grace. Efforts to bring about ecumenical agreement were advanced even further by Hans Küng's book on "Justification," which dealt with Karl Barth's justification theology. The work of Otto Hermann Pesch, a Catholic researcher, on the justification theology of Martin Luther and Thomas Aquinas has been of particular importance to the ecumenical dialogue on the issue of justification. The bilateral Lutheran-Catholic dialogue on justification since the late 1960s has also contributed greatly to a common understanding. One particular German study with the title *The Condemnations of the Reformation Era: Do They Still Divide?*,[1] which delves into the traditional doctrinal differences, deserves particular mention in this regard. The *Joint Declaration on the Doctrine of Justification* (*JDDJ*) of 31 October 1999,[2] together adopted by the Lutheran World Federation and the Roman Catholic Church, can therefore rightly be viewed as the product of decades of theological work on the doctrine of justification. These

[1] Karl Lehmann and Wolfhart Pannenberg (eds), *The Condemnations of the Reformation Era: Do They Still Divide?* (Minneapolis: Fortress, 1990).
[2] *Joint Declaration on the Doctrine of Justification* (Grand Rapids, Michigan/Cambridge, UK: William B. Eerdmans Publishing Company, 2000).

ecumenical understandings would not, however, have been possible without the renewal and deepening of the Catholic doctrine of grace and justification that was encouraged by the Second Vatican Council. This doctrine upholds the proprium of Catholic theology within an ecumenical understanding.

Dealing with the controversies of the Reformation era

From very early on, the dispute over Martin Luther's theology focused on the understanding of justification. This began with Luther's new view on the sacrament of penance. Today, we are better able to see how Luther's objection did not aim at doing away with the sacrament. Luther's main issue was instead: How are we able to have our sins forgiven? From the theology of his time, Luther would have heard that God forgives people their sins when they repent of their sins in a sincere act of love. It was the task of the priests to declare and to indicate through absolution the forgiveness of sins, a forgiveness that had already occurred through full repentance. The forgiveness of sins was therefore an effect of repentance. Here we can identify the nominalist theory that God does not deny God's grace to those who do what they are capable of doing. The justification of sinners would thus appear to be a consequence of people's repentance, which, itself indeed a gift of God, is already performed in the forgiveness of sins. In his intensive work on late medieval repentance doctrine, Luther began to understand that repentance, conversely, is anchored in a promise of God that people take on and embrace in their faith. Luther was influenced considerably in this by Bernhard of Clairvaux, and through him, by Augustine. Faith is the sole suitable response to God's promise in God's Word. Justification occurs only through grace in faith in the saving acts of Jesus Christ.

While the Lutheran and Catholic views did in fact converge significantly in the sixteenth century, Catholic theologians found Luther's views to be unsettling, criticizing him for denying the personal responsibility of people for their actions. The Council of Trent (1545–1563) therefore stressed the responsibility of individuals and people's ability to participate in God's grace. Those who are justified are to be involved in the unfolding of grace in their lives.[3] The Council of Trent expressed clearly that people cannot be justified through their works or due to their own nature without God's

[3] *From Conflict to Communion: Lutheran-Catholic Common Commemoration of the Reformation in 2017*, Report of the Lutheran–Roman Catholic Commission on Unity (Leipzig/Paderborn: Evangelische Verlagsanstalt GmbH/Bonifatius Gmbh Druck-Buch-Verlag, 2013).

grace. The only source of our justification is God's righteousness, through which he makes us righteous. The Council also stressed, however, that while neither faith nor works could earn anyone their justification, people do participate through their free will and consent to prepare themselves to receive the grace of justification and to multiply this grace through good works. With the forgiveness of sin, people receive virtues that are poured out through grace: faith, love and hope.

The dispute over these issues escalated once and for all when Luther and the other Reformers began to declare the justification doctrine to be the "first and chief article" and "guide and judge over all parts of Christian doctrine." "That is why a division on this point was so grave and the work to overcome this division became a matter of highest priority for Catholic-Lutheran relations."[4] This controversy would become the object of extensive research on the part of individual theologians and numerous national and international Lutheran-Catholic dialogues in the second half of the twentieth century. The results of these studies and dialogues were ultimately taken into account in the *JDDJ* by the Roman Catholic Church and the Lutheran World Federation.

Justification—the central salvation event in the faith of the Church

The understanding of faith and justification has developed considerably with Catholic theology in the course of the past decades. The Second Vatican Council (1962–1965) constituted a major demarcation point in this development. The Council made it possible to embark on a new direction in the classical doctrine of grace and justification, which had been shaped by the Council of Trent for several centuries. The central concern of Catholic theology can subsequently be seen in terms of forms of grace doctrine tied to salvation history and to personal dialogue. Justification appears here as the center and pinnacle of the event of grace. The decisive statement on Catholic justification doctrine can be found in the following passage of the church constitution *Lumen Gentium* (*LG*):

> The followers of Christ are called by God, not because of their works, but according to His own purpose and grace. They are justified in the Lord Jesus, because in the baptism of faith they truly become sons of God and sharers in the divine nature.

---

[4] Ibid., para 122.

> In this way they are really made holy. Then too, by God's gift, they must hold on to and complete in their lives this holiness they have received.[5]

While the Second Vatican Council did not present a revised doctrine of justification in contrast to the Council of Trent, the new orientation with regard to the central event of justification is easily recognizable. This central message can be broken down into a number of parts:

Christ alone is holy

This central Christological point unfolds within the context of ecclesiology, and particularly here in connection with the chapter on the universal call to holiness in the church. The main point of this section is that Christ is the one who sanctifies the church as a whole and who calls it to holiness. Christ delivered himself up for his people in order to sanctify them. Christ is the only way to salvation. In this context, the universal call to holiness means that it is not a matter of moral perfection or ethical heroism, and that people do not attain sanctification in such a way, but the ground for sanctification is the holiness, which is God, that is granted to the saved without their having earned it. God's will for reconciliation forms the basis for the grace of sanctification that Christ grants in his death and resurrection. The fullness of grace is Christ himself. Grace is unconditionally connected to Christ's act of reconciliation. The *JDDJ* therefore has it right in that: "Through Christ alone are we justified, when we receive this salvation in faith."[6] All assertions on the doctrine of grace and justification hinge upon this clear central Christological point.

Grace is God's eternal design, God's universal will for salvation that God extends to the individual

As we read in the Dogmatic Constitution on Divine Revelation *Dei Verbum* (*DV*),[7] the invisible God speaks to the people out of the abundance of God's love. God wishes for people's salvation, the forgiveness of sins and people's renewal. God alone is the gracious source of the will for salvation. Grace is God in God's will for salvation, which God communicates to the people. Grace is the merciful and loving leaning toward sinful people of God in

---

[5] *Lumen Gentium* at **www.vatican.va/archive/hist_councils/ii_vatican_council/documents/vat-ii_const_19641121_lumen-gentium_en.html** , para. 40.

[6] Op. cit. (note 2), 16.

[7] *Dei Verbum at www.vatican.va/archive/hist_councils/ii_vatican_council/documents/vat-ii_const_19651118_dei-verbum_en.html* , 2.

Christ. While a distinction does emerge here between grace and justification, it must be mentioned that grace, in accordance with classical Catholic doctrine, is always to be understood as a gift. This gift can, however, never be separated from the giver: Grace can never be separated and made independent of God. God acts from grace for the sake of human salvation. This inclination of God toward people is focused on the individual, whom God speaks to as God's addressee. Fully within the context of this Catholic understanding, the *JDDJ* states:

> This new personal relation to God is grounded totally on God's graciousness and remains constantly dependent on the salvific and creative working of this gracious God [...]. Thus justifying grace never becomes a human possession to which one could appeal over against God.[8]

Justification takes place through faith in Baptism

In the classical language of Catholic theology, this is a matter of justifying grace, which acts to sanctify people. This revolves around the event of justification itself, i.e., the forgiveness of sins that occurs in Christ's act of redemption, and the ensuing transportation into a state of salvific grace, which is more simply called here–in contrast to the classical language of grace doctrine–simple sanctification. What is meant here is that sanctification is a gift. It aims at participation in God's nature and essence. Faith and baptism are instrumental causes to this end. Baptism is clearly the sacrament of faith and not a human achievement. Faith and baptism refer back to God's word: "those who believe in Christ [...] are reborn [...] through the word of the living God (cf. 1 Pet. 1:23) [...] from water and the Holy Spirit."[9] Baptism is a confession of faith. Baptism is indeed geared toward growth in faith. Catholic theology, in this vein, speaks of an increase of grace in faith, which is to say to keep God's grace and allow it to unfold in our lives. In the context of a Catholic understanding, the *JDDJ* states: "Persons are justified through baptism as hearers of the word and believers in it."[10]

Faith is a personal decision

The *DV* has as its central statement here: "The obedience of faith is to be given to God who reveals."[11] This is a matter of emphasizing the holistic character

[8] Op. cit. (note 3), 27.
[9] Op. cit. (note 5), 9.
[10] Op. cit. (note 2), 5.
[11] Op. cit. (note 7), 5.

of faith. The text itself points here to the biblical idea of bringing about the "obedience of faith" (Rom 16:26; 1:5). Obedience is a term from the language of the early mission, describing conversion as submission to the gospel. Obedience and faith run parallel to one another, and it is not the message of faith but the performance of faith that is primary here. Obedience of faith refers to Christ's revelation and entails the reception of the message of salvation. The short text in *DV* is, of course, part of the tradition of church doctrine, in which faith represents agreement with the truths of faith set down by the church. The connection cannot be dismantled here:

> But the Catholic Church professes that this faith, [...] is a supernatural virtue by which we, with the aid and inspiration of the grace of God, believe that the things revealed by Him are true.[12]

Dei Verbum then applies this understanding to the new understanding of revelation, placing the main focus on the performance of faith, without eliminating tradition. The response of faith to God's revelation of Godself is thus not chiefly or solely an agreement with the articles of faith, but an opening up to God himself.

> To make this act of faith, the grace of God and the interior help of the Holy Spirit must precede and assist, moving the heart and turning it to God, opening the eyes of the mind and giving "joy and ease to everyone in assenting to the truth and believing it."[13]

Faith is thus a matter of personal dedication, carried out in love. Faith is our personal "yes" to God. In the *JDDJ* we read to this end that "to have faith is to entrust oneself totally to God."[14] The acceptance of the truths of revelation is incorporated into this faith. Again, we see here the newly established relationship between God's Word and faith: The Word of God is God's power for the salvation of all who believe. The proclamation of the gospel is geared toward the sparking of faith in Jesus, the Christ. Faith in Christ is nourished by the Word.

---

[12] First Vatican Council, *Dogmatic Constitution on the Catholic Faith, Dei Filius*, at **http://inters.org/Vatican-Council-I-Dei-Filius**, chapter 3.
[13] Op. cit. (note 7), 5.
[14] Op. cit. (note 2), 36.

Faith becomes effective through love

"Thus it is evident to everyone, that all the faithful of Christ of whatever rank or status, are called to the fullness of the Christian life and to the perfection of charity."[15] Faith precedes love, and only in love does faith become effective. "Every person must walk unhesitatingly according to his own personal gifts and duties in the path of living faith, which arouses hope and works through charity."[16] Love is thus not a human contribution to the work of redemption but a form of God's justifying grace itself. In the interplay between divine grace and human participation, God's grace is always given primacy. Love is itself a gift of God that takes on form in human beings. If people "receive all things with faith from the hand of their heavenly Father,"[17] they proclaim their love in this way. Understood this way, Catholic theology can speak of cooperation with God's will. But the relationship between cause and effect remains preserved here: God is love, God pours out God's love into our hearts through the Holy Spirit. Every person of faith must be willing to hear God's Word so that love can grow like a seed. Love is closely connected to justification in faith. The *JDDJ* explains the Catholic distinction in terms of the forgiving grace of God always being connected to the gift of a new life that is evidenced in active love with the involvement of the Holy Spirit. Love is received and realized through faith. This is why each person of faith must be willing to hear God's Word. Faith therefore comes first and provides the foundations. Love is then a subsequent way of expressing faith. It is through this gift of love that people can themselves live as justified and redeemed. God's love enables them to love God more than everything and to love their neighbors. As we read in the *JDDJ*:

> According to Catholic understanding, good works, made possible by grace and the working of the Holy Spirit, contribute to growth in grace, so that the righteousness that comes from God is preserved and communion with Christ is deepened.[18]

How can we speak here of cooperation? From a Catholic understanding, faith is an act of surrender and of faith, which also incorporates human reason and will. Faith results from God's grace. The human response, even as a gift of God itself, remains a movement toward God and personal consent, while not, however, constituting human action by means of one's

---

[15] Op. cit (note 5), 40.
[16] Ibid., 41.
[17] Ibid., 41.
[18] Op. cit. (note 4), 38.

own powers. The cited council texts speak in clear terms of personal consent. This is an act of the Holy Spirit that moves people's hearts to turn to God, and which opens the eyes of the mind: "God constantly brings faith to completion by His gifts."[19]

The communion that comes into being through participation in God is the consequence of God's justifying action

This is the goal of the event of justification, and this is why the church constitution places the topic of justification in the realm of ecclesiology. People's personal beliefs can only be completed in the community, as the justified are incorporated into the body of Christ. The basic idea that community arises through participation in Jesus Christ only unfolds of course in the context of the sacrament of the Eucharist. Through the Eucharist, the justified faithful gather together in communion with Christ and with each other. An ecclesiology of communion needs to be developed in this connection. Church is the community of justified sinners. The *JDDJ* puts it as follows: "Our consensus in basic truths of the doctrine of justification must come to influence the life and teachings of our churches."[20]

A short summary of Catholic justification theology

The theology of justification represents a key to the gospel of Jesus Christ. Righteousness is a term central to Holy Scripture, and as such it aims at a salvific relationship of God with people. God's love realizes God's all-encompassing will for salvation through Jesus Christ in the power of the Holy Spirit. The message of justification lends expression to the unconditional acceptance of people through God's grace. It is faith in Christ that brings about and forms the basis of full participation in God's act of revelation. This message is universal and is addressed to all, as all are called to communion with God. Faith in Christ's act of salvation can, however, only truly be lived in the communion of the church. The full need for God's grace and justification can be seen in people's inability to reestablish their broken communion with God. The church is thus a sign and instrument in Jesus Christ's work of salvation, and leads people to the kingdom of God. As a standard and measure of Christian faith, the doctrine of justification brings to the fore the gift nature of the Christian faith. This has consequences for the proclamation, doctrine and pastoral work of the church. While people

[19] Op. cit. (note 7), 5.
[20] Op. cit. (note 2), 43.

are justified without the works of the law, faith always involves human activity as well. Faith in Christ encourages and enables us to perform good works, carried out in love and hope.

A consensus in the basic truths of the doctrine of justification

The *JDDJ's* consensus in basic truths of the doctrine of justification is expressed thus: "By grace alone, in faith in Christ's saving work and not because of any merit on our part, we are accepted by God and receive the Holy Spirit, who renews our hearts while equipping and calling us to good works."[21] The expression "by grace alone" is, moreover, explained in that "the message of justification [...] tells us that as sinners our new life is solely due to the forgiving and renewing mercy that God imparts as a gift and we receive in faith, and never can merit in any way."[22] Only within this framework can the limits and dignity of human freedom be established. The expression "by grace alone" is interpreted to mean that people "depend completely on the saving grace of God for their salvation. The freedom they possess in relation to persons and the things of this world is no freedom in relation to salvation."[23] With regard to salvation, the relationship of cause and effect between righteousness and God's grace, justification and sanctification, are therefore clearly established. It is only within this God-given order that the freedom and participation of people can be suitably determined. The basic consensus established here includes the understanding that the denunciations once leveled at the doctrines of other confessions have lost their validity. This is a consensus in basic truths that allows for different concerns and accentuations. The sixteenth-century dispute has thus come to an end. The reasons to denounce one another are no more.

Questions

What in Luther's theology of justification do Catholic theologians find somewhat confusing and irritating?

How does Catholic theology comprehend the faith in justification that has already taken place in God?

[21] Ibid., 15.
[22] Ibid., 17.
[23] Ibid., 19.

Wherein lies the basic consensus between Lutheran and Catholic teaching on the doctrine of justification?

Bible Study: Ephesians 2:4–10

Cristina Grenholm

Martin Luther firmly believed that the liberating message of the gospel cannot be delivered only once but, rather, that it needs to be repeated. There are two reasons for this.

First, it can never be fully grasped. The dominating logic of life seems to be that one needs to work, strive and make constant efforts. Life has a tendency to hide the profound insights of the gospel. Life is always a gift that nobody can earn by working hard. Life is not the result of how much energy you put into it. This is not to say that our efforts cannot make the world a better place—that is indeed our calling. However, at the end of the day, whatever has been achieved has nevertheless not been done by us. It may have been developed by us and we may have helped people and plants to flourish but everything is actually given to us. This is a constant surprise and a great consolation. It is God who makes our days. Life is given to us and to the whole of creation by grace.

The second reason is that we not only strive, but we also constantly fail. We do not achieve what we intended to achieve, or what we sensed we were urged to do. Sometimes this is due to our own failures, and sometimes it is due to the structures that rule our world. We need to be forgiven over and over again. We need to be lifted up from a state of resignation when we are faced with all the things we cannot change.

Salvation is not for sale. Thus, we cannot buy it with any kind of currency—be it money or blood, sweat and tears. Salvation is not achieved through physical or spiritual effort, by observing strategic priorities, or attending inspiring conferences. Salvation is not for sale. Cost-benefit models do not apply. The give-and-take mechanism is irrelevant. It is based on a give-and-receive model, and we are always at the receiving end. Salvation is not for sale. It is given away.

The message needs to be repeated, but how should this be done? Should we always try to remember the words? No, the message of the gift of salvation itself needs to be given as a gift from one person to another. It is not the type of information that needs to be kept in mind. It is a reply to a need, an answer to a question, a whisper to someone who is unable to express their need. The gospel always comes as a surprise—it is always unexpected. Therefore, the need might not yet have been articulated, the question may not yet have been posed and those who cannot express their need may not yet have begun to long for a whisper from somebody else.

It is part of our calling as baptized disciples of Christ, of our shared priesthood, that we look for the moments when the gospel needs to be articulated. Salvation is not for sale—it is part of a constant flow of God's love that cannot be stopped, not even by death. There is hope, light and a new beginning for everyone in need and we are sent to one another as preachers of this liberating grace. We need to study the biblical texts that give us this message and pray that it will help us to become instruments of God's grace. The good news cannot be bought or sold—it needs to be expressed and shared.

Let us therefore turn to one of the central texts of grace: Ephesians 2:4-10

> But God, who is rich in mercy, out of the great love with which He loved us even when we were dead through our trespasses, made us alive together with Christ—by grace you have been saved—and raised us up with Him and seated us with Him in the heavenly places in Christ Jesus, so that in the ages to come He might show the immeasurable riches of His grace in kindness towards us in Christ Jesus. For by grace you have been saved through faith, and this is not your own doing; it is the gift of God—not the result of works, so that no one may boast. For we are what He has made us, created in Christ Jesus for good works, which God prepared beforehand to be our way of life.

A Bible study in three steps

This text is filled with words that are cherished in our tradition: mercy, love, life, grace, gift. In this Bible study we shall take as one of our starting points the conviction of the Reformers: that God speaks to each and every one of us. We are all approached by God. God does not direct Godself to experts only. We each have something to share with others. We are constant receivers of mercy, love, life and grace. Each and every one of us has been struck by this insight at crucial moments, although we may not have reflected on it in this way. Each and every one of us has been in desperate need of God's gifts, but may have been unable to express that need. Everybody can recall some occasion when the light returned or the burden was lifted off. We may also remember who or what the instrument was by means of which this happened. Let us make the word become flesh by sharing this with one another.

Start by reading the text aloud together. You may sit in a circle and read one verse each. Let the word circulate several times and listen to the text two or three times. Or let different voices read it once. Then take a few minutes to allow everybody to choose their key word with which to open the text. Let each person be guided by their inner self. There is no "correct" key word. One person may choose a word that has been important to them for a long time. Another may choose a word that stood out in the readings. Yet somebody else may just pick a word at random.

When everybody has identified their key word, share them with one another. If you are a small group, the whole group can listen to the individual choices and get a brief description of why each person chose that particular word. Be careful not to judge the choices. Listen to one another. If you are a larger group, you may want to share in groups of four or five. You may experience that the biblical text is expanded and broadened in your group. There are so many different words with which to open a text–it can be approached from many different angles.

Go back to silence and let your own key word guide you through the text. What does this key word open up? What is it that becomes problematic or difficult? Those who prefer to write something down may do so. You need to allow for an atmosphere of reflective tranquility but you should not make the time for contemplation demanding or stressful. Three minutes will be enough in most cases.

Now, let everybody talk to the person next to them and relate their findings to one another in pairs. If you have time, share what the story that you were told by the other person made you see or think.

Finally, it is time to approach the big issues of the day. Try Google search, look for international news, or find another way of bringing the world to your Bible study. Agree on something that challenges, provokes or calls you to action. The world is not only a market where things are bought and sold. Salvation in all its dimensions of liberation, forgiveness and empowerment is constantly given away, but there is also much in this world that prevents grace from flowing. Equally, that is precisely why salvation is needed.

Add the big issue of the day that you agreed upon to the key word and the text. It is possible that going back to individual reflection is not the easiest and most fruitful way of doing this. Instead, return to the pairings whereby people guided each other through the text by means of their individually chosen key words. Now, let everybody share what the triangle of text, key word and pressing issue of the day that the other person raised revealed.

Close your Bible study by sharing some of the things you discovered with the whole group. Just one phrase from the participants will provide you with a rich range of expressions of God's salvation that is never for sale, but constantly resonates in our lives.

List of contributors

Busi, Suneel Bhanu, Rev. Prof. Dr, Bishop emer., Andhra Evangelical Lutheran Church, Dean of the Department of Research and Doctoral Studies, Gurukul Lutheran Theological College and Research Institute, India

Grenholm, Cristina, Rev. Dr, Secretary for the Church, Church of Sweden Central Office, Sweden

Hinlicky Wilson, Sarah, Prof. Dr, Assistant Research Professor, Institute for Ecumenical Research in Strasbourg, France

Lahe, Jaan, Rev. Dr, Associate Professor of Religious Studies, Tallinn University, Estonia

Moyo, Chiropafadzo, Dr, Dean of Martin Luther Deanery and Director of Lutheran House of Studies, Evangelical Lutheran Church in Zimbabwe, Zimbabwe

Neuenfeld, Elaine, Rev. Dr, Secretary for Women in Church and Society, Lutheran World Federation, Geneva, Switzerland,

Oberdorfer, Bernd, Prof. Dr, Professor of Systematic Theology, University of Augsburg, Germany

Thönissen, Wolfgang, Prof. Dr, Director, Roman Catholic Johann-Adam-Möhler-Institute in Paderborn, Germany